Ojibwa
Warrior

Dennis J. Banks. Photo from the Banks collection.

Ojibwa
Warrior

Dennis Banks and the

Rise of the American Indian Movement

Dennis Banks
with Richard Erdoes

UNIVERSITY OF OKLAHOMA PRESS : NORMAN

Selected titles by Richard Erdoes

(with John Fire Lame Deer) *Lame Deer, Seeker of Visions: The Life of a Sioux Medicine Man* (New York, 1972)

(with Alfonso Ortiz) *American Indian Myths and Legends* (New York, 1983)

(with Mary Crow Dog) *Lakota Woman* (New York, 1990)

(with Leonard Crow Dog) *Crow Dog: Four Generations of Sioux Medicine Men* (New York, 1995)

(ed.) *Legends and Tales of the American West* (New York, 1998)

(with Alfonso Ortiz) *American Indian Trickster Tales* (New York, 1999)

Library of Congress Cataloging-in-Publication Data

Banks, Dennis.
    Ojibwa warrior : Dennis Banks and the rise of the American Indian Movement / Dennis Banks with Richard Erdoes.
        p. cm.
            ISBN 0-8061-3580-8 (alk. paper)
        1. Banks, Dennis. 2. Ojibwa Indians—Biography. 3. Ojibwa Indians—Civil rights. 4. Ojibwa Indians—Government relations. 5. Wounded Knee (S.D.)—History—Indian occupation, 1973. 6. American Indian Movement—History. 7. Civil rights movements—United States. 8. United States—Race relations. 9. United States—Politics and government. I. Erdoes, Richard, 1912– II. Title.

E99.C6B258 2004
977.004'97333—dc22

                                                                    2003065024

The paper in this book meets the guidelines for permanence and durability of the Committee on Production Guidelines for Book Longevity of the Council on Library Resources.∞

Copyright © 2004 by Dennis Banks and Richard Erdoes. Published by the University of Oklahoma Press, Publishing Division of the University. All rights reserved. Manufactured in the U.S.A.

1 2 3 4 5 6 7 8 9 10

*To all the brave men and women of our movement
who have passed on to the spirit world.*

Contents

CONTENTS

Illustrations

Unless otherwise noted, photographs are by Richard Erdoes.

Ojibwa
Warrior

CHAPTER 1

A Night to Remember

On a dark night you could hear the ghosts crying, the ghosts of three hundred women and children killed by the soldiers, so long ago.

—*Dennis Banks, Ojibwa*

May 8, 1973—Stand down at Wounded Knee. For seventy-one days we had held out against an army of U.S. Marshals, FBI, a corrupt tribal chairman's private gang of thugs called "the goons," and a bunch of vigilantes, cowboys, and ranchers eager to "bag themselves an injun." Elements of the 82d Airborne had been standing by in the vicinity—just in case they should be needed. The Feds had brought against us a swarm of armored cars, an occasional jet fighter to get a look at us, .50-caliber machine guns, M-79 grenade launchers, high-powered searchlights, and "Snoopy," their helicopter, to spy on us.

We had killed our last steer. We were down to one meal a day, sometimes a meal every other day. We had only rice and beans left, and even that was running out. No flour, no sugar, no cigarettes. Gladys Bissonette had found a can of some fatty seasoning used to make popcorn and a box of powdered spuds. She mixed these together with some odds and ends and managed to make a meal of it. We still had some root tea for the warriors. That was it.

Our lifeline had been the few miles between Porcupine and Wounded Knee, a sparsely wooded area that gave some cover to our runners who brought supplies to us in their backpacks every night. But now the whole place was full of marshals with sniper scopes and infrared night-vision scopes, non-barking attack dogs, and trip-wire flares, which could turn night into day. On top of that, the Feds had started huge brush fires to burn off the cover, making it easier for them to detect anyone going in or out. Supplies were down to a pitiful trickle. Starvation was staring us in the face.

Almost every day now we had fierce firefights. The Feds fired thousands of rounds at us. At night their tracer bullets made a big show, crisscrossing the village from all directions. We were almost out of ammo—our guys were down to about ten bullets per man. A good many of our warriors had been wounded. Miraculously, only two had been killed. Frank Clearwater had been sleeping inside the Sacred Heart church when a bullet crashed through the wall and hit him in the head. He never woke up. Buddy Lamont, a thirty-one-year-old Vietnam veteran, was killed near the Last Stand bunker. He had been pinned down by a sniper, rose up to see where the shots were coming from, and was hit. His death was a terrible shock for us, particularly for Kamook, my sweetheart, who was Buddy's niece. We tried to get to him, but the Feds' fire was so fierce that it took us two hours to recover his body. He had been shot through the heart. His body was still warm when I touched it. The pain for us was very deep.

Buddy's death was the end. Negotiations went on for a few days more, but we knew that it was over. The end had come. We had to surrender. Of the resistance leadership—besides me—only Carter Camp remained at the Knee alongside our spiritual leaders, the medicine men Leonard Crow Dog and Wallace Black Elk.

Kamook had gone with her sister, Bernice, to transport Buddy out of the perimeter to Pine Ridge to prepare the funeral. Against all promises made to her, Kamook had been arrested, handcuffed, and kept overnight in the tribal jail. But she came back to Wounded Knee. She walked on foot over five miles in the dead of night to join me during the last days. I had felt sad and lonely while she was gone. Now I was happy to have her back.

It was the fifth of May. I had to tell her, "The stand down will be on May eighth. Then the marshals will come in, and probably the goons too. So you must leave before then. I don't want you to be roughed up and hurt by those bastards. I don't want you to be arrested again."

Then Lou Bean told me, "Dennis, the police are waiting for you. The FBI is waiting too. The goons have sworn to kill you. You have to get out of here before the Feds arrive."

Kamook added, "An FBI agent wanted me to persuade you to give yourself up. He said the FBI would guarantee you safe passage to the nearest jail." We all laughed.

I said, "Thank you, no. I don't want that kind of safe passage."

Kamook left in secret before me. We had made plans how and where we would meet on the outside.

Then a few of us got together. We sipped the last of the coffee. All agreed that I should not surrender. My friends were sure that some of the FBI and the goons would create an incident and shoot me down. Henry Wahwassuck, a Potawatomi from Kansas, was a close friend and head of my security.

He said, "A few warriors have to go with Dennis and make sure he gets through the perimeter."

Len Foster, a Navajo and one of the earliest supporters of AIM said, "I'll go with Dennis. I'll protect him with my own life."

Henry asked, "Who else?"

Len suggested Percy Casper. "He's a good man, a Canadian Indian from British Columbia. You can rely on him no matter what." We also picked Frank Black Horse, a Lakota always ready for a fight.

I said, "That's it. That's all we need. And we are going to have a sweat to pray and purify ourselves."

So the night before the last, we went into the sweat lodge: Henry Wahwassuck, Percy Casper, Len Foster, Frank Black Horse, our two medicine men—Leonard Crow Dog and Wallace Black Elk—and me. Crow Dog ran the sweat. He brought out his pipe and told us, "With this pipe, with this tobacco, and with this prayer, I'm going to make you invisible."

That is what he told us. We all prayed that we would get out without being discovered, that we would escape using the darkness of the night as our shield. It was a powerful ceremony. The spirits came in and we felt good and confident. When we saw little lights flickering in the darkness, Crow Dog warned us not to shoot at them because these were the souls of our dead ones. And we heard a ghostlike crying and singing coming from the arroyo where the men of the Seventh Cavalry had butchered our women and children back in 1890. The Feds in their bunkers had heard the ghosts too, and it had shaken them up. Some of the marshals said later that an Indian on a horse had ridden through their camps and then suddenly dissolved into a cloud, into nothingness.

On the final night at Wounded Knee, we had one last meeting. I told my friends, "Tomorrow the Feds will come in armed to the teeth with their APCs. They say they just want us to disarm, to give up our weapons. They are lying. They will handcuff the men and take them in buses to the nearest slammer. I don't like handcuffs and leg irons on me. I will not surrender. The Feds have slapped $160,000 bail on me, and I could not possibly come up with that kind of money. I would have to go underground and lie low until it was time to surface."

Carter Camp, Leonard Crow Dog, and Wallace Black Elk decided to submit to arrest the next morning. They wanted the honor of being the last ones out of Wounded Knee, and they deserved it.

"I'll give you my forwarding address," said Carter. "Pennington County Jail, Rapid City."

Others came with me that night. I told the warriors to take their rifles and shotguns with them. "You never know when you might have to defend yourselves. The goons are out there."

We had to pick a safe way out of the Knee. We were tightly surrounded. Everywhere the Feds had roadblocks, and at every roadblock there was an APC (armored personnel carrier) and maybe a Jeep or two—also German shepherd dogs. The whole perimeter swarmed with marshals and FBI.

We finally decided to go out toward the north across the creek in the direction of Porcupine Butte. Some warriors had scouted the area and thought the north was not as densely held by the Feds as the south, west, and east. Then Lou Bean came up with a great idea—a group of women would cause a diversion at the south end of the perimeter to draw the Feds' attention to that point, while we headed north.

Night fell. It was about 9:00 P.M. when we were ready. South near a roadblock, Lou Bean and about twenty other women started a tremendous racket. You could hear the Feds' radios informing one another,

"Significant activity over there." Big flood lights, which they had used to scan all of Wounded Knee, were suddenly trained on that area. We grabbed our opportunity to sneak out. I will never forget the brave women who, throughout the seventy-one days of the siege, gave us their support.

The five of us were traveling light. We each had a small backpack. My four companions also had their rifles, and that was it. We went in single file. Len Foster walked point, then came Henry, me, Casper, and Black Horse. When the women thought we had safely gotten out, they quit making a racket, and the searchlights resumed sweeping the whole perimeter again, back and forth. We would run in a crouch about a hundred yards and flatten out whenever the lights fanned over us. Then we would jump up and run another hundred yards, hit the ground again, run again. That is how we got through those searchlights, but they were not the only lights we had to deal with. All of a sudden the Feds started shooting up flares dangling from small parachutes. They lit up the whole valley like a Fourth of July night.

We walked north across the creek. When we got beyond it, we could hear the Feds up on the hill in front of us. They were driving around in their Jeep and laughing. In the gully below were trip wires. The Feds had set them up with cans so that if you tripped over the wire with your foot, you set off those cans. They made a great noise you could hear from far off, telling the Feds where some Indians were trying to come through. Tripping a wire would also cause a flare to go up. I remember that Casper or Black Horse got his leg entangled and set off a flare. He was stumbling around. Henry got really mad at him, really pissed off, and told him in no uncertain terms to watch himself. We did not want to be stopped and get into an armed confrontation.

We were lucky. We got through that gully without incident and hustled along at a fast clip. Now and then Lenny, our point man, would scout ahead, telling us, "Wait right here. Let me make sure that we don't run into some of those pigs." He would go over the next hill and make certain no Feds were there. Then he would come back and tell us the coast was clear and we'd hustle on again. We would stay inside ravines as much as we could to avoid being discovered. Unfortunately, the ravines were not straight. They zigzagged all over the place. We would walk maybe three miles, but gained only one. All this took time—it took us maybe two hours to cover a mile and a half.

We finally got up to a high, open area with lots of trees, but where we had to go there was a stretch of about one hundred and fifty yards without any cover at all. At the end of that was a tree line. There was no help for it. We had to cross that open space while occasional flares turned night into day. So I said, "Okay, one at a time. Let's make a run for it!" We did, and suddenly there was that Jeep. It had two Feds in it and a German shepherd. We were in the vehicle's shadow and it covered us. Everybody hit the ground and flattened out while the Jeep drove right by us. They didn't even see us. I knew Crow Dog's medicine was working.

Man, my heart was pounding! I thought, "Is this what it comes down to!" We were out in the open and the tree line was still some seventy or eighty yards away. We just had to get into those trees. Well, we made it into the woods and felt a little safer. Then we heard an owl hooting. It was sitting in a tree trying to tell us something. In almost all Indian tribes the owl is looked upon as a messenger, a bringer of bad news. If an owl visits you it means that somebody is going to die. The owl kept hooting. I said, "It is warning us that there is danger ahead." We were walking toward Porcupine Butte, and the owl was flying ahead of us as if it wanted to show us the way.

Then Lenny said, "Instead of walking cross-country over all those hills for ten or eleven miles, why don't we take a shortcut? I know the country around here. There's a road over there, no more than a mile away."

I said, "Why not, instead of humping over every hill."

So we cut across, hit a fence, and climbed over it. Once in a while we could see the lights of a car on the road. Wounded Knee was way behind us and we felt good about it. It was about one o'clock in the morning and pitch dark. No moon. We were walking along the edge of the road. When we got to Porcupine Butte we looked for Ellen Moves Camp, who was supposed to meet us there with a car, but she was not there. We saw cars coming toward us a mile or two ahead, and we hid in the brush by the side of the road. While planning our escape, we had passed word to those who were to meet us to blink their lights twice every half-mile, but these cars did not blink their lights. We remained out of sight. We found out later that these were U.S. Marshals patrolling the whole area.

We made good time from then on. We climbed over another fence, moving fast. About five o'clock in the morning, we got to about a mile south of Porcupine Butte. We were on a hill and down below was the village with lights coming from some of the windows. We came to a big open area—I think it was a landfill or trash dump—and there was a white car sitting there. The lights were not on but we could hear the engine. More than that, we could hear loud laughter. It sounded like some skins hanging out with their girls.

Lenny asked, "What shall we do?"

I said, "Go over there and check them out. Maybe it's someone we could catch a ride with."

So one of the guys sneaked up to the car and checked it out. He came loping back and said, "They are inside the car. They are talking and laughing like they're having a big party in there."

I said, "Well, let's go and surprise them."

We walked up to the car and we were the ones who were surprised. Henry opened the door. A light went on inside and there they were— two U.S. Marshals in their camouflage suits with an AR-15 sitting between them. They were as shocked as we were. They took off in a hail of gravel that hit us in the face.

We knew that once they realized we were only a handful of fugitives, they would be back in a hurry. I told the boys, "Let's get out of here!" The area west of the highway was densely wooded, so we took off toward it. We were walking along the trees when we heard cars pull up. They brought dogs out to do some sniffing. Our adrenaline was surging. We ran on for maybe a half-mile, but somehow they kept up with us. We could hear them with their bullhorn telling us, "Come on out of there. Come on out. Throw your weapons down."

They had left their cars and gotten right on top of us. Real close. And we heard them talking. "How many were there?" "I saw two of them." "Fucking Indians!"

We could hear the dogs, but they did not pick up our scent. We threw our packs down and laid low there in the brush. The boys had their rifles cocked. I tried to keep calm. Finally, they stopped searching for us and left. We got up and scattered ourselves in the woods. That is when we got separated and lost touch.

It was getting light. I was alone. I heard barking and saw two marshals coming with a couple of dogs. They had not picked up my scent yet. They were just combing the woods because they knew someone was out there. I ran over a hill and the dogs must have seen the movement—they started barking and howling like mad. They were coming toward me, getting closer and closer. I knew that over the next hill was the school Our Lady of Lourdes. I ran over there, through the campus to the road, where I saw three mobile homes.

I knocked on one door and an Indian lady opened it. She cried, "Dennis Banks! Come inside quick! Where did you come from?" I told her and she said, "Wow!" She glanced out the window and saw the marshals coming with the dogs. The kind, stout-hearted lady pushed me into some dark cubbyhole, saying, "Stay there. Don't worry. I won't let these pigs come into my home."

The marshals let their dogs loose, hoping they would pick up my scent somehow. They didn't know it was me they were chasing. They were just after some nondescript, suspicious Indians. Otherwise, there would have been more Feds.

Porcupine, like most reservation towns, was full of skinny, mangy, hungry, and mean reservation dogs. They came running, tearing into those big, fat, overfed police dogs. It was one of the most vicious dog-fights I have ever seen. In a moment, there was just a snarling tangle of legs, tails, and teeth. The marshals were trying to save their dogs from being torn to pieces. They had lost all interest in me.

The nice lady fried up some eggs for me and gave me a big mug of "black medicine." She let me use her phone. I dialed a number in Rapid City where I thought Kamook might be, and I guessed right. A while later, Ellen Moves Camp showed up with Kamook. The marshals were gone and I could relax a bit. Ellen said they had been at Porcupine Butte hours before, but had been chased off by the Feds. They asked what had become of the boys, but I didn't know. We hung around there for another two or three hours checking the area, but didn't find a soul. We found out later that they had made it safely to the house of John Attacks Them, a friend of Casper's. John hid them, and a couple days later got them safely to Crow Dog's place at Rosebud. Kamook and I finally made it to Rapid City, where we stayed for a very short time with friends. I think that the power of the pipe and the sweat lodge, the songs and the prayers, protected us, and as Crow Dog had said, made us—in a way—invisible.

The manhunt continued and I was the prey. The Feds were determined to get me, not only for Wounded Knee, but also for other earlier civil rights confrontations. We could not go on hiding with friends in Rapid City. It was too close to Pine Ridge, too close to areas swarming with agents and marshals. We got hold of a car and headed south to Utah, but then we decided to head north—to Canada. We were joined by Ron Petite and his wife Cheryl, an AIM couple in a similar situation. They brought my nine-year-old son DJ, a child from a previous marriage, along.

Kamook, Cheryl, and DJ drove across the Canadian border without incident. Ron and I went across on foot through the woods, and they picked us up on the other side. By stages, and amid hair-raising adventures, we got all the way to the Northwest Territory, to Yellowknife on the northern edge of Great Slave Lake. From there we took a small floatplane some friends had chartered for us to a place called Rae Lakes. The place was named after a chief called Rae, who had settled there with a small band of Northern Dineh. The chief welcomed us and promised to help us in any way he could. We had arrived at the end of the world, at the northernmost edge of the continent. You could only get there by plane. There were no roads. No FBI agent, no marshal, no mountie would ever come there.

By then it was autumn and getting cold. We had brought enough groceries to last us three months. Boxes and boxes of stuff. We took a lot of salt to cure dried meat because we intended to hunt with the rifles we had brought. Rae's people showed us how to fish with a net, and we also did well with duck hunting.

We decided to build ourselves a log cabin. We had brought saws and axes—everything we needed. We finished the cabin and moved in, living as people had done a hundred years earlier. We were entirely cut off from the rest of the world. I liked it, just the five of us alone in nature with the nightly concert of wolf songs.

I had plenty of time to reflect upon my life. To think back on how it all started, how I had gotten from a traditional childhood on an Ojibwa rez in Minnesota to the big city, to the founding of AIM, to Wounded Knee. How had it all begun?

CHAPTER 2

At the Center
of the Universe

*Once we were happy in our own country and we were seldom hungry;
for then the two-leggeds and four-leggeds lived together like friends;
and there was plenty for us and for them.*

—from *Black Elk Speaks*

The place in which I drew my first breath is gone now, overgrown with weeds, but the foundation is still there. The woods that were filled with the sounds and songs of birds and animals are silent now; and by the time I had grown up, there was little left of our once vast reservation.

I was born on April 12, 1937, at Federal Dam on the Leech Lake Indian reservation. Bertha, my mother, told me that it was very cold on the eleventh. Water, which had seeped into the cracks of trees, turned to ice and broke them apart with a sound like a sharp cry of pain. It was the kind of cold that can freeze the marrow in your bones. I was born five minutes after midnight on the twelfth. My grandmother, Jenny Drumbeater, helped to bring me into this world. My mother said that it seemed I was fighting my way out of her womb. I have been fighting ever since.

I was not born in a hospital but on a creaking bedstead in my grandparents' house. It was just a wooden two-bedroom house with a living room and kitchen—a typical reservation dwelling of those days—

without electricity, running water, or indoor plumbing. For light we had kerosene lamps with shiny tin reflectors, for heat a potbellied stove, and for cooking an ancient cast-iron kitchen range. Always next to it was a bucket of fresh water from the creek with a dipper hanging from a nail driven into the wall. Outside stood the two-hole privy.

There were seven of us living in that house, including my older brother, Mark, and my sister, Audrey. So it was pretty crowded. We had no insulation and in the winter all our backsides froze. During those cold months we put two feet of rammed earth around the base of the house to keep the icy wind out.

Though I was not born in the traditional manner of a hundred years ago (inside a wigwam of birch bark, the mother-to-be kneeling on a layer of dry grass, bracing herself against a staff planted firmly in the earthen floor), my grandparents saw to it that some of the old taboos concerning birth-giving were still kept. They would not allow my mother to look at anything ugly or at a deformed person or animal so that I should not be born deformed or blemished. I am also sure that they would not have let her step over a tree felled by lightning, for that might have brought on convulsions during her birth pangs. I know that my coming into this world was made known by a gunshot, because that was the custom at the time. The placenta was first placed high in the crotch of a tree where the dogs could not get at it, and later it was ceremoniously buried.

Traditional people put a newborn's navel cord inside a beaded rawhide pouch, which they fastened to the cradleboard. Some individuals have kept their navel cord for their entire lives; others dispose of them in various traditional ways. It was said that keeping a navel-cord pouch for at least a while would give wisdom to the child. I don't think I ever had a navel-cord pouch—at any rate nobody ever told me that one was made for me.

But I know that a big feast was given to celebrate my birth, and that a naming ceremony was held at my grandparents' house. Only the closest relatives and friends were present. They feasted on wild rice with deer and moose meat. They smoked the sacred pipe and spoke about sacred things. I was handed around the circle from one person to another, and everyone had good words to say to me.

One way to find a name for a newborn was to have the grandfather shoot an arrow into the air and then search for the place where it had come down. From the things he found there—a plant, an animal track, a rock—he picked the baby's name. But Nowa-Cumig, my Ojibwa name, came from Grandfather Drumbeater's dream. The name, as he told me, means "at the center of the universe" because the land on which I was born is the place where Gichee-Manitou, the Creator, made the whole western hemisphere from a tiny lump of earth.

At that long-ago time, Grandfather explained, a great flood covered the world with water. Wazushk, the muskrat, dived down to the bottom of the foam-speckled waters and came up with a tiny lump of earth in one paw. He placed it upon the back of the Giant Turtle floating on the surface. And the Creator made the little lump of earth grow and overspread the turtle's back until it became a continent, the Red Man's home. I think that Grandpa might have dreamed that one day I would fight for this earth and all the creatures living upon it, and for the survival of our Anishinabe people. Therefore, he gave me this name. He told me that it was sacred and that I had to live up to it.

My names were entered in the tribal enrollment book and also in the agency registry of the Bureau of Indian Affairs (BIA). Otherwise, except for a few close relatives, the world took no notice of my arrival. My mother did not even go for a check-up after I was born because the nearest hospital was at Cass Lake, forty miles away, and we had only a horse and buggy for transportation.

I have very few memories of my father, Walter Chase. He had entered the military and then married and raised another family. I have since met my brothers and sisters from that family. We occasionally write and visit one another.

I am proud of who I am. I am a "Shinabe," an Anishinabe, from the land of the Ojibwa people, a member of one of the largest tribal nations in North America.

I was born into the Pillager Band of our tribe. Five generations ago we had a great chief named Ogama. I am his direct descendant. One day I am going to go back and claim my inheritance. I am going back to insure that a way of life and thought, which was created hundreds, or even thousands of years ago, continues. That is a responsibility that goes with being born.

Grandma Jenny belonged to the Turtle Clan. Our band has seven: the Crane, the Loon, the Pelican, the Turtle or Fish, the Bear, the Marten, and the Deer Clan. Each clan has a specific and important part to play in the life of the tribe. Members of the Turtle Clan are people of strong mind and deep understanding. They are sometimes called "star gazers" because they meditate on the nature of the universe and the meaning of human existence. They are often called upon to settle disputes within the tribe.

When I was a child the elders of our family were my maternal grandparents, Josh and Jenny Drumbeater. Grandfather Josh was a headsman and a leader in our area of the reservation. The people in his family have a long history of drum-making. They are famous for being good singers—the kind of folks that go to ceremonies, clinging to old ways. Our ceremonial drums are large and elaborately decorated; it is considered a great honor to make these drums. I remember at age five or six singing around the drum with Grandpa Josh and the other elders.

My grandparents were traditional tribal people, but our old saying, "the lodge belongs to the woman, the woods to the man," was not quite true in their case. Both Josh and Jenny took part in the outdoor life of fishing, sugaring, and the harvesting of wild rice. I recall, when I was a small boy, going to camps where there was a lot of smoke and cooking. The men gathered wild rice while the women parched corn and steamed the rice. This happened in the fall. After winter was over, we went to the sugaring camp. The snow was still deep on the ground as we set up our camp in old white army tents where we had to sleep. I was so cold that I cried.

During the time of my earliest childhood, our extended family lived in two houses. One was Grandma's house, which had three rooms off the kitchen, plus a dining room. Grandma was always in the kitchen cooking. With my grandparents, Josh and Jenny, lived their sons and daughters, their grandchildren, Aunt Sarah, me, my older brother, Mark, and my sister, Audrey. Most Indian homes were crowded—we didn't mind. We were used to it.

We had a couple of cows, four horses, and a whole tribe of cackling chickens. Grandpa used to go logging. Every day he left with his ax. He worked hard and did everything by hand. He also had trap lines and would go each day to check his traps for rabbits. Grandma liked to fix rabbit stew for us. Grandpa could also hunt beaver, squirrels, and deer—plenty of wild meat. The house was filled with muskrat and beaver hides as well as deer skins. We lived close to nature, in rhythm with the seasons—fishing, hunting, trapping, ricing, sugaring, berry-picking. Grandma's home was always filled with the scents of these seasons.

I was brought up by my grandparents. I looked up to them and felt secure and comforted by their presence. It felt so good sitting at their feet and listening to their old stories, which I loved to hear. Grandma smoked a long-stemmed pipe with a bowl of sacred red stone, the Indian's flesh and blood, which came from the ancient quarry in north-western Minnesota. Grandma used Indian tobacco made of red willow bark and various herbs. The distinct, fragrant smell of its smoke agreed with me and delighted me even when I was a small boy.

Winters were very cold. Grandpa Josh would get up at five in the morning to light the fire. I remember horses from Old Agency pulling heavy logs over to us for firewood in our old iron stoves that we used for heating and cooking.

We lived at Headquarters Bay, at some distance from a village called Federal Dam. If we wanted to go anywhere from our place we had to use a small boat to cross a wide creek. Then we mostly used buckboard wagons drawn by horses to get around. On the rez, cars were still a rarity.

Our rez, one of seven in Minnesota, was called the Leech Lake Chippewa reservation. There are more Anishinabe reservations in neighboring states. The rez of my childhood was beautiful. Federal Dam was at the northeast corner of the reservation, where the water from Leech Lake flowed over a dam into the Mississippi River. Leech Lake is very large, with six hundred and forty miles of shoreline. Lake Winnibigoshish, the second largest lake on the rez, is smaller, though still pretty big. The whole country all around is like a history lesson of our people. The lakeshore is dotted with ancient Indian villages and camps, which have become settlements and towns over the years.

The lakes are surrounded by many small streams and waterways, dense forests, woodlands, and open meadows. The woods are full of pines, birch, oak, and—most important to us—maple trees, for making syrup. Game was still plentiful while I was growing up. Hunting, trapping, and fishing still played a large part in our tribal economy. Occasionally we ran into a moose, bobcat, or wolverine. It was said there were still a few wolves somewhere, though I never saw them. The lake echoed with the quacking of thousands of ducks and the mournful call of the loons. At night we listened to the hoot of the owl.

Then there were the bears. One time my mother and I were picking blueberries side by side. All of a sudden we heard a loud roar, and off in the distance we could see a big brown bear. Everybody was so excited and also a little scared. Grandpa Josh had brought his shotgun. He never fired at the bear, but we all gathered around Grandpa, huddling close for protection. From there we watched the bear. He was after the same things we were—*blueberries!* We stood still while he ate his way through the wild bushes. Every once in awhile he would look up at us, standing up to get a better view. Then he would hunker down to the delicious business at hand. The bear went through the blueberry patch at a fast pace and came quite close to us once. We made a great deal of noise to scare him off, but this did not stop him from stuffing himself while coming still closer. Finally he stood up for the last time, stared at us for a long minute, then shuffled off into the woods. He was not at all scared of us and maybe he was as curious about us as we were of him. It was a great thing for a kid to remember.

In some ways we were very poor as we had to do without a lot of things that most people take for granted. We owned one luxury item— a battery-powered radio the grownups listened to for news of the war. I don't remember having any store-bought toys. The ones I played with, old Josh or Jenny made for me. It was rare to have candy or sweets. Maple sugar was our candy. Except for what nature provided in her bounty, we lived on commodities. Once a month a big government truck would come with supplies—potatoes and flour, canned beans, bacon, and pork. We had to buy them with ration coupons. The quality of the food was pretty bad—powdered milk, powdered eggs, lard, powdered this and that.

Many times when I was young, we did not have any clothes except what we were wearing. I remember my mother taking us to town to the welfare office to ask if she could get a clothing order for us. After waiting and waiting, we saw her come out crying, and she told us that the welfare people had said no, she couldn't get an order. Then we had to stay in town overnight with no place to go. We slept huddled on a bench, and the next day we walked the thirteen miles back to our house because we didn't encounter a single car or buggy willing to pick us up. I remember the incident because it was such a long walk, and my mother had to carry me part of the way. She was crying the whole time. I don't remember anymore how or when we got clothes as we grew out of them. A lot of people came to our house to buy some of the fish we caught, and I believe the money we got from selling fish bought some clothes.

I remember on another occasion going with my mother to get some relief from the welfare. We were having a very hard time. I listened to an argument she had with one of the social workers. This man drilled my mother about who was living in our home, how many people, was the house sanitary, what sort of environment was it for children, and on and on. My mother did not reply to this. Instead, she said, "I don't have to answer this. I came here with my son to seek help. If you will not help, then we will just leave." And we left. Her last words to the social worker were, "You have to be dead around here before you will ever get help."

Since the days of my childhood, the reservation has changed. Originally encompassing almost a million acres, the reservation has been constantly chipped away by Congressional Acts. It has already been reduced to a fourth of its original size. When we were living at Federal Dam, the Leech Lake reservations had a population of 1,800 to 2,000 Anishinabes and around some 500 whites. At the turn of the twenty-first century, we have about 3,500 Indians and something like 6,000 whites. They outnumber us by almost two to one. Over time, much of the land has been sold to outsiders. Large stretches of lakefront have been turned into lots for middle-class vacation homes overlooking the beaches. The reservation looks like a checkerboard, some land owned by whites, some owned by our people.

The conditions keep changing in ways that do not benefit the Native peoples. Indians are forced to take out fishing and hunting licenses on our own land, putting us—as far as the law is concerned—on an equal status with white sportsmen, even though fishing and hunting is the major part of our livelihood. And with the coming of gambling casinos, people who used to trap or make maple sugar are dealing blackjack or tending roulette wheels instead. Our traditions and values are destroyed inch by inch.

But all of this happened in the future. Long before TV, computers, and casinos, there was an Indian school at Onigum close to Federal Dam. When I was four or five years old the school moved, and so everybody had to go to the new school at Walker on the west side of the lake. My mother moved us to a small settlement outside Walker called Old Agency.

We had to get to our new home by boat. It took us a long time. We did not go directly across Leech Lake—we went from Headquarters Bay to Whipholt, where we had some relatives, and camped there for a couple of days. Then we took the boat from there to Stony Point fifteen miles away. We docked there and walked two-and-a-half miles to Old Agency carrying our things. From start to finish, it took us almost three days to get there. Some of the way we got to travel on horseback. I sat behind Grandpa with my arms around his waist.

We settled down in our new home at Old Agency, way out on a peninsula with a winding dirt road where we would play. My mother was a hard worker and a good housekeeper. She was always busy in the kitchen or setting nets for fishing. There was so much for one parent to do. I can still see her bent over an old-style washboard doing the laundry, hauling water, cutting wood, cooking, and baking. She always had a warm fire waiting for us on a cold day. But it was Grandpa Josh and Grandma Jenny Drumbeater I felt closest to. The two of them together were my family as my mother slowly grew more distant from her children.

My mother was afraid of snakes. I used to pick up snakes, put them inside my pocket, and take them into the house. We would be sitting at the table and suddenly one of these snakes would wriggle out. My mother would exclaim, "What in God's name is that?"

I would answer, "One of my friends."

She would cry, "No, no, no! Get your friends out of here!"

I would scare my sister with them, and then my brother and sister would gang up on me and chase me out of the house.

I spent much time on or near the lake. It was very big. I went out in the boat with my family, watched them set nets. I liked to wade by the shore. The water was alive with black, gray, and spotted leeches. That is why they call it Leech Lake. My mom and everybody else were scared of and disgusted by them, but I would pick them up to look them over, letting them curl around my fingers and try to latch onto my hand.

I would go swimming, and I had to look over my whole body after getting out of the water because some of the leeches were very small. They would latch on between my toes or on my belly button or in the crack of my butt. It never bothered me but leeches drove the women-folk into hysterics. Leeches are not poisonous; they are just a nuisance. The first time I saw one it was hanging on my belly, a long black one. When I came out of the water, my mother was screaming and so were my brother and sister. You seldom feel it when they latch on, and when you pull leeches off, the bigger ones don't want to let go. You have to convince them to come off with a little tug.

We did a lot of wading and swimming at a place called Stony Point. It had huge boulders jutting out into the lake and a beautiful sandy beach about a half-mile long. It was a favorite place for us Indian kids to swim, but it has become a fancy resort for white people.

Since we had moved closer to the centers of bureaucracy, the Health Service began to take notice of us. I remember some very strange-looking white female creatures in starched white dresses with weird little white things on their heads coming to our house. These were the first nurses I had ever seen. They came with their trays of needles, Band-Aids, and little bottles. I was afraid of them because I would inevitably end up with a sore arm or sore buns.

A funny thing happened one time. The nurse who came that day had, on a previous visit, given me a shot in my rear end. So when she came again, I bent over in my most cooperative way and bared my little ass for her. She laughed and said, "No, not today."

When I was a child most of our people spoke English rather than our native language. My Aunt Sarah understood our language, but she hardly spoke it to us. Grandpa and Grandma spoke it to each other. My mother understood it, but she had gone to Flandreau Boarding School where speaking our native tongue had been forbidden, so she talked to me mostly in English. Even so, I could speak and understand Ojibwa, at least in part. Later at the white-run boarding school, the teachers made me forget it. It seemed as if our ancient language might disappear and our old religion with it.

I knew only a little about our spiritual beliefs. Grandpa taught me to make tobacco offerings. Tobacco is our holy plant, our greatest medicine. It is sacred to all Indian tribes. The smoke ascending from the pipe's bowl connects the human being with the Creator. I always carried a bag of Duke's or Bull Durham with me wherever I went and sprinkled a little on the ground, not knowing exactly why, but doing it nonetheless. That was what I was supposed to do.

Once when I was older, I was taken to a wake. For the first time I saw a dead body, the body of a person I knew. I had a strange nightmare about this death because I didn't understand it. Later, I could understand it when stories were told to me about going to the Spirit World. I watched the Elders put some kind of structure over the grave. It looked like a small oblong house barely big enough to cover the grave. It was about eighteen inches high and had a little platform at one end on which people offered spirit food for the departed. All the little houses faced east to west; I remember going over to the burial grounds to put some food on a little tray on the west side.

At the wake, some of the old people spoke for a long time in the Anishinabe language, and then there came the drum of the Midewiwin, our ancient religious society. It was decorated with beadwork all around its sides, and wedged between four curved staffs with eagle feathers tied to their tips. I can see this drum in my mind now, after all that time. With the drum came the singers. Their songs were so beautiful to me. I tried to get as close to them and the drum as possible. Their powerful magic touched my young heart.

There is one other memory from that time at Old Agency that has remained vivid. When I was about five years old, there lived an old, half-blind woman at the edge of a clearing near us. I do not know how she spelled her name, but it sounded like De-be-shonce. She must have been in her seventies. She would walk down the road holding a scarf in front of her eyes to shield them from the sun. She used to talk to the trees every morning and sometimes in the evening. The grownups told me, "Don't go to her house. She is crazy."

We young kids, the four- and five-year-olds, would go over there in the morning or the evening and make fun of her. We used to hide in the bushes to watch her. She would come out of her house with a bag of tobacco in her hands, go to that special tree of hers, and sprinkle the sacred tobacco around the base of the trunk. She would gently touch the tree and speak to it in the old language, and chant and sing to it. She was giving thanks to the Creator and thanking the tree and all living things. We kids thought she was weird, so we hooted and whistled at her. She just pretended not to hear.

Forty-five years later, I was at a Sun Dance in Washington State at Yelm with the Pullayups. On the second day of the Sun Dance, a young man came up to me and said he was having trouble with his wife. He had two young boys with him. I said, "Let's talk it over later. We're going to have a sweat now." He gave me some tobacco during the sweat. It was early in the morning. When we came out of the sweat, the sun had just risen. I told this man, "Listen. After today's dance is over, you and your wife will sit down with me and we will talk. Bring your kids."

I left him standing there and, with his tobacco in my hand, went over to a big tree nearby. I sprinkled some of the tobacco around the base of its trunk. I put my hands upon the tree, and I felt as if it were alive and I could feel its heart throbbing. I started praying. I asked the Creator for guidance in running the Sun Dance, to help those who were being pierced to endure and transcend. I prayed for the survival of all the green growing things, and for the winged ones, and the four-leggeds, and for the survival of our Indian people. I prayed, "Grandfather, help us during this day and all the days of this sacred dance." Suddenly I heard laughing. It came from the man's kids. They were giggling out loud, and I knew just what they were thinking—"Uncle Dennis has gone bananas. He's talking to a tree!"

I called to them, "Come here, I'll tell you what it's all about."

But they cried, "No, no!" and they ran away back to camp.

Later their father told me, "Dennis, my boys tell me you are acting very strange."

It took me forty-five years to really understand what that old blind woman, De-be-shonce, was doing. I bitterly regret that I never had the chance to go back while she was still living and tell her how sorry and how thankful I am now for what she had shown me. How soothing, in retrospect, to listen to the soft lilt of her voice in prayer. I loved her singing even though I laughed at her, and I now know how close she was to the Great Spirit.

I was even grateful to the two little boys who had made such fun of me because they made me see that beautiful old, blind face again in my heart, bringing it all back so clearly.

Time went by. I saw men go away from the reservation to fight the white man's war. Some never returned, leaving their bones in faraway places with unpronounceable names. I began to experience a sense of abandonment. My mother seemed at times distant and uninterested in taking care of us. She would go into town and not come back for four or five days. She would be off somewhere for longer and longer periods, and I felt her absence deeply. I was taken by a feeling of loneliness, but my grandparents and my mother's sister, my Aunt Sarah, were still there to console me. Even old De-be-shonce dropped in once in awhile to speak kind words to me, feeling her way around with the help of a walking stick. Eventually my mother remarried and faded farther and farther away into the distance. And finally came the terrible day when the yellow bus arrived.

CHAPTER 3

The Yellow Bus

The old boarding schools that Indian kids were forcibly taken to were concentration camps for children where we were forbidden to speak our language and were beaten if we prayed to our Native creator.

—Dennis Banks, *Ojibwa*

There is one dark day in the lives of all Indian children: the day when they are forcibly taken away from those who love and care for them, from those who speak their language. They are dragged, some screaming and weeping, others in silent terror, to a boarding school where they are to be remade into white kids.

It happened to me in 1942. I was young and did not know what was in store for me. An agent from the Bureau of Indian Affairs—a large-bellied man smelling of cheap cigars and beer—came into our home waving a bunch of papers, yelling, "Where are those kids who'll be going?" Everybody was crying. I was too small to understand, but I sensed that something bad was going to happen.

My older brother, Mark, and my sister, Audrey, also had to go. Aunt Sarah packed some boxes of food for us to take along. The BIA man shoved us out of our house ahead of him. What was happening to us was also happening in most of the other homes nearby. White men were herding kids and parents toward the agency building. In front of it, a big yellow bus waited to carry us away.

They took Mark and Audrey into the bus first. I was clinging to Grandma, who was crying. I didn't want to go. Grandma gave me a little bag of snacks, then somebody pulled me into the bus. A large group of parents and relatives watched us go. They were all weeping. I was crying too, but was slightly reassured because my brother and sister were with me and I knew most of the other kids. Audrey comforted me, saying, "We're going away to school, but we'll be back. Grandma will come and visit us."

Then I really was frightened because I began to understand that we were going away for a long time—not just a few hours. The bus had a radio that was squawking with all the war news. My sister fixed me a sandwich. I thought we were going to Walker, the only real town I knew, but they were taking us to Pipestone, Minnesota, a full two hundred fifty miles away. More than eleven years would pass before I would see my relatives again.

It was getting dark when we finally arrived at Pipestone. My first sight was of the big, gray stone buildings, grim and forbidding. Then I saw the schoolchildren who were already there. They were all dressed the same—little soldiers in khaki uniforms. All the girls from the bus were taken into one building and all the boys into another. I cried out to my sister, "Audrey, don't go! Come back!" But there was so much noise that she did not hear me.

They fed us something and lined us up. Some of the teachers, who were called "boys' advisors," put us in barber chairs and dusted us all over with some awful smelling white stuff. It was DDT. They rubbed lots of it in our hair. I suppose it was to kill lice. We didn't have any lice, but they assumed we did. Then they shaved our heads down to the skin. I had worn long hair down to my shoulders; I felt uncomfortably naked without it.

We continued through the line where all our clothes were taken from us. They issued each of us a government khaki uniform and stiff black shoes, which immediately started to chafe above my ankles and soon rubbed me raw. I remember the years of Pipestone as the years of blistered feet.

After that we lined up to receive bedding and then they took us to the dorms, which meant still further separation. Mark was put with some older boys, and I found myself among strange kids in a large, stone-cold hall. I quietly cried myself to sleep.

When I woke up in the morning I could not remember where I was. We lined up in three rows, the biggest boys in the back and the smallest in the front. I saw Mark standing in the back row, but could not find Audrey. I finally saw her standing near the kitchen. I broke the line and started running to her, but was stopped by the boys' advisor and pulled back. They told me I had to stay on the boys' side. Audrey had seen me, however, and waved to me. I waved back.

We were marched two by two into the dining hall, where I had my first breakfast at Pipestone. We got our plates and found a table, but had to stand behind our chairs until the table was filled up. Only then were we allowed to sit down and eat. I was really hungry and got up for more food, but the advisors chased me back to the table. I was taught to raise my hand and ask politely for seconds.

That was the beginning of a life of innumerable rules. I only saw Audrey from afar standing with the girls; I wished so hard that I could be with her. They were marching us back from the dining hall to the main building when I broke away, trying to reach my sister. But the advisors had sticks and used them to drive me and some of the other boys back into line. One of those advisors thrashed me with his stick.

One of our advisors was Mr. Smith. He had been a drill sergeant in the army. He had a harsh, grating voice and he never talked—he barked. He was always talking about the army, which made *men* out of dumb boys. He lectured us on how the army built character and how a soldier stood as high above a civilian as a human being stood above a chimp. There was also a Mrs. Smith. In contrast to her husband, she was a nice, kindly lady. We boys were divided into groups of ten, with her in charge of my group. She always came over to talk to us and give a little comfort. She tried hard, but we kids came from a such a different world that she could not really communicate with us.

Our schedule was always the same. We woke up at six in the morning, went down to the mess hall, then to school, and finally to dinner, and then the dorm again—over and over. In between activities, we were given dust mops and told to clean the whole place, wherever we happened to be. I was with thirty to forty first-graders. Altogether, there were about five hundred Indian kids in that school.

Every time I had a chance to see Audrey, I would ask her, "Where's Mom? When is she coming? When can we go home?" Then I would start to cry because Audrey was a substitute parent for me and a comfort, but the time I could spend with her was limited.

From time to time my mother would send letters to Audrey and Mark, and they would read them to me. Always the letters would say, "Tell Dennis that Mom loves him." But not once in the nine years I was at Pipestone did my mother visit. Though most kids went home once a year for summer vacation, nobody ever came for us. I was lonesome—not so much for my mother after awhile—but I missed the woods and lakes, which remained vivid in my mind. I yearned for Grandpa Josh and Grandma Jenny Drumbeater and always wondered how they were. Sometimes, as if in a dream, I thought I could smell their sacred tobacco.

It took six months before I could begin to adjust to my new surroundings. I could never really accept them. I didn't understand why I had to be there. During my first year in school, sleep was my only escape. I could not wait to go to bed. I pretended in my daydreams that I could fly—fly through the air to my old Indian home.

I made some friends. There was Fred Long, whose nickname was "Bojack," Fred Morgan, George Mitchell, "Spoon" Willis, and "Pee-Wee" Brown. They were all Indian kids my own age, and they were especially close to me because they too never had any visitors and could never go home for the summer. For nine years we were always together. I felt happy with them. The bond between us was so strong that we are still close friends, even now—fifty-three years later. But even with their friendship, sometimes the yearning to be away from that stone-and-brick heap and the longing for home was so strong that I could not stand it. Four times I ran away and four times I was brought back. The school's punishment for running away was the "hot line." I had to run between two rows of other kids, who held sticks and switches. As I passed through the line they lashed out at me. It was like Code Red in the military when you were disciplined by your fellow students. But that wasn't the only sting I felt.

Later on as an adult, I realized that Indian kids were sent to Pipestone and similar institutions to separate us from our families as a matter of government policy, to separate us from our language and traditions in order to Christianize us—or "acculturate" us, as they called it. We had daily indoctrinations in Catholic beliefs. In English classes the aim was to make us forget that we were Indians. There were no pictures on the walls of Native Americans or Indian heroes such as Sitting Bull or Geronimo. Instead there were pictures and posters of white presidents and generals. Nothing could be seen that would indicate we were in a school for Indian children.

I could speak some Chippewa when I arrived at Pipestone, but after nine years in that place I forgot it because we were forbidden to speak our native languages. Our teachers only allowed us to speak English.

Their efforts to acculturate us extended even as far as our history books, which depicted Native people as murderous, mindless savages. In one of these books was a picture of a grinning Indian scalping a little blond white girl, one of those cute Shirley Temple types. I began to hate myself for being Indian, and made myself believe that I was really a white boy. My white teachers and their books taught me to despise my own people. White history became my history because there was no other. When they took us once a week to the movies—the twelve-cent matinee—I cheered for Davy Crockett, Daniel Boone, and General Custer. I sided with the cavalry cutting down Indians. In my fantasies I was John Wayne rescuing the settlers from "red fiends." I dreamed of being a cowboy. My teachers had done a great job of brainwashing me. They had made me into an "apple"—red outside but white inside.

There was a place called the "stink dorm." Any boy who wet his bed was put in there for a week. One summer day we had iced tea—I drank so much of it that I peed in my bed that night. I was embarrassed, but I told my friends about it and they tried to help me hide my bed sheets. Somehow the advisors found out about it and called my name, "Dennis Banks to the stink dorm!" They shouted that at lunch time so the whole school could hear them. Everybody knew what "stink dorm" meant, and they laughed at me. I had to stay in that place with some other bed-wetters for seven long days. It was a humiliation I never forgot.

After three or four years in this place, I gave up all hope of ever going home in the summer. Forty or fifty among us never did. We took care of the campus when the other kids were on the rez with their families—we mowed the lawns and painted the dorms and hallways. The school employees would also get us to work for them, doing their yard work. In the summer of my eighth year, Grandpa and Grandma came with some other members of the Drumbeater clan. Their visit triggered a rush of memories and longing to get back to Leech Lake where I had left my heart. After my grandparents went home, I tried to run away. The authorities caught me two days later and threw me in jail. Then I had to go through the beatings again.

In spite of the beatings and the futility, I was determined to try again. I was not alone in wanting to get as far away from that place as I could. All my friends wanted to run away—there were eight of us and we all had the itch to go. We decided to stage a great breakout. We knew that State Highway 75 ran north a long way into the unknown, but some of the older boys told us which towns we would have to go through. We planned our escape for the morning, and we went to breakfast and concealed as much food as we could, stuffing our pockets with it—enough, we thought, to last for a few days. We also swiped some loaves of bread from the bakery.

We also provided ourselves with civilian clothes. New boys arriving each year at Pipestone had to give up their own duds in exchange for khaki uniforms; the stacks of confiscated clothes were kept in a special room. It was locked, but we managed to pry a window open and get in, grabbing whatever we could find. We then gathered out back, discarded our uniforms, and put on the street clothes, which of course didn't fit and probably made us look pretty odd. It didn't matter. We ran behind the main buildings to the corner of the campus, dodged through the nearby cattle farm from which our school got milk, then disappeared into the cornfields.

The first day we didn't dare stop but walked all night. It was freezing cold that late in the year, and we had forgotten blankets. We finally found a farmhouse, crept into the barn, and burrowed into the hay, close together to get ourselves warm.

The next day we took off again, walking down the road. Our food was already gone. We tried to hitch rides but nobody seemed inclined to pick up eight bedraggled Indian kids. The school sent two cars out after us. I was almost relieved to see them because, whatever the punishment, they would at least feed us when we got back.

And punished we were. They made us drop our pants. We were lashed with the strap, ten licks for each of us. Then we had to run through the hot line. I tried to dodge the blows but every one of the boys in the line managed to strike me at least once. When we made it to the end of the hot line, they shaved our heads and made us wear girls' dresses everywhere for three days. Despite such humiliations I ran away nine times, always heading north. Always they caught me.

When I was eleven years old, I was transferred to another boarding school at Wahpeton, North Dakota, a junior high school. I stayed there for three years. I was afraid to leave Pipestone, horrible as it was. It had become very familiar to me, and my friends were there. Besides, Wahpeton might be worse. And it was.

"Wahpeton" is a Sioux word meaning "those who dwell among the leaves." It is the name of one of the Dakota Sioux tribes. Like Pipestone, Wahpeton was run like a military institution. On Memorial Day, for instance, we marched stiffly in our uniforms and caps with our wooden play guns over our shoulders, marching to the sound of the band. Always before us waved the Stars and Stripes, our conqueror's flag.

I never had a chance to say, or even think about, what I wanted to be when I grew up. But I did know that I wanted to play basketball, and I soon made the C team. I loved to pile into the bus and travel with my teammates. I loved yelling and screaming, the excitement of pulling off wins, coming from behind—the thrill of us Indians beating a team of white boys. I liked that very much.

At that time I was still confused about who I really was. I envied the white kids for their money, for their feelings of superiority, and I longed for their whiteness. But I also knew that I was Indian, and I enjoyed my pals, enjoyed beating these teams of white boys and then feeling superior to *them*. It would take time to resolve this conflict within myself.

I was at Wahpeton in the seventh and eighth grades. I was becoming a big boy but not quite there yet. However, my emotions were there. I wanted to be part of the game and did not want to be left behind.

After the eighth grade I was transferred again—this time to the big Indian boarding school at Flandreau, South Dakota, on the Santee Sioux reservation. Just as at Wahpeton, there were kids from many tribes—Ojibwa, Winnebago, Potawatomi, Sac, Fox, and Lakota. I was only there for about a year. By then I was sixteen years old, in the ninth grade, and I finally decided that enough was enough. I made my last escape. I ran away with Bojack—we are friends to this day. We walked from Flandreau one night all the way to Pipestone, Minnesota, eighteen miles along the railroad tracks. Then we caught a freight train. The freight car took us all the way from Pipestone to Willmar, where we jumped out and hitchhiked to Bemidji. From there we finally made our way to the Leech Lake reservation area, and I looked for my mother. I found her near where I had been born. She was remarried and had other children with her new husband.

I needed to talk with my mother. I had felt so rejected by her. I thought that by sending me away to boarding school, my mother had tried to get rid of me. I felt betrayed in those early years. I did not know then that it was government policy that forced Indian kids away from their families. It had never been explained to me, so I thought my mother was somehow to blame for the years I was forced to live away from home.

When I came back nine years later, I never asked her why she didn't come and get me. She did ask me if I had received the many letters she had sent, and of course I had. But I never asked the question, "Why didn't you come for me?" I should have. I know now that I judged her too harshly. She was a victim of the system. Her life consisted of unending hard work and my father wasn't there to help her. She needed someone to love and look after her; she needed a husband. But in spite of everything, even before I understood, I loved her.

At sixteen I considered myself a man. The sense of a family to go home to was a thing of the past. I felt the strongest links of family to Grandpa Josh, Grandma Jenny, and my mother's sister, Aunt Sarah. When I went into the military a year and a half later, I listed my grandparents first as my nearest kin to notify in case of injury or death, then my Aunt Sarah, and my mother after her. At any rate, an important but painful part of my life was over. I was eager to discover what would come next.

CHAPTER 4

Interlude

A reservation is a parcel of land inhabited by Indians and surrounded by thieves.

—Gen. William Tecumseh Sherman

The two years after I ran away from boarding school and came back to the rez was the one time I was really involved in the traditional life of my people. When I got back I was taken around and introduced to all my relatives, many of whom I had not seen for years. I met my cousins, Aunt Sarah's boys, and I joined her family. I stayed at Aunt Sarah's house and she and I became very close.

My first winter back was spent getting reacquainted with the reservation and the people, and with pitching in to help with the chores around the house. Before winter set in, we needed to chop a lot of wood, maybe five or six cords. Chopping wood was an endless chore. Wood was our only source of heat and fuel for cooking. We dragged in dry wood, sawed it up, chopped it into chunks, and stacked it by the house. In winter we'd get up around five every morning to get the fires going and start our chores. The house was a small, simple two-bedroom structure with a good-sized living room. With all of Aunt Sarah's family and me, we were pretty crowded. There were seven of us living together in that house, and I liked that. To me it meant a lot because I had a home and a family. Sometimes I even shared my bed with a cousin and experienced what sharing in a family meant.

That winter I also began to learn things from the older men on the rez. They taught me about the different trees, plants, and herbs. When spring came, I remembered the old natural rhythm of life—from sugaring in the early spring to the rice harvest in the fall. It all came back to me.

Along with those memories came the shock that I had forgotten most of my native Anishinabe language. At school, English overpowered everything—I had to think in English to avoid being punished for accidentally speaking in my own language. The suppression of our native languages was a tragedy that affected several generations of Indian children forced into the BIA boarding schools. It brought several tribal languages close to extinction. After all those years, when I listened to my relatives speaking our language, it touched a resonance in me. But most of it I couldn't understand. Grandpa Josh and Grandma Jenny would be talking in Indian and they'd ask me to say something, almost making fun of me. I'd say a word in English and then say it in Indian, and they laughed as they corrected me. Years later I tried to study my language but I never became fluent in it.

For a while I enrolled in the high school at Walker to get my diploma. It was not a BIA boarding institution, but a public school. Up to that time, I had only gone to school with Indian kids, never with white students. And on my first day there, I had an uneasy feeling that I had never experienced before. I was surrounded by white kids, and it made me uncomfortable. For the first time in my life I could sense that there was a difference between these students and me. They kept to themselves and excluded me from their discussions in the hallway or lunchroom. We had a lot of reservation kids at that school but only three were in my class. I didn't have any white friends at Walker. There was a wall between us and them.

I was still interested in sports and wanted to participate regardless of whether the other kids were white or Indian, but the racial segregation at Walker was not easy to avoid. The bus picked us Indian kids up every morning. A couple of times I missed the bus from the rez and had to walk the thirteen miles to school. One time in the winter I had to cross the lake. It was three miles across and I ran all the way. There were thin spots in the ice so it was a little scary but also exciting. Though I could not participate in school sports, I got plenty of exercise.

The first winter I stayed at Aunt Sarah's, I put in a trap line for rabbits. Every morning before I went to school I would go out and check the traps, which were about a mile from the house, and bring in whatever rabbits I found in the snares. Then I would go to school. When I came back I would check the traps again. I was getting five or six rabbits a day, which I would skin and dress myself. Or I would leave them outside in the cold where they wouldn't spoil.

There were usually three or four dogs or cats around, and by the time I got back with the rabbits, the dogs would be following me. One time I had seven or eight dogs after me, and one of them managed to grab a rabbit and run. I chased him then thought, "Well, he deserved it," and let him get away. All the dogs fought over that rabbit—it was a free-for-all with tremendous snarling, growling, and howling. When I cleaned the rabbits, I would throw scraps to the dogs and cats. The cats got all the guts. Sometimes we would cook the heads; sometimes the dogs got them. We had rabbit stew almost every night. That was my little contribution to the family, and it made me feel good.

I didn't get into trapping for muskrats because I did not have the big traps that needed to be set up in the water. I never trapped beavers because I felt they were more purposeful creatures; whereas the only purpose rabbits had was to be caught in my snares for the soup pot. I wanted to protect the beavers. I enjoyed watching them building their dams.

I remember tracking a porcupine once for about two miles, watching him crawl up a big tree. I told him not to worry. I didn't have the heart to shoot him. I once shot and killed a porcupine and still felt very badly about it. I left it there and kind of apologized for what I had done, but took a bag of quills from it because the women used them for decorative embroidery. Aunt Sarah had said, "You should have brought it home. We could have cooked it. Porcupine makes good eating." Until that time it had never occurred to me to be eating porcupine.

I hunted. Grandpa Josh taught me, "If you meet an owl or a fox when you start out on a hunt, it means bad luck. You might just as well go home. Never kill an animal wantonly. Don't say anything that could hurt the feelings of a deer. Don't boast, 'Today I'll bag two deer!' The Great Spirit who created the deer does not like it. Rather, sprinkle sacred tobacco around your kill and thank the deer for having given itself so that people may live."

Hunting is best when the leaves are falling and the deer are fat. When they held a deer fry, a family would invite everybody over for big cookouts. Always the dogs would be there. They lucked out every hunting season. We would have to hang deer and other game from high tree branches so that the dogs and cats could not get at it. They got enough scraps to gorge themselves without getting at the best parts.

Much later, when I came back from the military, the old happy hunting days were at an end. The BIA and the state began to regulate everything. Under Public Law 280, we had to take out fishing and hunting licenses and compete with the wealthy tourists who dominated what had been—for all our known history—our livelihood. Constantly we felt this oppressive federal presence and we resented it. Grandpa Drumbeater hated the BIA and insisted he would go on in his old accustomed way, never taking out a hunting or fishing license "like some goddam white tourist!" He flatly ignored the new law, and he looked down upon those who obeyed the white man's crazy regulations.

The sugaring season started around the end of March, when there was still lots of snow on the ground, and ended during the last days of April. Our family has its own maple grove we return to year after year, but the groves are not "owned." The concept of ownership, either of land or of whatever grows or lives upon it, is not part of what Native people believe. If one particular family has done its sugaring in one place for a generation, then others will not intrude into that place. But when a family does not do its sugaring there for a year or two, others can make their maple sugar there. The Drumbeater clan had a big sugar camp near Federal Dam. We had about one hundred and fifty trees to tap. Sugaring was part of our subsistence and livelihood.

During the first spring back on the rez, I spent two weeks at the sugar camp doing much the same thing I had done as a little kid before I was sent to boarding school. Remembering back to when I was a kid who was so proud to help, I thought about those early impressions of life. I collected the sap from one-gallon cans on the trees, emptied them into five-gallon buckets, and then I put the empty cans back on the trees. The older boys took the five-gallon buckets to where we had a big fire. Grandpa Josh was in charge of the big pot on that fire where sap boiled down into maple sugar. As children, we watched the boiling and bubbling as the syrup thickened, and we begged for a little curl of syrup on a piece of birch bark. We dropped it into the clean snow to turn it into snow candy. I recall Grandpa Josh telling me to put a pinch of tobacco on the fire before eating the year's first maple sugar, and to do the same before eating the first fish or wild rice of the season. So that was our sugar camp.

The year I returned to the sugar camp, I was the big boy and did the heavy work. I chopped the wood for the kettle fires, built lean-tos, hauled water, dragged around the full five-gallon buckets, and snared rabbits for our simple camp meals. I breathed in the unforgettable scent of the wood fires and the rich, mouthwatering aromas of good things bubbling in the big, soot-covered pots. I watched the women cooking every day—I liked to hang around them while they made pan bread and biscuits.

But the main reason for being there was syrup and sugar. The sap was collected, boiled, evaporated, and refined. It had to be closely watched while boiling. Just as soon as it began to "make eyes," it had to be taken off the fire and worked with a kind of wooden board that looks like a small canoe paddle. If you boil the sap, you get maple syrup; if you keep boiling it, you get sugar cakes that can be ground into sugar. In our homes we used this natural sugar.

We had to bundle up in the evenings because it was always very cold at that time of year. One thing I liked about our sugar camp was when we wrapped ourselves in blankets to go sit around the fire in the darkness, listening to the elders tell the old tales. There was always a lot of storytelling. Some of the old-timers told stories of how bears would come into the camp to lick sap from the trees. Then the men would put some sugar cakes well outside the camp so that if bears were attracted by the sweet smell of boiling sap, they would find these stashes of sugar cakes and not bother us. That was our offering to Brother Bear. It is strange how we coexisted out there, but that is how it was done. And I know if I ever again organize a sugar camp in the spring, I'll put out sugar cakes for the spirits and the bears. I have many good memories of those sugar camps—of the sugar, the snow, and the stories—to last me for the rest of my life. We usually stayed out there for about ten days after the sap began to run. Then everybody would put the cans back in the shack until the next year.

Last summer, some forty-five years after my first spring back on the rez, I went back there. I found our old one-gallon cans lying around, most of them rusted out. I took two home as a reminder of those long gone days. Families no longer camp out there. A few people still tap the trees, but they're no longer bothered by the men with their badges and green uniforms who came to the sugar camps. They swaggered around with their clipboards and told our families which trees we could tap, that only the trees they had marked were for us. They would ask how many gallons of sap we had and mumble something about taxes. They had not imposed taxes on us, not on the Drumbeaters, but it was the assumption of control over our affairs that we resented so much. Every time I see a badge, it represents to me the police, a bureaucrat, or some government agent trying to control us.

Much of our activities, fishing in particular, centered around the lake. In late summer we would set up our fish camps. Again, nobody "owned" any part of the lakeshore, but families fished at the same spot over the years. Others did not intrude on that part of the shore. During my childhood I went along with my family to our fishing camp. The whole family would be there—my grandparents, my mother, Aunt Sarah, and all the kids belonging to my mother and my aunt. I would watch the bigger kids spearing fish and observe my mother setting out nets. I remember the nets filled with fish, and, small as I was, I tried to help by taking the fish out of the nets and putting them away. In the evenings we would have a big fire to roast or fry our fish. The old people would tell stories until we fell asleep.

When my grandparents were young the nets were still made by women who spun the cords from various plant fibers. But by the time I was a toddler, almost all the nets were factory-made. A dozen or so stones were tied to the nets to serve as sinkers, and big stones were used to hold the nets down across the lake bottom. Some nets were up to three hundred feet long. They had to be dried after each use. Almost everything that had to do with the care of nets was done by women. It was they who repaired, cleaned, and dried the nets.

We ate many kinds of fish, but the only fish we smoked were the whitefish. We split the fish down the back and removed the bones and guts before we placed the fillets upon racks to smoke over slow fires. Fishing was not only done with nets—we fished with hooks, spears, and traps. Just as with our hunting and sugaring rights, our fishing rights were restricted when agents from the Bureau of Fisheries made us pay for fishing licenses. There was nothing left that didn't have the government's handprint on it.

One of the most important events on the reservation was the wild rice harvest, which takes place in the early fall. The rice grows near the lakeshore or in slow-moving streams. We always went to the same place near Headquarters Bay where our families had traditionally harvested rice. Ours was only one of many ricing camps around the lake. The camp of the Drumbeater Clan consisted of between twenty and thirty people. Everybody went to the ricing camps, even the smaller children.

During the rice harvests before Mark, Audrey, and I were sent to boarding school, we had to stay back in camp. Even though we were so young, we tried to help take care of the campsite. There was always an older man who would stay behind with us to protect us from bears that might be attracted by the food in the camp. That food usually consisted of roast duck because ducks were always around the rice. Grandma Drumbeater was the boss lady who kept the whole camp busy—cooking, cleaning up, and washing clothes.

The rice had to be harvested just before it was totally ripe. If we waited too long, the rice kernels would drop from the stem into the water. We could lose a lot of the harvest by waiting too long.

I remember the first time I stood on the dock watching the boats go out for rice. The rice sticks out of the water, which is about ten feet deep. Stalks of wild rice can be fifteen or even twenty feet tall. There are always two men in each boat—one sits in front with a long pole to move the boat along while the other bends the rice stalks to knock the kernels into the boat with two sticks called "knockers." He pulls the stalks in with one stick and hits them twice with the other, knocking most of the rice kernels into the boat. A lot of rice drops back into the lake, and that is as it should be—it replenishes the rice field.

The rice stalks have sharp slivers on them that fly around during the knocking, so we had to wear bandannas around our faces to protect our eyes. If you got a sliver in your eye, you would have to tell someone about it quick and they would get it out for you. If you rubbed it, the sliver would just push itself further into the eye and get stuck. That was the first lesson ricers had to learn.

When the boat was filled it was time to go back to shore. The men would row back to the dock and we would all help lift the rice out and load it into big bags. After the rice gathering was done, all the bags were laid out to dry. When the rice was dry, we poured it into big buckets and the men and women would stand around them together loosening the hulls. Then the rice would be put into big frying pans to be parched. Afterward, a woman holding a big screen basket full of rice would stand against the wind and toss the rice up into the air. The hulls would fly off in the wind. The woman had to wear a bandanna to protect her eyes, and she sang a special song about the rice. Sometimes two or three women would sing along. The men would sit around the drum, which was beaten in rhythm with the singing.

Wild rice is not just a delicacy. It is our sacred food. It is saved up for winter ceremonies when we bring out food for the spirits. It is a wild plant, an uncultivated plant, the Creator's gift to our people.

The ricing would last for about ten days. At the end of the season we had huge gatherings. We would put on our finest quilled and beaded outfits—beautiful buckskins, bustles, ankle bells, and vests and jackets with beaded designs. Some men would wear a sacred eagle feather tied to their hair. Dances would go on for days. We always held a great ceremony to give thanks to the Great Spirit.

There were also social events. Fifteen or twenty rice camps were located in the Federal Dam area alone, and there were many more camps all around the shores of both Leech Lake and Cass Lake. There was a lot of visiting back and forth between camps and chances for boys and girls to meet, a beginning of relationships. Men and women of all ages sang and danced, and the young people and little children were all included. I remember my mother getting me dressed to dance when I was only four years old. I had on a wonderful head roach made of porcupine hair decorated with the quills and a round-dance bustle made of feathers. I can still hear the tinkling of my dance bells. Our rice harvest festivals are unforgettable.

Wild rice was a blessing in still another way. It bought for us our clothing, shoes, and other things we needed. It played a very important part in the Ojibwa economy. We took half the rice home, and the other half my mother and grandfather took to town to sell. Sometimes rice buyers came to the landings and bought directly from the camps. The price fluctuated between twenty-five and thirty cents a pound. Nowadays the price would be about one dollar and twenty-five cents or more per pound. People loved our wild rice. It is more nutritious then regular rice and tastes better.

Of course, the government agents would be there too, weighing the rice, tagging it, fixing the price, and trying to get a piece of the action by buying our rice to sell through government channels. But there were white buyers who ignored the BIA and its regulations. Now, in addition to regulations, we have some competition. White growers have begun cultivating a genetically engineered variation of wild rice and selling it as "wild rice," but it does not taste the same. Something is missing from it. Our wild rice has *always* been there; the wildness is there. The rice beds are still right where the Creator planted them.

I had been lucky. In my youth I had had the chance to glimpse our old traditional life, but it was only a glimpse. Already, during my two years back at home, that way of life—of interdependence and harmony with the natural world—was coming to an end. After eleven years at boarding school, I had come home to a bad situation. The white sportsmen had killed off the game. Our rice had to compete with commercially cultivated "wild" rice. There were no jobs for Indians. Many of our people were sick. The food available to us was bad and insufficient. Suddenly we were living on junk food, drowning in Coke and Pepsi.

It seems the makers of soft drinks discovered that Indians were good customers for the stuff. My younger sister, Terry, from my mother's second marriage, always used to have a Coke or Pepsi in her hand. It is addictive. You've got to have it. Overindulgence in soft drinks brought about an outbreak of diabetes. People started dying of it. Terry passed away at forty-two years of age from the disease. It was heartbreaking to see our people dying in this way. In the end, the doctors chop off their toes. Then they chop off a foot; then they cut off a leg from the knee down. After that it's from the hip down until you die from gangrene. I believe this comes from the food and drink that has replaced our old traditional fare.

Because the reservation seemed to be going to hell, I became restless. I wanted to cut loose and travel. Someday, I thought, I will be getting on a Greyhound bus. To me that was the ultimate high in traveling—getting into that huge bus and going with the roar of the engine, the shifting of gears, and looking back to wave at somebody waving at me. I think back to all those times when I was young and watched buses go by, waving and hollering and hoping somebody on that bus would wave back at me. I figured, some day it will be me on that bus, and if somebody waves up at me, I am going to slide the window open and wave back. And I'll yell, "Come on, let's go! Pick yourself up, go where you want to go!"

When I bought my first bus ticket, though it was only from Cass Lake to Bemidji, it got my adrenaline surging, and I thought, "Wow, man, I want to save this forever!" I meant the ticket stub. Dreams come true. Throughout my life I have traveled many miles around this earth and have been in the strangest places. But at age seventeen, I thought only of getting away and going to a place different from the place I was in.

I stayed on at Federal Dam on the rez even though I didn't know what to do with myself. I felt a yearning for something spiritual but had no clue what this could be. I started going to wakes, not even knowing who the deceased was, because I just wanted to hear the songs. And when they started chanting in Indian, I knew that is who I was. That was me. Songs mean much to me. I am a good singer now. For many years I did not sing at all—I just sat around the drum with Grandpa Josh feeling my heart beat in rhythm with the drums and listening to the ancient chants. There were songs learned from birds, in visions, and in dreams. We had no concept of people being "songwriters." The melodies come from the spirits and are only captured by those most closely connected to them. Such songs belong to the people rather than being someone's private copyrighted property.

The drum is the heart of Indian music. In Mohawk country a man talks to his drum, asking for its help during a ceremony. People will dance, adding the sound of their feet to the rhythm of the drum. It is the instrument around which people gather. I always felt that drums were living beings. As people gather in a circle around a drum, the power of the circle moves outward from the drum to the people and draws them into the circle. Then the people are as one. Both spiritually and politically the drum represents a power. So that was something I could have to comfort me as I set out into the unknown, the memory of our songs and the drum. The roots of my spirituality come from there.

I hitchhiked twice to Minneapolis to visit my sister Audrey, who had settled there. I ran into my old friend Floyd Westerman, who had just enlisted in the Marine Corps. We talked about the guys we knew who were already in Korea or in Germany. So I enlisted in the Air Force. For me, as with many other Indian kids, it was the only way out, the only chance for three meals and a warm place to sleep. I went home and talked to my mother about it. She said, "Fine, if that's what you want to do." I was only seventeen and had to have my parents' permission to join up.

Before I left, my Uncle Jim came to me and gave me a little pouch to wear around my neck. He said, "Keep this with you at all times," and I did. My Air Force buddies thought it was a good luck charm and kidded me about being a superstitious heathen. A medicine bundle has great spiritual meaning for its wearer. Prayers go into it, and it is worn for spiritual protection. Mine was a small medicine bundle on a cord around my neck. I took good care of it.

On the night I went into the military, a ceremony was held by all the people living near us. Men and women sang, and some smoked the pipe for me. As I savored the smoke and the fragrance of the sacred red willow bark tobacco, I closed my eyes and recalled Grandma and my childhood. Three men sitting on the ground were smoking the sacred pipe. I never spoke to them but I knew they were smoking and praying for me. I got down beside them, knowing that they were smoking for my coming back safe and in one piece.

CHAPTER 5

Machiko

Because there was a seed, a pine has grown here on these barren rocks. If we yearn for each other, what can keep us from meeting?

—from the *Manyoshu, Book of Ten Thousand Leaves,*
Japan, eighth century

After passing an entrance exam, I joined the Air Force in April of 1954. Before going into basic training I arranged for my mother to get half my pay. She got it every month, and I was glad to be able to do this much for her.

First I was trained at Lackland Air Force Base in Texas, then I was transferred to Fort Sam Houston. From there I went to Barksdale Air Force Base, which was a huge camp in Shrevesport, Louisiana. I was there for seven months traning as an aerial photographer. At first I worked as a cartographer, transferring photographic information to maps, then moved on to actual aerial photography. I went through a ninety-day course for photography and graduated to do this kind of work for real. Because the information was classified, the FBI did a background check on me. I received a top secret clearance from the Air Force. Soon I was handling top secret material involving aerial shots of Korea, Manchuria, China, and parts of the Soviet Union.

I found it easy to adjust to military life. I guess my years at boarding schools prepared me for another round of obedience and discipline. I shined my shoes and did all the things you are supposed to do in the military. I was into that level of toxic fantasy. I wanted to fly planes; I wanted to "kill a commie for Christ." The patriotism in me was so strong that I defended the military and its policies, including whatever the government was doing overseas. I defended the war in Korea and was ready to defend any war the U.S.A. might be involved in. I was so patriotic, it was ridiculous. I dreamed of being the general of the whole goddam Air Force.

While I was still in basic training, I met a guy by the name of Ken Kobayashi. He was of Japanese descent. We were both assigned to the Second Air Force, and we became close friends. We knew another guy, a Chinese kid named Gim Toy—the three of us stuck together through our entire military careers. Both guys were from California—Gim was from the Stockton area, while Ken was from Redondo Beach. I think the initial friendship was linked to the color of our skin. I felt somehow related to them. We just naturally gravitated toward one another.

We all got our assignments to the same base in central Japan. This was my first time out of the country. They moved us through California, then we boarded the ship *USS Breckenridge* with four thousand other GIs going to Japan. I got a KP assignment for thirty days on that ship. I hated day-after-day KP. And I was seasick for the first three or four days out from the constant rolling of the waves. I couldn't sleep, and if sleep did overtake me, I was still sick when I awoke. I closed down. I knew I didn't like navy life, and I didn't care to learn much about it. A navy ship is a navy ship, and all I cared was that it was taking us to Japan.

From the beginning I was in love with Japan. When we arrived I was sent to a small base in Osaka called Itami Air Base. They had old-time twin-engine B-26 reconnaissance bombers they used for aerial photography of Manchuria and Korea. We got all our equipment, settled in, and went through a week-long orientation about Japanese people, their culture, the history of the war with Japan, and what we were doing there as occupation forces. They told us that certain places were off-limits to us. We were instructed that there were rules we had to abide by. Even though the country was under U.S. military occupation, we were still subject to Japanese law as well as our own Air Force regulations. We were not supposed to become involved with the Japanese people on a personal level. The watch word was "no fraternization!"

Well, naturally these rules could not be enforced because many of us had to work with Japanese people. I spent a lot of time on base on my duties, but on my time off I was getting acquainted with Japanese culture, talking to people, asking questions, going to museums, and absorbing as much as I could. I began to pick up the language. I studied Shinto and Buddhist beliefs. I liked to attend the festivals held at Takuraska north of Osaka. I fell in love with the whole country. I knew I was there to accomplish a military mission, but in my heart I somehow felt that something on a very personal level was happening to me.

We were surrounded by bars that were right off base. We called them the Thousand-Yard Strip—saloons, pawnshops, clip joints, and whorehouses. It was said that if you didn't hock your watch, drink a gallon of beer, and get laid, you were not a man. There was one bar where the guys from our squadron went called The Top Hat. I started going there too. I didn't like whiskey then, and in fact didn't like hard liquor at all. But I began to like beer. In the excitement of this new place, there was peer pressure to act macho. You had to get drunk and have mindless, paid-for sex. I had had sex before—in high school—but it was a bashful thing, playful even, not a rowdy, drunken affair. But I was curious. I kind of wanted to go to one of these whorehouses, but not so much for sex. I wanted to see what a whorehouse was like.

The military is a training ground. It teaches you things in your off-hours just as it does on base. Even while you are a kid you start hearing about joining the Air Force or Navy or Marines. They tell you you're going to see the world, have a woman in every port. Then when you are actually there, you're supposed to be macho and use women as sex objects.

I talked to Gim and Ken about it. "What should we do first, guys?"

Gim Toy was a museum kind of guy. He said, "Well, there are some theaters and museums we should go to." I knew what I wanted, and Kobayashi was a cross between what I wanted and what Gim wanted. Yes, I wanted to go to the theater and the museums, but I wanted to meet people, to see who they were in all aspects of life, to touch them and visit with them. Of course we saw them working as houseboys, as construction workers, and in offices on the base. But I wanted to explore. The Thousand-Yard Strip was a good place to start.

So we got our passes and walked down the road. Of course there were girls calling out to us, "Hey GI, do you want some Coca-Cola?"

They were girls who worked in the bars. Their job was to get you to drink and spend money at their bar. But there were other girls who would call out, "Hey GI, do you want a short time?" That was the first time I heard that expression. The guys from the base told us, "They were asking you for either a brief time or all night!" A short time was maybe half an hour with them: you pay for some sex then leave. All night obviously had a different price tag.

But we didn't go in there. I was just absorbing all kinds of impressions. Not every store or station was a bar; not every house was a whorehouse. There were little bakeries, a small grocery shop, toy shops, pharmacies, and a lot of rickshaws.

Itami sits in the hills near Osaka. In fact, all of Japan is hilly and mountainous. The country's few flat areas are used for farming. There was a particular smell around Itami. It wasn't constant but you would get a whiff of it sometimes, and you would know there were "honey buckets" nearby. A honey bucket was a container full of human waste that had been dug out of the toilets to be mixed with an additive, then used as fertilizer in the rice fields. On base the showers and toilets were just like in America, but Japanese toilets were different. You had to squat down on a little commode that had no apparent bottom to it. All the waste would go straight down into a holding container. From the outside, the farming community would dig it out and use it for fertilizer. I found out that human waste is a great recycled agriculture enhancer in a country without cattle and animal manure. But when I first saw a Japanese toilet, it kind of repulsed me.

I explored alone sometimes, and other times I hung around with Ken and Gim. We went on different excursions—hiking or to the movies, and of course to the Thousand-Yard Strip. On our first outing when one of us said, "Let's go have a beer," into The Top Hat we went. We were greeted by three girls who introduced themselves. As we sat down with them, it was understood that they would be company for us as long as we spent money on them. We tried to talk—they with their broken English and me with no Japanese at all. There was music and dancing and a comfortable feeling. I watched another girl behind the bar bring drinks for us. She was very pretty.

There was a mystic quality about being with women my age who were of a different race but with the same color skin. We began to talk about little things like where I was from, about music, and whether we knew how to dance. Ken was able to talk a little Japanese with the girl sitting next to him. Gim was engaged in conversation in much the same way I was. Right then I sensed something inside me that would never leave me. Even though it was a bar setting, these people saw me as a human being.

Well, naturally I was a GI, and they saw that first. But there was never, "Give me money," or anything like that. If we spent a dollar or two dollars, that was all right. Five dollars was all right. And if we went in there and spent just fifty cents in four hours, that was all right too. I was never propositioned by any of those girls. That first time, we stayed for perhaps an hour and a half. Then Gim said, "Let's go," so we drank up, said good-bye to the ladies, and walked out.

We had originally set out for the train station to go sightseeing. But there we were on our first encounter off the military base with three "nationals" who didn't know us before, and we were excited about it. We never did make it to that train station. Gim was talking about cameras, and I was still talking about the girls. "Ken," I said, "those girls were nice. I want to visit there some more." We eventually made it to the photo shop where Gim bought a camera, and then we found a place to buy some apples and oranges to munch on. By this time it was getting late and we had to be back at the base by 9:30. We were on our way back when I said, "Let's just pop back into the bar and see what's going on." It was pretty crowded. The girl I had been sitting with was sitting with another GI. I thought, "Well, that's her job." I looked at the girl behind the bar again and caught her eye. She just looked and kind of smiled a little bit. I disappeared through the door and I thought about our first evening out.

I thought about racism. Here in this country, I didn't sense it, and I didn't see whites surrounding me all the time. And I liked it. I enjoyed the company of the people of this country, the people I was falling in love with.

The next morning I went to the library on base during break. There were all kinds of books on the Japanese language and I thought, "Well, I'll learn it." Of course when anybody goes to Japan, they buy these little books entitled *How to Speak Japanese in Five Easy Lessons*. Ha! "I'll buy that and get somebody to help me." And so I did.

I told Ken and Gim, "I'm going back to that bar tonight."

Gim said, "Yeah, me too, but first I'm going to go check out this museum. It's only open until seven."

So I went back to the bar alone. I ordered one beer and talked with another girl for maybe a half an hour. Then I went out to walk around. I followed a side street that went up where I could see people working in the rice fields. Three hours went by while I sat watching from the edge of a canal with my feet dangling over the water. My attention was absorbed by men balancing the honey buckets on their necks and shoulders, and the women working knee-deep in the fields. I could hear them speaking, feel the culture of these people. Way off in the distance I could hear some kind of Japanese string music. This feeling that there was a purpose for me other than the military began to move through me.

I kept going back to The Top Hat. The young girl who was bartending greeted customers as they came in. So when she greeted me, I asked what her name was. She replied, "Machiko." I told her my name, and she said, "You're new, GI?"

I said, "Yes. . . ."

Then she spoke to everybody else in Japanese. "*Mena-san, kodi wa American Indian.*" Later on I understood that she said to her friends, "This is an American Indian." They all came over to talk to me and shake hands with me, then we sat down a little while together. Behind us the jukebox played rock and roll, Hank Williams, country western— such a contrast to the music that floated across the fields and canals from the *koto*, the *biwa*. It was about my second week in Japan. I kept asking her questions about herself, but she wanted to know more about me. There was such an aura of joy around her.

I didn't even go to dinner the next night. I went straight to The Top Hat, right back to her. We'd talk and talk, and dance a little bit. She showed me how to dance the box step and jitterbug. Today those are still the only steps I know. She would do these little things that made me feel so cared for. I would be smoking a cigarette and she would flick ashes off my shirt, or she would straighten my tie while talking with me, caring about me. She was sixteen and I was seventeen, and we were falling deeply in love. Something wonderful was blossoming for me.

After about two weeks, I thought about her all the time. So one Friday I told her that I was getting a three-day pass and could be gone from the base two whole days. She said, "Do you want to see my parents? I live with them over at Takarazuka about two hours from here."

I said, "YES! Yes, yes." I packed a little bag and that night we went. I stayed with her until she finished her work at The Top Hat around midnight. We went up to the train station in a hurry because the last train was about to leave.

A couple hours later when we arrived at Takarazuka, she told me she felt it might be better to show up at her parents' house in the daylight. She said, "Tonight we'll go to a motel." Of course I thought that was a great idea. We had to wake up the motel clerk to show us to our room. As was the custom, we took off our shoes and went in through the wood-and-paper sliding doors. The inside was like a traditional Japanese home with futons and a hibachi in the middle of the living room with a table over it. Machiko served me some hot tea and then said that she was going to have a bath. She asked me if I would join her.

I had never exposed myself naked to a woman much less bathed with one, and I wasn't sure I understood what she meant. She was saying, "Come on, hurry up, take off your clothes," yet there was nothing sexual in what she was suggesting. Until that time, I didn't realize that in Japan it was natural to be undressed and to bathe together. We took off all our clothes and stood totally naked.

There were these little stools to sit on to wash yourself up. We sat down, lathered all up, then took more hot water and poured it over ourselves. Then we got into this big hot tub for maybe a half-hour or so. The water in the tub was so hot I thought I would die. I tried to jump out but she laughed and pulled me back. It was hotter that a sweat lodge run by Crow Dog, which can be almost unendurable. After a time, we got out and lathered up again, really scrubbing ourselves clean.

We did this whole process twice. She scrubbed my back, which embarrassed me a little. I almost grabbed her hand to tell her to stop, that I would do it myself. But she teased me out of it and slapped me on the butt, saying, "Come on, you're a GI. You're supposed to be tough." She acted like she thought I was afraid of the water because it was too hot. I was looking at her; she was so beautiful. I was seeing her for the first time, naked and relaxed in all her loveliness.

I met her parents, kind simple folk who smiled and bowed to me. I bowed back just like they did. They served me fragrant tea in tiny cups.

They couldn't speak English but seemed to approve of my friendship with their daughter. I realized I was falling in love for sure, even after just two weeks with Machiko. Machiko Inouye. I found that I not only loved her for herself but also for being Japanese. A passion flooded over me for her country with all the sights, sounds, and smells. All of it opened up vividly to me. I asked Machiko to go with me to different places. We would ride the trains together, do our shopping, and take in the sights around the countryside. We even went to see traditional Kabuki plays.

She was the first woman to care for me, to bathe me, to cook for me, to listen to me, and sing with me. She knew something about American Indians. And even though she couldn't speak my Anishinabe language, she learned a few Indian songs and she taught me some Japanese songs. We would sing together.

We rented a little place of our own close to the base soon after our trip to Takarazuka. I would go there every evening after work and return to the base each morning. We spent six months at Itami Air Base. She never asked what I did. All she knew was that I was a GI.

For men in the military, relationships with women are very insecure. You are subject to forces beyond your control. Some total stranger with gold braid on his sleeve can tear your world to pieces with a flick of a pen. I knew what a relationship with a woman could lead to for a GI, but here I was getting myself involved deeper every day.

After six months our unit was transferred to Yokota Air Base, which was a huge Strategic Air Command (SAC) Base outside Tokyo. There they had the big bombers, B-47s. We were assigned to the 548th Reconnaissance Tech Squadron to do more aerial photography work. I asked Machiko to move up there with me. A friend of mine, Joe Golgosky, also had a Japanese girlfriend, who was named Judy. Machiko and Judy were close friends, so we all moved to Yokota together. We rented a whole house and stayed there for the next three years. I used to bicycle the six or seven miles we lived from the base.

I loved my life there with Machiko. She was fascinating. Through her, I began to learn more and more about the Japanese people. For the first time, I heard about the native aborigines, the Ainu, but I wouldn't become acquainted with them until twenty more years had passed.

One morning in 1956 we got an early wake-up call, "Hurry up, hurry up! Get moving!" We were told there would be a demonstration against

Tachikawa Air Base by Japanese "troublemakers," but we already knew what it was about. The air base, which was about thirty miles from Yokota Air Base, was going to be expanded into an SAC Base. The plan was to extend the runway by at least one thousand yards to make way for the B-47s and B-52s that were coming in. To facilitate this, a great chunk of useful farmland had to be condemned and destroyed. A Japanese court fought the move, and a mass public demonstration was to take place against this takeover by the U.S. Air Force.

The farmers had begun to organize and the students were organizing behind the farmers. It developed into a strong opposition to the U.S. Military. Soon there was a growing number of farmers, students, Buddhist monks and nuns, and ordinary Japanese citizens banding together in demonstrations. As the crowd of demonstrators grew larger and larger, our command post told us that we were going on full 24-hour alert with combat readiness.

On this particular day, they called us at three o'clock in the morning to tell us to grab our gear and go stand out there at attention with the rifles and live ammunition they had issued us. We were only a short distance from where the line of demonstrators was forming. Our officers stationed one man every ten feet around the perimeter of the entire base. I stood at the end of the runway that was to be lengthened. Ken Kobayashi was to my right with Sergeant Johnson on the other side of him; to my left was Gim Toy. We stood at attention for what must have been two or three days in a row.

An officer had told us that if any of the demonstrators set foot on the base itself we had to shoot, first a warning shot. If that didn't stop them, we were to fire on the demonstrators. "You have to shoot them," he said. We could not understand this. These people were nothing more than nonviolent demonstrators. This was their land that our Air Force was trying to take away. Here I was, living with a Japanese girl, and many of my friends were doing the same. Our sergeant had a Japanese wife. Sergeant Johnson said to the Captain, "Shoot at what? You want us to shoot to scare them? You want us to shoot over them with a warning shot?" The captain replied, "Shoot to kill." It was 1956. There was no war going on, but that was the order.

Ken, the sergeant, and I talked about the predicament that we found ourselves in. "What do we do? I said. "These people—this is their land, and if they come over the fence, it is still their land. I don't know that I could shoot a Japanese for wanting to occupy his own land."

Sergeant Johnson said, "Well, if anything happens, I'll just fire a warning shot, but we are not going to shoot anybody for *this*. I'll be damned if I'll do that. I will help defend the United States of America. I did take that pledge, but I haven't seen anybody try to invade America lately." That was the kind of talk going on among the GIs assigned to this mission.

About ten o'clock on the third morning we heard the drums. We were standing on the base's side of a big cyclone fence about ten feet high. On the other side of that were the Japanese National Defense Forces. Beyond them was a row of police. We were facing four or five thousand demonstrators. Out in front were Buddhist monks and nuns in their orange robes beating huge drums—the *taikos*. The rhythmic pounding grew louder and louder. I had never heard so many drums in my life.

Off in the distance, a mass of orange-robed people had appeared, chanting and hitting the drums—thousands and thousands of people. There must have been four or five thousand of them. I had seen monks and nuns before, but not this particular sect. Their heads were shaved. When they reached the front of the demonstration, they all kneeled down maybe fifteen feet on the other side of the police. They continued to chant "*Nam myo ho ren ge kyo*" for several hours. We were at parade rest, talking together about all this.

Years later I would understand what that chant means even though there is no literal translation of it. When you have a good feeling such as the birth of a baby, you chant. Or if you hear of the death of somebody, you chant the same words in a sorrowful voice. Of if you see something beautiful, you say it. It means beauty. It means peace.

There we stood in opposition to these people, us holding our M-16s and our sergeant with his BAR, his Browning automatic rifle, fed by its belt of ammo. All of a sudden a commotion broke out way over to our right. Then the yelling and screaming began, coming closer and closer. We could see the Japanese police rushing the demonstrators. The helmeted Japanese Defense Forces seemed to be there to back up the police. We had seen students moving toward the fence when the police suddenly charged them with weapons and heavy sticks. The Buddhist monks and nuns sitting still on the ground in front of us were chanting when the police rushed them in a frenzy and started cracking skulls with a terrible sound as if they were striking coconuts. The monks and nuns did not fight back. It was a terrible thing to witness. I saw elderly nuns with blood streaming down their faces.

Sergeant Johnson suddenly grabbed his BAR and fired a round into the air. Then he hollered, "Stop it! Stop it! Halt!" The police stopped beating the people and turned around to face us. The Japanese Defense Forces turned around as well, not knowing what to do. In that critical moment, when I saw them turning around to look at us, I grabbed my rifle, cocked it, and pointed it up in the air. Almost all the other GIs did the same thing. I believe that by firing his weapon, Sergeant Johnson may have saved hundreds of lives. In that confused moment anything could have happened, but what everyone saw was Sergeant Johnson running toward the fence, shouting in Japanese, "Stop the beatings! Stop it! Stop it!" Then all was quiet.

Off in the distance behind us I could hear the sirens coming. The military police heading toward us had heard the shooting. Sergeant Johnson must have let off at least fifteen or twenty rounds. He returned to where we were and said, "Kobayashi, this thing accidentally trip-fired, and it went off like that. That's what happened."

Kobayashi said, "That's what I saw."

Sergeant Johnson said, "Airman Banks, this BAR trip-fired. I finally jammed it up and stopped it."

I said, "As far as I know, Sergeant, that's what I saw, too."

The military police arrived and came running toward us with their guns drawn. First they talked excitedly with Japanese interpreters asking what happened. The interpreters pointed at us. Then the military police came over to us and one of them said, "Sergeant, what happened here?"

Sergeant Johnson said, "I went to put my rifle down like that, and all of a sudden it started firing. I grabbed it and managed to stop it."

The MP asked Ken, "Did you see anything?"

Ken said, "I was standing at parade rest. I saw Sergeant Johnson put the rifle down, and it just started firing."

The MP looked around and said, "Did anybody else see anything?"

I said, "I saw the same thing."

They turned around, went over by the fence to confer, and came back. "All right, you guys, listen. We're going to take you out of here and bring in somebody else." They picked about five of us and gave us a ride out of the area, then we returned to our barracks. They didn't question us any further.

I felt sick at what I had seen and ashamed of the uniform I was wearing. I remembered Sergeant Johnson firing and yelling for the beating to stop—I had looked past the Japanese Defense Forces then and could clearly see the monks who were trying to help the injured. They were carrying them away to safety. That terrible scene has remained with me all of these years. I shall never forget those demonstrators were peaceful people literally being beaten to death. Since that time, during my struggles in the American Indian Movement, I have seen BIA police wield their clubs at Indians like that. Each time my memory flashed back to what I saw that day in Japan.

Machiko and I had been together for two years when she became pregnant. It was inevitable. After our little baby girl, Michiko, was born, I felt wonderful. We decided to get married in the old Japanese way and went to a Shinto priest. Machiko looked so beautiful in her wedding kimono. We drank to our mutual happiness from tiny cups of sake.

I took the marriage document back to the base and tried to arrange for us to have a civil ceremony as well. They said, "We do not recognize such marriages. And we are not allowing members of the armed forces to marry Japanese subjects." I said that we had already been married. "The hell you are!" was the reply.

"Hey," I said, "We have a baby now and our child needs help." They said that Machiko could fill out an application to be married, but it wouldn't do any good. We had to fill out all this paperwork. I was called in by the OSI, the Office of Strategic Investigations, and told that I could not marry her because her family were members of the Socialist Party in Japan and that she might be a Communist. I was baffled and angry. I told them Machiko was not in the least bit interested in politics.

They said, "We are denying your marriage application—and we are also taking away your top-secret clearance."

I didn't care about the top-secret clearance but I was shattered by the announcement. I realized that I had been living in a state of self-delusion. Air Force life had made me mentally lazy. As a GI, I was doing mostly nothing—just taking a vacation from thinking. But it was the hour of awakening. I had been guarding the ramparts of the American Empire, but now I felt like those Crow and Arikara Indians who, after scouting for Custer and fighting on behalf of the whites, were pitted against their own brothers, the Cheyenne and Lakota. My Japanese family members were called "gooks," "slopes," and "slant-eyes" by whites, and those who suffered from these names were people just like me. Was I not a "slant-eye," as all American Indians are? The American Air Force, which I had thought of as a friend, turned out to be an enemy.

I started drinking in a destructive way—whiskey with beer chasers, are called "boilermakers." I began to change, to get rowdy drunk along with the rest of the GIs. I still had Gim Toy and Ken Kobayashi as friends, and we've been friends all these many years since that disastrous time.

I was determined that I was never going to return to the United States again. I did not want to return, for I was so much in love with my wife and child, and the country and its people. I had extended my tour of duty for two years, but then suddenly they ordered me back to the United States. I said, "No, I'll take my discharge right here in Japan." They insisted, "No, Banks, you have to go back to the States to get your discharge."

I grabbed Machiko and the baby and went AWOL. We moved to another place, but they found us and court-martialed me. I was found guilty. They took away my stripes, suspended my pay, and put me in jail for thirty days. When I got out, I managed to find Machiko again. We moved to a new hiding place until two months later when they discovered us and took me away. This time they sent me to the States in chains. My image of the United States was already shattered, my belief in America crushed, my duty and obligation finished. I wanted nothing more to do with the military or the U.S. government. I just wanted one thing, and that was to stay with my family in the country I had come to love. I had even started to speak the language. But I was on a plane bound for the States.

We stopped in mid-ocean at the Midway Islands, and I attempted to escape. But they arrested me again, handcuffed me, and put me on the plane back to the States. Someone had assured me that when I got back I would get my mustering-out pay, one thousand two hundred dollars.

They said, "If you're so stuck on that Jap, you can turn around and fly back." I had told Machiko to wait for me. I didn't know how long it might take, but I intended to go straight back as quickly as possible.

They didn't give me the money. They gave me pieces of it in little installments over a period of time. There was never enough to buy that ticket. I wrote Machiko that I was going to have to work somewhere for awhile to earn the money to come back for her.

I was staying in Stockton, California, where I started working with Gim. I was hoping to scrape together enough money to get back to Japan, but the money was never there. I got so depressed about the whole situation that I started drinking again. I always wrote Machiko, "I will be coming. I will be back," but it never happened. I was only able to afford the barest necessities of life and the price of a bottle.

The weeks turned into months, and months to years. After a period in Stockton, I went back to the reservation. I had written my mother to tell her about my wife and baby. My relatives thought I would be bringing them back with me. They all said, "Dennis, where is your wife, Machiko, and the new baby?" Then I had to tell them the story about how all our plans had been destroyed. I would still write to her and she would write me back. Two years went by. The figures of Machiko and the baby were fading in a fog. I went on drinking. Eventually I moved to Minneapolis and started getting involved with various Indian issues there. I began to settle down. I met another woman, and my life took some new twists and turns over the course of the next few years.

Fourteen years later I was in a position of leadership during the siege at Wounded Knee, South Dakota. Some videographers from Japan were documenting what was happening there for Japanese television. They were doing a story on me, and we met together for several days. I don't know, but maybe Machiko saw the footage on TV, because a call came in from Japan to the place in Minneapolis where I had an address. The people who were staying there didn't get her message to me until several months had passed because of the trials that followed the long siege at Wounded Knee. The message said that our child, Michiko, was fifteen years old, going to high school, and that everything was okay. The number must have been taken incorrectly, because when I tried to call her back I got a hotel. There was no one there by the name of Machiko Inouye.

Five years later, I finally went back to Japan. I knew the places where Machiko had lived and her parents had been. I went back to her parents' place. They had moved some twenty years before that. I looked up her last name, but there must have been more than three hundred people in that province by that name. It was like looking in America for a person named Jones or Smith. I got on the phone and called fifteen or twenty different people. I went to the school Machiko had attended and left word there in case there was ever a reunion of the 1953 class.

All this was very emotional for me. I ran into one of her friends, who said that Machiko had remarried, of course, and that she had raised our daughter. Michiko had grown into a young woman herself and was at a university in northern Japan. At that time, she was twenty-four years old. That was the saddest part for me. I was anxious to locate Machiko and then my focus shifted to Michiko. But I did not find her.

I went again to Japan ten years after that, in 1988. I had released a book out there about my life, and I put out a call for Machiko to contact the publisher. No call ever came. I even went back to the little place we had rented, but it had been torn down. Even the old grocery store where we used to trade was gone.

I acknowledge that I have a child somewhere in Japan. It brings me sorrow that I never found her. It must be the same for children looking for their parents. I travel back and forth to Japan quite often now, about twice a year. Every now and then a young girl will come up to me and say, "My father is an American Indian." Shivers run through my whole body. But then she is not Michiko at all, but someone else's child.

I am hopeful that one day I will see her. Someday, if fate is kind, I will finally find the ones I lost in that ill-fated time.

CHAPTER 6

We AIM Not to Please

*Things won't ever be the same again—and that's what the American
Indian Movement is about. We are the shock troops of Indian sovereignty. We intend to raise questions in the minds of all—questions that
have gone to sleep in the minds of Indians and non-Indians alike. AIM
is the new warrior class of the century, bound by the bond of the drum,
who vote with our bodies instead of our mouths. Our business is hope.*

—Birgil Kills Straight, Lakota

The years after Japan were incredibly hard. Friendships that went back
a long time helped me survive the Indian ghettos of St. Paul and Minneapolis. Old friends from the boarding school who had gone into the
military helped one another hang in there—guys like Fred Morgan,
Bojack, George Mitchell, and Floyd Westerman. As the years went by,
we would inevitably run into each other along the way, usually in St.
Paul's "Indian Town." Life was as tough as could be, but always we kept
going. I think all of us rode the rails at one time or another. In those
days, jobs were few and far between. Still we survived, mostly in the
slave-labor markets of Minneapolis, Chicago, and Milwaukee. Nothing
changed our friendships. We supported one another in our struggles
and we laughed a lot of those damned hard times away.

We all were drinking in those years, not really caring what the
booze was doing to our health, sometimes going on binges for days and
even weeks. But when we were together, we had good times. Often we

spent the night talking of the old days, laughing and remembering all the crazy things we used to do. We had all served in the military and, during our get-togethers, would talk about our boarding school buddies who had never come back from the wars in Korea or Vietnam. Many times we cried. We eventually all lived on Fourth Avenue, the center of Indian life in Minneapolis.

Every year, the arrival of spring meant the opening of a season for hunting Indians, who provided slave labor for both the Twin Cities and the state of Minnesota. Together with the first robin came the annual renewal of the "quota system," which meant that the police had to arrest a certain number of Indians—usually about two hundred every week—to provide unpaid labor for the work house and various city projects. Every Saturday night at nine o'clock, the police arrived to conduct their manhunt. You could set your watch by the arrival of the paddy wagons.

The cops concentrated on the Indian bars. They would bring their paddy wagons around behind a bar and open the back doors. Then they would go around to the front and chase everybody toward the rear. As soon as you went through the back door, you were in the paddy wagon. The cops' favorite targets were Bud's Bar on Franklin Avenue and the Corral, which was less than a hundred yards away. They rounded us up like cattle and booked us on "drunk and disorderly" charges, even if we were neither.

During the early sixties, I got caught in that dragnet maybe twenty-five times. Monday mornings I would sometimes end up at the work house or they would put me to work on a farm. Once this happened to me three weekends in a row. I would go back to the same bar and get caught again. We were sent out to clean up stadiums and the convention center, which would take two or three days. Then they would tell us, "Okay, you guys, you can be released now." It took me a while to realize that the police raided only the Indian bars and never the white ones.

For Indians, doing time in jail is almost a traditional rite of passage. About 1 percent of the Minnesota population is American Indian, but more than one third of all prison inmates in the state are Indians. We wind up in the slammer because we are Indians, because we are too poor to raise bail, and because we cannot pay for an attorney. We have to deal with a public defender who, in most cases, persuades us to make a quick plea-bargain deal.

Inevitably, I, too, wound up in the penitentiary. In 1966 I was indicted on burglary charges. I called it my "sixteen bags of groceries case." At that time I was married to Jeanette, a beautiful Indian woman I met during a visit to my sister Audrey. I fell instantly in love with Jeanette. She brought four children from a previous union into our marriage, and we had four more of our own. So I had to provide for a family of ten including myself. I had a miserable, minimum-wage job that could not support us, so I stole to put food on our table.

My partner in the escapade was a white man named Bill. We were arrested for stealing sixteen bags of groceries. He managed to get an attorney, while I had only a court-appointed public defender. When we were up for sentencing, it quickly became obvious that Bill was not going to be sentenced to the same time I was. I got five years, whereas he was sentenced to two years of probation and was released immediately. At first I thought this was because he had an attorney. It didn't occur to me that it was because I was an Indian who had been saddled with a white judge and a white arresting officer.

I was stuck at Stillwater, the Minnesota state prison, from early 1966 to May of 1968. Inside the pen, I began to read about Indian history and became politicized in the process. I would read the papers and see that demonstrations about civil rights and the Vietnam war were going on all over the country. I realized that I desperately wanted to be part of a movement for Indian people, but we had no organization to address social reform, human rights, or treaty rights. We had nineteen Indian organizations for social welfare and gathering clothes. These were needed, but there was no movement specifically addressing the police brutality that was an everyday fact for Indian people or the discrimination in housing and employment in Minneapolis. Nor were there ever Indians speaking at those big rallies I saw on TV about the war in Vietnam or minority issues. Helpless in my prison cell, I felt that the chances for creating an effective Indian rights organization were passing us by.

I had plenty of time to research the issues of American Indian civil rights since I was in a maximum security prison for two-and-a-half years with nine months of that in solitary confinement. This nine-month period came about because I did not want to spend all my time making twine and Minnesota license plates. I refused to be a typical prison inmate. I was different from the others, so they locked me up in a cell by myself. I started to educate myself while in solitary and found that there was a lot of social and political unrest happening on the outside. I began to follow the anti-war movement, the marches and protests, the Students for a Democratic Society (SDS), the Weathermen, and the Black Panthers. Inside Stillwater, I made a commitment to myself that there would be an Indian movement.

When I got out of prison in May of 1968, I no longer had a family. With eight kids on her hands, Jeanette had been forced to look for support elsewhere. Maybe this was fate—removed from all family obligations, I was free to found an Indian civil rights organization. I called up my old friend George Mitchell, who had been at the boarding school with me, and said, "George, I want to get a movement going, and I would like you to help me." I figured that, between the two of us, we could put together a series of meetings to get the Indian community in Minneapolis behind an effort to begin making the changes that we needed.

George and I swung into action in the summer of 1968. We contacted all of our relatives, friends, acquaintances, and people from the reservations as well as from the Indian slums in the city. We went from house to house with five hundred leaflets we had printed, handing them out to every Indian we could find. We told them, "We need to have a meeting."

Our first meeting was set for eight o'clock on the evening of July 28, 1968, in the basement of a rundown church. In those days about forty or fifty people would come to any given Indian meeting. Usually you could not get more than that to come unless there was some kind of handout—toys, clothing, or a feed. Then you could get more, but few people were going to meetings to deal with the important issues. We thought that no more than fifty people would come. I went out and bought a hundred plastic cups, some Kool-Aid, coffee, and fifty donuts. We borrowed some chairs, and hurried to the church to prepare for the meeting. I wrote on a scrap of paper the kinds of issues I thought we should discuss—prisons, courts, police, treaties, the government. By six o'clock, already ten or fifteen people—besides the ten who had been helping to organize the meeting—had shown up. Between six-thirty and seven, about fifty more people arrived. Before long the donuts were gone. By eight o'clock the place was packed. Almost two hundred people had gathered to listen and to begin making their voices heard.

I opened the meeting. I told these people that I had called them together because I felt that we needed to talk as a group about issues that concerned us all:

> People are fighting battles in the streets of Chicago. They're fighting to stop the Vietnam war and bring about changes in the political party system. They're fighting in the streets of Alabama to change the situation for blacks. The SDS movement is trying to change the whole structure of the universities. What the hell are we going to do? Are we going to sit here in Minnesota and not do a goddamn thing? Are we going to go on for another two hundred years, or even another five, the way we are without doing something for our Indian people?

As the meeting went on, people began to speak up. One man spoke of the police brutality and said, "When do you propose to go down there to Franklin Avenue, to all those Indian bars where the cops inflict abuse on our people every night?"

I told him, "We could go down there tomorrow morning."

He said, "No, let's go down there right now, tonight!"

People started to get excited and speak up. I knew that this excitement was going somewhere. The man in a hurry to get things done was Clyde Bellecourt, a Loon clan member from the White Earth reservation. During that first meeting he spoke with such intensity that his enthusiasm swept over us like a storm. In that moment, AIM was born.

I said, "Our top priority is to do something about the police brutality that is going on every day. Tomorrow we'll start our protests."

"Hell, no," said Clyde. "We start right now, this evening." And that is what we did. Clyde had some previous experience from organizing the "Red Ghetto People" in 1964 in Minneapolis. We immediately made Clyde the first chairman of AIM. I became the first field director. Together with George Mitchell, Harold Goodsky, and a number of determined women—among them Francis Fairbanks and "Girlie" Brown—we formed AIM.

We had an organization, but we did not yet have a name for it. George Mitchell came up with Concerned Indian Americans, and for a short time we went with that until somebody pointed out that the initials spelled "CIA." We had to find a better name for our newborn organization. During one of our first meetings, a woman stood up and said, "You always aim to do this and to do that. Why don't we just call ourselves 'AIM'?" Clyde, George, and I came up with a number of names that had the word "movement" in them. We finally settled on "American Indian Movement."

There was great enthusiasm to get our meetings going. We were on a roll. The people wanted action, and our first priority was to deal with police brutality. In Minneapolis, only 10 percent of the population was Indian, but 70 percent of the inmates in the city's jails were our people. We painted three old cars red. Clyde had one, George had one, and I had the other. With these cars, we immediately established an Indian patrol to prevent the police from further harassing our people. We patterned it after the patrol created by the Black Panthers in Oakland.

I rejected violence and some of the methods involving force adopted by the Panthers, but I knew that AIM would do what we had to do to achieve our ends. A cartoon that had been taped on one of the desks in the AIM office around that time showed Dennis the Menace running around the room with a flyswatter. He had a look of determination and had apparently used this little weapon of his with a minimum of success. The caption read, "AIM, DENNIS, AIM." It was a reminder to me of the need to reconcile the issue of nonviolence with our determination to achieve our goals.

As AIM began to work as a group, raising questions that had been dormant in the minds and hearts of Indian and non-Indian people alike, we questioned our beliefs about "necessary violence" and whether we should arm ourselves. I didn't want AIM to be seen as a group that advocated violence, but, on the other hand, I felt that our people should not face heavily armed, racist cops empty-handed. There was just too much evidence of racism in the streets, and sometimes a show of strength can actually prevent violence. Racism was considered by most Americans to be only a black/white issue, a view that ignored the Indian as a significant minority.

AIM went to the chief of police to point out the particular brutality toward Native people on the streets of Minneapolis. He said, "Naw, there's no racism here."

We told him, "We can prove it to you. We will bring you films and photographs that show your people using excessive force *all* the time and acting in a sadistic way."

We bought walkie-talkies and began wearing identical red berets so that we were easily identifiable to other Indian people. We got into our red cars and drove down to the bars, where we stationed ourselves at the front doors. When the police turned onto Franklin Avenue, we would yell, "Here they come!" We had two cameras to film footage of the police storming into the bars, rounding up people, making arrests indiscriminately, and hitting people with their nightsticks. We shot the scene from inside our cars, always taking care to avoid being noticed by the cops. We then had evidence on film and tape that the cops only rounded up Indians and not a single white person. Later, the booking sergeant confirmed what we already knew: one hundred fifty Indians had been arrested that weekend. Our next step was to empty out those two bars just before the police would arrive. We pulled out the drunk patrons and gave them rides home. By the time the police arrived, there was nobody left to arrest. After we started our red car patrols, the number of arrests dropped dramatically.

At our first meeting, we had nearly two hundred people show up. Two years later, AIM's membership had grown to five thousand. By 1973, there were seventy-nine chapters, eight of which were in Canada. With this expansion, we began to do a lot more than just confront police brutality. We had an attorney from the Legal Aid Society available every Thursday evening at AIM's office to help people in need of legal assistance. We established a program to improve Indian housing. We rented a hauling trailer to help Indian families move. We improved communications between Indian and non-Indian communities. AIM set up its own radio program on Station KUXL to broadcast news of Indian concern. The station also published its own bi-monthly newsletter. Eventually, we established our own alternative school for Indian kids—the Red School House.

Minneapolis soon became too small for AIM. In 1969, we took part in the National Education Conference. One young man came up to me and asked if I would go to Cleveland and make a presentation at their Indian Center. His name was Russell Means. I told him I would. Some months later, we formed the Cleveland chapter of AIM. According to Russell, he asked me, "What can I do to join AIM?"

I answered, "You just did!" That's how Russell remembered it. He was an Oglala Lakota from Pine Ridge, South Dakota, a very charismatic and spellbinding speaker. Women adored him. One of our Minneapolis guys used to joke that "Russell was a victim of white broads with the hots for good-looking, long-haired savages." AIM people always had a sense of humor. Russ went on to become a very effective AIM leader.

Before long we received a call from a Milwaukee man who said he wanted to set up an AIM chapter in that city. He was Herb Powless, an Oneida of the Six Nations of the Iroquois Confederation. Herb soon took on a leadership role and we became lifelong friends. AIM had begun to spread out, to become a nationwide organization.

As an AIM leader, I was in the public eye. People looked up to me. I was "news." But I was still hitting the bottle. I stopped drinking on New Year's morning of 1970, after having gone through a terrible night of d.t.'s. It was snowing and I had come home early. It was the worst night of my life. I felt as though I had done nothing worthwhile in my life, that my image as an Indian civil rights leader was a sham. The thought of what booze was doing to my mind and body overwhelmed me. I had been having terrifying nightmares. The whole night I lay on the floor thinking that I was going to die, that this was the end. I started to pray to every god I could think of. I prayed to Buddha, to Rama, to Jesus Christ, and to the Great Spirit, "If you let me see the sunrise one more time, then you can take me. But if you don't take me, I will give up this old way of life, and I will walk a good path."

The snow kept falling. I went to the window, still out of my mind. Then I realized that I had left the door wide open and that a lot of snow had drifted into the apartment. I was wearing only my shorts and I was freezing. I managed to close the door, crawl under the covers of my bed, and go to sleep just as the sun was coming up. Later I woke up and saw that the whole place was trashed. There was garbage all over. The kitchen was littered with dirty dishes and spilled coffee. Furniture was knocked over. I could not figure out what had happened. In the days before, I would wake up in the morning with a six pack of beer and immediately start drinking. But on that snowy morning, I was hungry. I began frying up some eggs, thinking, "What has happened here? What kind of party did I have?" I opened a can of beer, but as soon as I got it to my lips I remembered what I had gone through the night before. I told myself, "No, never again." I poured all the beer down the sink. I have not had a drop of alcohol since that moment.

There was one more change I needed to make. I saw my reflection in the mirror—a gray flannel suit, white shirt, and necktie, looking like a respectable middle-class white man. "That's not what I want to be," I thought. I threw the necktie away and let my hair grow long. I began a new life.

(From left to right) Dennis Banks's mother, Bertha Jane Banks, with her mother, Maggie King-Banks, and sister, Sarah Teresa Banks, in October 1918.

Dennis Banks *(middle row, fifth from left)* at Pipestone Indian School in Pipestone, Minnesota, in 1947.

Housing conditions on the Rosebud Sioux Reservation, South Dakota, in 1970. Similar conditions prevailed at the nearby Pine Ridge reservation.

John Fire Lame Deer *(second from left)*, Lakota, on top of Mt. Rushmore reclaiming the South Dakota Black Hills for the Lakota tribe, 1971. To his right stand Lehman Brightman, Lakota, and Minnie Two Shoes.

John Fire Lame Deer praying with peace pipe at Mt. Rushmore, 1971.

Henry Crow Dog, Lakota.

Indians on top of the presidents' heads at Mt. Rushmore, 1971.

John Fire Lame Deer during a Yuwipi Ceremony, Rosebud, South Dakota.

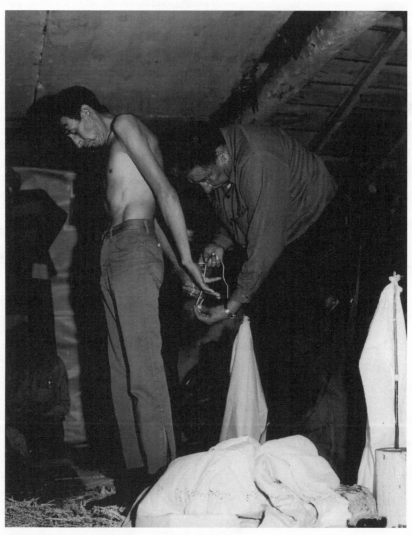

Johnny Strike being tied up for a Yuwipi Ceremony.

Leonard Crow Dog, Lakota, tied up in a star blanket for a Yuwipi Ceremony, Rosebud, South Dakota.

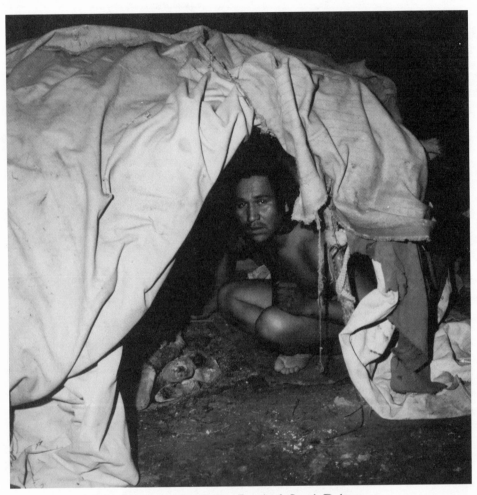

Leonard Crow Dog in a sweat lodge, Rosebud, South Dakota.

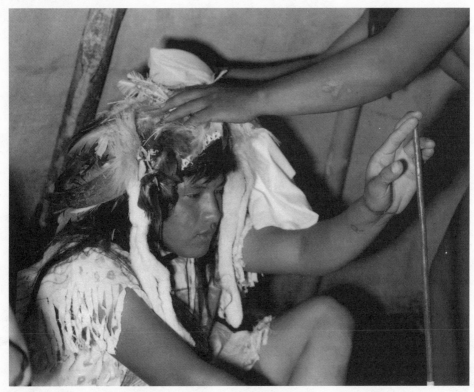

A healing ceremony performed by Leonard Crow Dog, Rosebud, South Dakota.

Henry Crow Dog smoking sacred pipe.

Henry Crow Dog eagle dancing.

Dennis Banks, Ojibwa, Sun Dancing at Pine Ridge, South Dakota, 1972.

Sun Dancer at Wounded Knee, South Dakota.

Russell Means *(center)*, Sioux, Sun Dancing at Pine Ridge, South Dakota, 1971.

Chief Bill Eagle Feathers, Lakota, Sun Dancing at Winner, South Dakota, 1969.

Dennis Banks *(on right)* Sun Dancing with an eagle bone whistle at Pine Ridge, 1972.

Merle Left Hand Bull Sun Dancing with an eagle bone whistle at Rosebud, South Dakota, 1971.

Pierced Sun Dancer at Crow Dog's Paradise, South Dakota, 1971.

Pete Catches, Lakota, Sun Dancing at Winner, South Dakota, 1969.

Dennis Banks at the takeover of the Bureau of Indian Affairs (BIA) building, Washington, D.C., November 1972.

Russell Means at the takeover of the BIA building, Washington, D.C., November 1972.

(From left to right) Vernon Bellecourt, Clyde Bellecourt, Lakotas, and Russell Means speaking in the assembly hall of the BIA building, Washington, D.C., November 1972.

Floyd Young Horse, Lakota, in war paint at the takeover of the BIA building, 1972.

Clyde Bellecourt.

Outside the BIA building during the takeover, 1972.

Floyd Young Horse guarding an entrance to the BIA building during the takeover, 1972.

"No Indians Allowed" sign, saloon at Scenic, South Dakota, 1975.

Demonstration in Custer, South Dakota, February 1973. The Chamber of Commerce building in the background was later burned. Photo by Ken Norgard's Canyon Camera Productions.

State troopers subduing protesters at Custer, South Dakota, 1973.

Passive resistance at the Custer protest, 1973.

State troopers dragging a young Lakota woman at the 1973 protest in Custer, South Dakota, through the snow, ripping her blouse off in the process.

CHAPTER 7

Crow Dog

The earth is a living thing. Mountains speak, trees sing, lakes can think, pebbles have a soul, rocks have power.

—Henry Crow Dog, Lakota

AIM was going strong. We had a movement, we had an agenda, and we were spreading out. More and more people joined us, but in my heart I knew that something was missing, something that should be at the center of what we were doing. There was an empty space in me somewhere and also in AIM. I wondered about that empty space for several months. Then one day, I remembered the songs I had heard before I was taken away to boarding school, the prayers, the old woman who talked to trees, and the fragrance of the sacred tobacco. I realized that AIM needed a spiritual basis. Spirituality is the heart and soul of Indian life, but we AIM people had been raised in white boarding schools, had lived in the Indian ghettos of big cities, had done time in prison. We did not know what we should believe in or how we could find sacredness.

I began searching. I took a four-day weekend and drove north to the reservation. I went asking for a medicine man. I knew where Eddie Benton had lived. He was the closest to being a medicine man that I knew, but he was gone. Nobody could tell me where he was. I went to the place where I was born. Grandpa Drumbeater had passed away. I talked with one of our elders, King Bird. He told me the ceremonies were still taking place, but they were hidden from view. I did not know where they were being performed. I drove back to Minneapolis, then met with some Lakotas I knew. I ran my problem by them. They told me, "You know, there is Crow Dog, out there at Rosebud. And Lame Deer. There are Chips and Fools Crow at Pine Ridge, if you really want to talk to some medicine men." So I took off for South Dakota.

I arrived at Rosebud in the wintertime. The piercing wind was icy cold, snow covered the ground. I went to the Tribal Council building and asked, "Where can I find Crow Dog?"

Somebody told me, "He lives eighteen miles south of here. Follow the sign that says 'Ghost Hawk Park,' then cross a bridge and follow the river. You can't miss it."

I drove out there, and on the left side of the road I saw a huge tire, higher than a man and painted white. Giant letters on it read, "Crow Dog's Paradise." The entrance to the place was formed by two especially long tipi poles crossing each other. A buffalo skull was tied to the top. I drove through the poles up to the house. It was homemade—a jumble of tree trunks, tar paper, old car windows, and what looked like a piece of siding from an old wooden freight car. There was an outhouse, a brush shelter for outdoor cooking in summer, a horse tied to a tree, and a lot of friendly dogs barking.

I knocked on the door. Old man Henry Crow Dog opened it. He was a full-blood. I had never seen a man before with such a classic Indian face. He looked like a photograph taken a hundred years earlier. He was tall and lean. He asked, "What do you want?"

I said, "I want to talk with you." He told me to come inside. His wife, who had a broad, sweet face, was sitting on an old rickety chair smoking a cigarette. She said her name was Mary Gertrude. She and Crow Dog spoke to each other in Lakota. When she had finished one cigarette, it did not take her long to start another from a carton of Pall Malls at her side.

Henry said, "Sit down!" So I sat there and they completely ignored me for almost an hour as they went about their business. Finally he made some coffee and Mrs. Crow Dog offered me some. Then he asked me, "Can you take us to town?"

I said, "Sure."

They put their shoes and coats on, and he said, "Let's go!" We went to town, not Rosebud as I thought, but to Winner, which was fifty miles east of where he lived. They did some shopping, and Henry invited me to stay for supper. Once we drove back to their home, his wife started cooking dinner—fry bread, hamburgers, and some more thick, black coffee.

He asked me, "Where are you from?"

I told him that I was a Chippewa from Minnesota. He asked me a lot of personal questions. He asked if I had ever been in a sweat lodge. I said, "No."

"Have you ever been in a Sun Dance?"

"No."

"Have you ever given flesh offerings?"

"No."

He whispered something to his wife and they both laughed. He continued, "Do you know how to put up a sweat lodge? Can you make one?"

I said, "No."

Again they laughed. "Well," he said, "you don't know any of those things. You don't know the sweat lodge, you don't know about the Sun Dance or flesh offerings. Do you at least know how to put up a tipi?"

I said, "No."

He growled, "Then we have nothing to talk about." Then he asked if I had a pipe.

I said, "No, but I grew up near Pipestone. I can *make* pipes."

He looked at me as if he could not believe it. "You can make pipes?"

I said, "Yes. I learned how to carve pipes as a boy."

He shook hands with me and said, "Then we *do* have something to talk about. You don't know anything so why did you come?"

I told him, "I need spiritual help."

"Okay," he said. "Tomorrow we start, but you have to chop some wood. Tomorrow we'll go into the sweat lodge." So we ate, and I spread my bedroll near their old wood stove and fell asleep.

The next morning while we had breakfast, Henry told me, "We'll go out and you chop some more wood." He took me to where he had his sweat lodge. It was made from willow sticks planted upright in a circle, bent inward and tied together at the top to make a little hut shaped like an igloo. The framework was covered with tarps and blankets and stood as high as my chest. The lodge had an entrance covered with a flap. Henry pointed to a nearby spot and told me, "Bring the wood here, chop it smaller, and start a fire."

I looked around me. Everything was covered with snow. I asked, "How can we build a fire in all this snow?"

He said, "Here is a shovel. Dig out this whole area. Then we'll start the fire."

He left me standing there and went back into his house. It was freezing and I was shivering. If you have never experienced a South Dakota winter, you don't know how cold it can be. I shoveled the spot out, chopped a lot of wood, then went back into the house and told Henry, "I did what you wanted me to do."

He led me back outside, then said, "Okay, put these rocks on the logs, start the fire, and stay here and watch it. Come and get me when the wood has burned down and the rocks are red-hot." Then he walked back into the house.

I wanted to follow him because it was so cold, but he repeated, "Stay and watch." After a time when I felt that everything was ready, I went in and told him. He said, "Take your clothes off and put this towel around you." I did, but I kept my shoes on because I didn't want to walk out there barefoot. Henry insisted, "Take your shoes off too."

So we went out again, and man, it was cold with nothing but a towel around my hips. We stood in front of the fire and Henry chanted his prayers. He put up a buffalo skull for an altar and placed a bucket of water near the entrance. Then he told me to go to the fire and bring the rocks into the lodge, one by one, with a pitchfork that leaned against a tree. I brought the rocks in, placing them one after the other inside a round pit in the center of the lodge. I had never been so cold in all my life, and I had been mighty cold before. I felt as if the cold would crack my bones. My teeth were chattering and my feet began to freeze.

I crawled back inside the lodge. The floor was covered with sage, and Henry had his pipe with him. He closed the flap over the door. The lodge was pitch dark except in the center where the rocks were glowing red. Henry poured water over the rocks, and instantly the icy cold turned into intense heat. Searing steam rose up from the rocks, making my flesh feel as if it were being scorched. When I tried to breathe, my lungs seemed to have caught fire. I thought this white hot heat was beyond what I could endure. The heat raised blisters on some parts of my body. I tried to crawl out, but he pulled me back. He prayed and sang in that blazing furnace. Finally, he said, "Open the entrance flap." At once cold air rushed into the lodge. The relief I felt was indescribable. But then the flap was closed, more water was poured over the rocks, and again I felt as if I were being burned alive.

At the second round, or as Henry called it, "the second door," I asked him to let me go outside. I crawled out and just lay in the snow for two or three minutes until Henry said, "Okay, come back in now."

I was thinking, "No, no, I don't want to go back in there," but I did. Another round and I was again writhing in pain. ("Rounds" are the four times during a sweat when the door flap is opened to let outside air come in and bring a little relief.) At the end of the third round, Henry lifted the flap, and I went out to lie in the snow once more. This time when I went back into the lodge, I felt uplifted and exhilarated. This seemed to me like a tremendous beginning to a deeper kind of life, but on the other hand I thought, "Maybe I can't go this way. Maybe it's too much for me."

I stayed with Henry and Mary Gertrude for four days. By the second day I was ready to tell him, "I want to have another sweat."

He said, "Then you've got to chop some more wood." We repeated the rituals that come before the sweat. This time I kept my shoes on until the last minute for fear of getting frostbite. I managed to last three rounds of that second sweat without leaving the lodge. I was proud of that and felt very elated. I gave Henry and his wife five pounds of coffee as a farewell gift, then went back to Minneapolis.

Those ceremonies at Crow Dog's led me to the path I knew would be right, not only for me but also for the American Indian Movement. That first meeting with Henry Crow Dog happened in early 1969 when I was thirty-two years old.

After I got back to Minneapolis I told Clyde Bellecourt what I had experienced. "Clyde," I said, "We have to find a spiritual direction for the American Indian Movement. Many of our people are churchgoers and consider themselves Christians. We are Indians and there is a Native religion out there, our own religion."

Clyde thought about this for a few minutes in silence, then he said, "I see what you mean. I agree with you."

So we both drove out to South Dakota to Crow Dog's Paradise. For the first time we met Henry's son, Leonard, who is probably one of the most powerful medicine men of our time. We attended a Yuwipi ceremony, which is a "finding-out" ritual that includes a sacred rock ceremony and a dog feast. It is one of the deepest and strangest ceremonies I have taken part in. During the Yuwipi, things happen that simply cannot be explained by modern Western science—things that frightened me at first because I was not yet ready to understand them.

The ceremony took place inside a room at Henry Crow Dog's home. The Yuwipi man, Leonard Crow Dog, had his hands tied behind his back with rawhide thongs. Next he was wrapped tightly like a mummy in a large star blanket, which covered him completely from head to foot. A long rawhide rope was wound back and forth around his body, binding him securely. He was gently laid face down upon the sage-covered floor in the center of a rectangular sacred space outlined by tiny tobacco bundles called "chanli" that were tied onto a long string. I could not imagine how he could breathe wrapped up like that.

The man sitting on my left told me that the sponsor of the ceremony had some very heavy questions to ask, such as where to find a certain missing boy. The spirits would give the answer to Crow Dog, who would then relate it to the participants. An altar had been set up with a buffalo skull, a staff with an eagle feather tied to it, four-direction flags, and other sacred objects. We all were sitting against the wall, men and women, and each one of us got a sprig of sage to put in our hair over one ear. We were told that this would encourage the spirits to come in and maybe talk to us. Heavy blankets covered all the windows and every little crack where a sliver of light might seep through. All pictures and anything else that could reflect light were turned around or covered. We even had to take off our watches and jewelry. Then the lights were turned off, and we found ourselves in total, profound, and absolute darkness.

The praying, drumming, and singing began. It was pure magic. Soon, little lights were flickering all over the place, circling around our heads, dancing on the ceiling. Ghostlike voices whispered in our ears as gourd rattles flew around the room. I felt eagle wings brushing my face, and I knew that a healing was taking place, that someone was being cured. The ceremony lasted about three hours. When it was over, the lights were turned back on, and there was Crow Dog sitting in the middle of the room untied. All the ropes that were used to tie him up were rolled into a neat ball, and the quilt in which he had been wrapped was lying neatly folded at his side. After Crow Dog related to us what the spirits had told him, the sacred pipe was passed around our circle, and everyone took four puffs. This ended the ritual part of the ceremony.

We were all asked to stay right where we were sitting. Mary Gertrude brought in the food as is done for all ceremonies. She served us a hot soup from just one large kettle. As the kettle was brought to where Clyde and I were seated, I immediately noticed the head of a small dog in the soup. We were given pieces of the dog to eat. This was part of the ceremony.

I understood the healing, but I didn't understand the meaning of eating dog or what it had to do with the rest of the ceremony. I guessed that it was some kind of sacrifice to help cure the sick person or to obtain the answer to a question, but I didn't know for sure. I had been told that it wasn't proper behavior to ask about the meaning of all that happened. I wanted to take the very smallest piece of dog meat I could find because I knew I must eat it, but everyone was looking at me. I decided to take the piece that was in front of me. I chewed it. It did not have a particularly wild taste to it, but it had a red meat flavor. That was the first time I ate dog.

Still, I had a nagging question. What was the meaning of this? I felt that deep inside of me, I knew the essence of these rituals. But each person who experiences a ceremony can only talk about what he or she *perceives*. In some ways we may not be able to interpret it all in our minds or to put it into words, but spiritually we understand it one way or another. So the essence of what I learned then remains with me today.

It is difficult to answer if someone asks, "What is it like to purify yourself inside a sweat lodge?" Each person's experience is different. When I went into the sweat lodge for the first time, there were two reasons for it. The first was to find out what it was like; the second was to build a foundation, a spiritual center for the American Indian Movement. Therefore, I had to understand each step of the purification process and its meaning—such as how to construct a sweat lodge, which direction it faces, what the various parts symbolize, and why women on their moons are not to enter a sweat lodge. All of this has to be understood. Usually the man who conducts the sweat explains such things to those who don't know them.

When I was in a sweat for the first time, I was very apprehensive and wondered, "How long is it going to last? How hot is it going to be?" That first time I panicked as I felt the intensity of the heat and I could not convince my body to accept it. At that time I could not bear the heat, but many years later, I can go into that same sweat lodge with even more of the hot rocks. I can absorb and embrace the heat. The sweat lodge has been transformed for me from a scorching hell into a temple.

Early on I understood this was what AIM needed. There was a void in our lives at that time—that void was our lack of spiritual connection. When we found it, we were embraced by it. It was as if a spiritual marriage had been performed.

There were some Ojibwa AIM members who said, "We should all go to spiritual leaders from our own tribes."

I told them, "I have already tried that. I just don't know where to find them because they keep themselves hidden."

Ceremonies *were* being performed at Leech Lake, but at that time they were jealously guarded and done in secret. Today our Anishinabe people have openly returned to their spiritual roots, and are reviving our ancient rituals.

In 1969 and 1970 that wasn't the case. Their secrecy was the reason I went to Sioux country, to the Lakotas. Their reservation was even poorer than ours, but they had a richness of ceremonial life that I was irresistibly drawn to. It was there for those who searched for it. The Lakotas had sweat-lodge leaders and pipe-owners in almost every household. The Crow Dogs gave AIM a lot of spiritual help. Through them, we met other Lakota medicine men like Wallace Black Elk, Bill Eagle Feathers, John Fire Lame Deer, and George Eagle Elk, all from Rosebud, as well as Pete Catches, Frank Fools Crow, and Ellis Chips from Pine Ridge. Even young Lakotas who were not medicine men were active in the traditional singing and dancing, and were able to speak their language. I fell in love with and married a young Lakota woman named Kamook. Our marriage sealed the bond between me and the Oglala tribe of Pine Ridge.

Young Leonard Crow Dog became AIM's spiritual leader. Because he joined AIM, his teachings are alive in many tribes throughout the United States. He stayed with us through hard times, through the "Trail of Broken Treaties" and the seventy-one day siege of Wounded Knee. He knew the risks he was taking—that he might be incarcerated or even die. He accepted all that and handled it magnificently. Native people still love him for what he did for us.

The most sacred and profound of all Plains Indian ceremonies is the Sun Dance. As Lakota medicine man Pete Catches used to say, "It's the granddaddy of them all." It is a ritual of self-sacrifice as well as a celebration of the renewal of all life. In 1970, I made a solemn vow to give my flesh and my suffering to the Sun Dance. A year later Clyde Bellecourt, Russell Means, and my old friend Lee Brightman journeyed to the Lakota reservation at Pine Ridge to take part in a Sun Dance with me, in the ceremony that transcends all others.

The dance has been misunderstood and misrepresented by outsiders in books and in movies. They have called it barbaric and savage without knowing any of the meaning behind it. For many years, the dance was forbidden. Those who performed it were put in jail. But the dance remained alive in the hearts of the people, who continued to perform it secretly in out-of-the-way places, hidden from the eyes of government agents. It thrived in adversity.

The Sun Dance is not an initiation rite or show of bravery. It is not a ritual that will make you a member of a tribe. By taking the pain that is part of the dance upon yourself, you can take away sickness and suffering from a friend or relative. Your sacrifice can bring a beloved son or brother back alive and well from war in a faraway land. It can help your tribe to survive.

Medicine man John Fire Lame Deer told me, "White Christians let Jesus do the suffering for them. We Indians take it upon ourselves. If we give Wakan Tanka, the Creator, a horse or tobacco, we would be offering him something he already has. Only our own flesh belongs to us. How can we give anything less?"

So we stood, the five of us, on the Sun Dance ground, surrounded by our Lakota brothers and sisters. In the center rose the the sacred cottonwood tree, the Tree of Life. Four of our direction flags fluttered from its branches. At its base rested our altar—a large, painted buffalo skull. In the clouds above, a wild eagle circled over us. With wreaths of sage on our heads and around our wrists, we danced, blowing rhythmically on our eaglebone whistles, making a sound like the twittering of a hundred birds. For three days we danced, staring at the blinding light of the sun, moving in a trance, seized with ecstacy.

On the fourth day we were pierced. It was Lame Deer who pierced me. With his pocket knife he made a slit in my chest above the heart and passed a wooden skewer through it. One end of the skewer was imbedded in my flesh; the other end was fastened to a long rawhide thong connected to the top of the sacred tree. A surge of elation made me forget the pain. At the end of the dance, the skewer ripped through my flesh as I tore myself free. I keep to myself for whom I made this sacrifice.

I have adopted the Sun Dance way of life. I have never regretted following it. My children are Anishinabe and Lakota: all Sun Dancers. It was one of the greatest moments in our lives when the Sun Dance and AIM became one.

CHAPTER 8

On the Warpath

There is a prophecy in our Ojibway religion that one day we would all stand together. All tribes would hook arms in brotherhood and unite. I am elated because I lived to see this happen. Brothers and sisters from all over this continent united in a single cause. That is the greatest signifi-cance to Indian people—not what happened or what yet may happen as a result of our actions.

—Eddie Benton-Banai, Ojibwa

As long as American Indians were polite and soft-spoken, and acted with decorum, they got nowhere. African American civil rights had been gained by protests. Clyde and I decided that in order to get any-where AIM had to become confrontational—confrontational but not violent. AIM walks with the Canupa, the sacred pipe of peace. If we were to put the pipe away and only carry the gun, our movement would come to nothing.

By 1969 I was completely absorbed in the study of American Indian struggles. I gathered up as much information as I could get my hands on—I could not get enough of it. Sometimes I would read on the sub-ject until two or three in the morning. I soon realized that the struggle for our land was at the heart of our many problems. In some areas, tribes were already fighting to get back territories that had been taken from them. The Pitt River Indians of Northern California were in the forefront with their struggle to reclaim their ancestral lands. Fights for

Native hunting and fishing rights were a part of these land struggles. I was determined that AIM should take part in this battle.

In November we heard of the takeover of the island of Alcatraz. Clyde Bellecourt called me at home and said, "Hey, DJ, did you hear the news tonight? A bunch of Indians occupied Alcatraz."

Alcatraz is an island in San Francisco Bay known as "the Rock." It was established as a federal prison in 1936 but closed down in 1963. When the Indians took it over it was an abandoned, uninhabited relic.

Clyde, George Mitchell, and I agreed, "Well, let's go!" We called the other AIM members for a meeting the next day, saying that we planned to go and support those people on the Rock. Somehow we scraped together the money for airfare.

Within the week, about fifteen of us arrived in San Francisco. It was around the end of November 1969. We called my friends Lehman and Trudie Brightman, who lived in the Bay Area. Lee was head of the United Native Americans and published a newspaper on Indian issues. He was a powerful speaker in those days. He arranged for a us to take a boat to Alcatraz to meet with the people out there. He loaned me his sleeping bag so that I could stay on the island for a few days. We would be joining American Indians from many different tribes and some Indian students from Berkeley. Those who had orchestrated the takeover of the island hoped to retain the massive, abandoned eyesore for an American Indian educational and cultural complex.

The government seemed to have little interest in Alcatraz until the occupation began, judging by how isolated, barren, and ominously stark it was. Indian people, however, were enthusiastic to restore the crumbling old relic. It seemed fitting somehow that this former prison should bene-fit Indian people, because among the first political prisoners incarcerated there was a group of Hopi fathers who refused to comply with the government's forced boarding-school practices. The Arizona boarding schools those men had opposed were part of the same oppressive system that had torn me and so many other Indian children away from their homes and families for their entire childhood. Those seventeen Hopi men stood up for their children in spite of the heavy consequences. The 1969 takeover of Alcatraz was a continuation of that "stand up" attitude for Indian empowerment.

The occupiers had a vision—on that naked pile of stones there were to be gardens and habitat for birds and animals. It was a great dream.

There wasn't an official leader of this occupation, although there were some remarkable people involved. The main spokesperson there was a Mohawk by the name of Richard Oakes. He had traveled the country studying the problems of various reservations and working as an activist whenever he was needed. An ironworker by trade, Richard then worked in the San Francisco Bay Area Indian community. He was a family man, easygoing and bright—a born leader. He was to pay a high price for his dedication to the demonstration on Alcatraz. His daughter, Yvonne, died on the island when she slipped and fell from an unfenced tier of the prison.

It was on Alcatraz that I first became acquainted with a young Santee Sioux poet and activist, John Trudell. He and his wife, Tina, had been working tirelessly on environmental issues and water conservation on reservation land. I was struck by John's eloquence. He had a way of cutting to the core of a problem. Clyde and I were glad when John joined AIM and became one of our leaders.

We met thirty or forty people on the island. We were given a tour of the whole place by some of the Indian security. I saw a subbasement where hard-core convicts had probably been confined. Behind a door with a tiny slit for observing prisoners was a dark, horrible space with a drainage hole in the middle. There was nothing else, not even a cot to lie on. There were six rooms like that one.

I decided to stay on the Rock for a couple of days. My bed was on the second tier of one of the cell blocks. It was extremely cold and damp at night. I thought about all the prisoners who had been caged in the cells at Alcatraz all those years. So many died there. How they must have suffered in the dampness and cold. I curled up that first night, and a chill went through my whole body. I went to sleep thinking about my confinement in the Minneapolis state prison system—how I had vowed never to go back to any prison after that. And here I was, sleeping in a cold cell intentionally.

I noticed right away that there was a lot of happiness amid those dripping walls. The comradeship was warm, people were high-spirited, and there were joyful sounds of drumming and singing. The occupation of Alcatraz lasted from November 1969 to June 1971, when the government took the island back by force, dragging Indians in handcuffs off the island. Alcatraz has since been made a tourist park.

When we returned to Minneapolis after spending a few days on the Rock, Clyde, George, and I talked about the need to be more aware of national affairs concerning Native issues. The winds of change were upon us. I could smell it and feel it. Our time on Alcatraz had woken us up to the realization that we were part of a larger movement and that the reclaiming of tribal land had to be on AIM's agenda. We planned to justify a series of takeovers with the Treaty of 1868, under which land that had fallen into disuse by the government would be available for Native people to reclaim.

Early one morning seventy of us took over an abandoned naval station at the northern edge of the Minneapolis/St. Paul International Airport. It was manned by only one security guard. We moved to occupy the empty buildings, knowing that we were in for a fight. Finally one morning a loud banging woke me. I had been sleeping in one of the small rooms downstairs. I looked outside to see a large number of marshals and police trying to knock down the doors. I ran to the third floor where the women and children were sleeping and woke them up. The women took care of evacuating the children.

Meanwhile, the police took over the first floor, forcing us to the second. By their sheer numbers, the police and marshals were able to take over the second floor. They just kept coming. We barricaded ourselves on the third floor, but soon there was a pitched battle between fists and clubs. I got hit from behind while I was fighting one man and started to rise again, dazed, when I got slammed again with a nightstick. I was out for the count. When I came to, I was being dragged from the building. Once I got back on my feet, I walked unaided to the paddy wagon. Clyde and Jerry Roy put up a hard fight against a half-dozen cops but were finally clubbed down. The wagon took us to the federal building in St. Paul.

There were some busted heads that day. We had some big lumps on our scalps. I had two. I remember sitting in the holding cell that day as the marshals taunted us with insults. The police had won this round, but in fact we could still laugh about it. Even on the way to jail we had been singing.

A similar takeover was led by my friend Herb Powless, chairman of AIM's Milwaukee chapter. With twenty-five of his people, he occupied another federal site—an abandoned coast guard station on Lake Michigan near McKinley Beach. Herb stressed to everyone that this was a peaceful takeover, but his group would not leave until forcibly removed. As I had done, Herb claimed the site under the Treaty of 1868. Milwaukee police arrived on the scene in two squad cars, but they promised to leave the AIM occupiers alone as long as everyone remained nonviolent.

A year later AIM still occupied that site. It had been converted into a halfway house for Indians with alcohol problems who were going through detox. There were eight permanent residents and the capacity to house many more. Also, AIM had established an Indian community school for elementary- and junior-high-aged children. It had ninety students. Herb remarked, "The only thing I regret is that we didn't take over a larger facility!"

We also made headlines with the 1970 occupation of Mt. Rushmore. That mountain is part of the sacred Black Hills and, according to legend, home of the Thunderbirds. Within the Black Hills are some of the holiest sites of both the Lakota and Cheyenne. To have the mountain defaced with the likenesses of Washington, Lincoln, Jefferson, and Roosevelt has been like rubbing salt in our wounds. For us the giant faces were the images of our conquerors, planted in the very heart of Indian country to mock us. This takeover was not started by AIM—it was the idea of three feisty Lakota ladies living in Rapid City, South Dakota. Richard Erdoes audiotaped two of them, Lizzy Fast Horse and Muriel Waukazoo, while they were on the mountain. They said:

> This idea of coming up here originated with us. We printed up some handbills about the movement to inform the reservation community of Pine Ridge what was happening. We took those handbills from home to home, telling people not to say anything about it. So the Indian population of Rapid City and the folks on the reservation knew about the occupation of Mount Rushmore a month before it happened, but the white people never knew about it. We just didn't let it out.

Lizzy Fast Horse went on to say:

There were only us three women. We thought other people were coming up, but they didn't. I guess they were scared. There was lightning all the way up, so we were thinking about Crazy Horse, and we knew he was with us. We were really scared that the rangers would arrest us. For a few days we were handing out handbills to the tourists below in the parking lot. But then Lee Brightman and a group of his people came up to support us. We got braver and braver, and now we're not afraid of anyone.

Lee Brightman's great-grandfather was killed at the Battle of the Little Bighorn, Custer's Last Stand. Lee took over the leadership on the mountain while medicine man John Fire Lame Deer became the group's spiritual guide. The group had grown to twenty-three. Besides Muriel Waukazoo and Lizzie Fast Horse, other Sioux women also climbed the sacred mountain. Among them were Ruth Hunsinger and her daughter, Davine, Minnie Two Shoes, Verna Gannon, and Jean Erdoes, Richard's wife. Everyone camped above and behind the carved heads in a little hollow surrounded by pines. Lizzy Fast Horse related:

We painted "Red Power—Indian Land" in large red letters on a big rock. We draped a huge flag with the words "Sioux Indian Power" over the forehead of one of the presidents. Pretty soon some rangers with flashlights came up and ordered us off the mountain. They were afraid that we would dump red paint on the faces of the presidents. We just laughed and said that that was a pretty good idea, come to think of it, and we scattered into the woods. There was a rumor that rangers up on top of the mountain had guns, so everybody hid out all night. The rangers occasionally tried to make an arrest but always without success. One of our young men told them, "If you arrest me, you will have to carry me all the way down."

The rangers gave up trying to arrest that young man. It was said that Wallace McCaw, superintendent of Mt. Rushmore National Monument, requested a company of armed forest rangers to defend him. He said he believed that "the AIM radicals wanted to put their feet on my desk." A story from that time is still told about how some of the guys occupying Mt. Rushmore formed a human chain by holding unto one another for dear life so that the one at the end could pee on Teddy Roosevelt's nose in a gesture of contempt and defiance. That part of the protest was a "for men only" party.

Lame Deer had brought an eagle feather staff, and a few AIM members scrambled up to the highest point of this so-called "Shrine to Democracy." Chuggy Fast Horse hammered the staff into a crack in the highest rock, thereby reclaiming the Black Hills for the Lakota people.

A reporter from the *Rapid City Journal* asked Lame Deer, "What is the significance of this staff?"

Lame Deer replied, "The lower part of the staff is painted black, which stands for night and darkness. It is the black face paint of war. It means that I am putting a blanket over the mountain by painting this staff. These president's faces are shrouded and dirty until the treaties concerning the Black Hills are fulfilled. The upper part of the staff is red, which represents the sun, the day's light, and the red face paint of gladness. It means that this land someday will be ours again."

After that Lame Deer renamed Mt. Rushmore, "Crazy Horse Mountain." Later a few others, among them Russell Means, John Trudell, and I, made our stand on the four bald, monster heads. By then most of the original group had left.

The protest on top of Mt. Rushmore only made the local news. The first big splash AIM made nationwide was the "Plymouth Rock and *Mayflower II* Demonstration." This event was originally the idea of Frank James and other Wampanoag Indians who had proclaimed Thanksgiving as a day of mourning for American Indians. James was president of a federation of New England tribes. He intended to use the 350th anniversary of the Pilgrims' landing, which would insure a large crowd, to demonstrate in a "dignified and responsible manner" in order to draw attention to the repression and poverty of American Indians. This was to be done by members of the local tribes—the Wampanoags, Narragansets, and Passamaquoddies—who had been, as Russell Means put it, the "first victims of the Wrath of the Wasp." The Wampanoags had invited AIM to come and help make this a really big protest, and, of course, we came.

On this occasion the AIM group was led by Russell Means, Clyde Bellecourt, John Trudell, Floyd Westerman, and me. It happened on November 26, 1976, and turned out to be not quite as "dignified" as

Frank James expected. AIM lent the event a distinctively militant flavor. We made sure that we made an impact. The action began when some three hundred Indians from about twenty tribes gathered around the statue of Massasoit, chief of the Wampanoags, on a hill overlooking Plymouth Rock and the harbor.

We made some fiery speeches. Frank James shouted, "We want people to know that the Pilgrims stole our corn and that all that love and brotherhood stuff between Indians and white settlers is a lie!" I called the Pilgrims' landing the greatest land grab in history. At the same time, local whites held their annual *Pilgrim's Progress* parade and feast.

A replica of the *Mayflower II*, which brought the first English people to New England, was anchored not far away. I told Russ, "With all the attention on what is going on here, let's go and take over that ship!" As about thirty of us swarmed up one gangplank, a crowd of terrified tourists ran down the other. It was easy to take the *Mayflower* because there was nobody guarding her. Bill Miller, an Indian from Michigan, lowered the old British royal banner. Somebody else hauled down the American flag and rehoisted it AIM-style—upside down.

I climbed up the rigging as high as I could go, all the way to the top of the mast. I made a speech from the crow's nest to the crowd that had gathered at the wharf. Then we noticed the life-sized figures of Pilgrims placed here and there on the upper deck. A dummy of the captain was sitting near the wheel. Clyde grabbed it and climbed up the mast to where I was perched. As he took hold of one arm and I of the other, Clyde yelled, "Here is the captain of the *Mayflower*. You can have him!" We flung the dummy into the sea, where it bobbed up and down. At the same time, our young AIM men began throwing more of the Pilgrim dummies overboard. Down below people were clapping and cheering.

The dumping of the dummies brought a dozen policemen on the scene, eager to clear the ship. We did not give them much of an argument. I did not want anybody hurt, and we had already made our point. We had held the ship for two full hours. We had made history—we had made our most famous symbolic gesture by taking over the *Mayflower II* in the name of the American Indian Movement.

After that, Russell Means staged another media event as only he could. As the headlines in the Boston Globe put it, "INDIANS DUMP SAND ON PLYMOUTH ROCK!" Russell, with the help of Clyde and Slow

Turtle, together with some Wampanoags and AIM people, spoiled a planned Thanksgiving feast by burying Plymouth Rock under several feet of sand from the beach. We had about twenty people with shovels working until the whole rock was covered. Russ summed it up by telling a crowd of reporters and onlookers, "This is a new kind of Boston Tea Party. Only this time the Indians are for real!" Later on that night, John Trudell and few others sneaked in again and painted old Plymouth Rock bright red.

Next after Russ's speech, we marched to Plymouth Plantation, where the locals were running around dressed up like seventeenth-century Pilgrims. We spoiled their little costume ball by walking into the big dining hall and creating a scene. One man, who seemed to be the "head Pilgrim," asked his unexpected guests to sit down and take part in their turkey dinner. I was angry, knowing that this "feast of brotherhood" was in reality a celebration of the Pilgrims, armed with matchlock guns and steel weapons, killing peaceful Wampanoag Indians.

I yelled, "We won't eat this crap!" and grabbed one end of a long table covered with plates of food. I gave it a heave and turned it upside down, spilling plates, bowls, glasses, bottles, and a lot of turkey wings and drumsticks on the floor. Floyd and Russ did the same. At this, the Pilgrims lost their composure. It was quite a party, and we got our message across.

Later, after all the commotion I heard a little boy at a Pilgrim parade ask his mother, "Where have all the Indians gone?"

"Oh, they're not part of it," she told him.

CHAPTER 9

Yellow Thunder

The dark agony of a silent man was suddenly transformed into an issue an entire nation must face.

—The *Nishnawbe News*

On Valentine's Day 1972 in the city of Gordon, Nebraska, a fifty-one-year-old Lakota man, Raymond Yellow Thunder, was beaten to death "just for the fun of it." Leslie and Melvin Hare, two white sons of a wealthy rancher, grabbed Raymond from the street and beat him to the ground. They dragged him into the Gordon American Legion Post No. 34, where a dance was in progress. The Hare brothers stripped Raymond Yellow Thunder naked from the waist down and forced him to dance at gunpoint to provide "entertainment" for the crowd. Then the Hare brothers beat him again. They were joined by two other men: Bernard Ludder and Robert Bayless.

As the manager of the Legion Post later testified, "Leslie tromped him good."

Then the brothers invited the spectators to participate, saying, "Go ahead and hit him. It's fun!"

One of the white women thought it would indeed be fun and got in on the act. After a while, people got bored with beating and kicking Yellow Thunder and gawking at his nakedness, so the Hare brothers dragged him back out to the street again. On February 20, Raymond Yellow Thunder's dead body was discovered stuffed into the trunk of the Hares' car. According to one report, Raymond's body was found inside his own pickup truck.

The Hare brothers were arrested on second degree manslaughter, a charge for which nobody in that part of the state had ever spent a day in jail—if the victim were an Indian. The brothers were immediately released without bail pending trial. Raymond's relatives were denied their right to view the body, which had been quickly sealed in a coffin without any preparation for burial. The prosecutor called the brutal murder "a cruel practical joke done by pranksters." He also referred to the killing as an "incident."

When Raymond's relatives pried open the sealed coffin, it was found that his brain had swelled badly from bleeding and that his body bore marks of having been beaten with fists, boots, and a heavy instrument such as a hammer or tire iron. The prosecutor remarked, "It wasn't as bad as they made it out to be. He wasn't castrated."

To that, an Indian woman replied, "Oh, is Raymond Yellow Thunder still alive then?" The case might have been dismissed like so many other crimes against Indians had AIM not stepped in.

Raymond Yellow Thunder was a kind and humble man. He was a member of the Oglala Sioux tribe and a grandson of the famous chief, American Horse, who had fought Custer at the Little Bighorn. Raymond loved kids and would often baby-sit the children of his relatives. He worked as a ranch hand near Gordon but spent the weekends at Porcupine, South Dakota, on the Pine Ridge reservation. On these occasions he always brought bags of groceries for his little nephews and nieces, even though he had little money and none to spare. He was loved by all who knew him, but no one in a position of authority made an effort to bring his murderers to justice. His three sisters wanted his body exhumed. They wanted the Hare brothers to stand trial for murder. But to the authorities, Raymond Yellow Thunder was just another dead Indian. Neither the Oglala Tribal Council nor the FBI was interested in pursuing the case.

AIM was holding an Indian leadership conference in Omaha, Nebraska, when the news of Yellow Thunder's murder came in. One of Raymond's sisters who lived on the reservation at Porcupine had a nephew named Severt Young Bear, a great singer who later became an outstanding member of the Movement. He decided to come to us for help. At the same time, Birgil Kills Straight, another Pine Ridge man, called us to say that the men who had murdered Raymond Yellow Thunder were still running around free. All of the AIM members who were present decided right then to put our hearts and all of our resources into getting justice for this murdered man. We formed a caravan on the spot, filling two buses and some cars. We started toward Pine Ridge, picking up more people on the way.

As we were traveling from Omaha to Pine Ridge, I thought about how much I wanted to present myself and my AIM companions to the people in a way they would remember. I dressed up for the occasion with a concho headband that was to become a trademark for me. I announced that I wanted everybody to be dressed well. A couple of times I got on the bus's P.A. system and said, "This is Dennis. I want you to look good and proud when we get to the rez."

When we arrived at Pine Ridge, we held a big meeting. The place we were in was packed to overflowing with Pine Ridge Oglalas, AIM people, and Indians from other nearby tribes. We were treated to a hero's welcome. I told the crowd that we would no longer tolerate being abused and murdered. I said:

> If AIM cannot protect our people, it might just as well pack up and disappear. The attitude of white rednecks in South Dakota and northwest Nebraska is that they can kill an Indian just on a whim and get away with it. But they should know *now* that if they point a gun at us and pull the trigger, somebody might get it into his head to shoot back. AIM will take any and all steps to ensure justice for our people. We are prepared to die in this cause.

We had a discussion on whether to go to Gordon armed or unarmed. AIM's spiritual leader, Leonard Crow Dog, held an all-night ceremony. He said that the spirits had told him to carry the Sacred Pipe instead of the gun, to go to Gordon with the power of Indian sacredness. We all agreed on that.

We started out for Gordon, Nebraska, from Porcupine, South Dakota, on March 6, 1972. First, Crow Dog prayed and sprinkled sacred gopher dust over us—the same medicine Crazy Horse had always used before going into battle to make himself bulletproof. Then our caravan got moving. It consisted of one chartered bus and about two hundred cars. It was a sight to be seen—our biggest demonstration yet.

As we neared Gordon, panic spread among its white citizens. As one newspaper put it, "they went bananas." Out of the town's population of two thousand, more than two hundred residents jumped into their cars and trucks and fled. Some of those who fled locked and barricaded their stores and houses, others left their homes wide open with their breakfast still warm on the kitchen table. We had alerted these folks that we were coming—peacefully. We had called the Justice Department in Washington, D.C., the governor of Nebraska, the BIA, and Gordon's city fathers. We also called the Highway Patrol to escort us into town. Our caravan went down Broadway and made its way through the business district. The streets were empty, though there was a small cluster of men throwing beer cans and bottles at us. We ignored a firecracker that one of them tossed in our direction.

Some local Indians had parked an old flatbed truck in an empty parking lot next to a concrete platform. We used this to set up our microphones and loudspeakers. We spoke to the crowd that had gathered and to the press. We took over the town hall and the mayor's office without any opposition. We impaneled an ad hoc grand jury to hear complaints from Lakota men and women. One juror was a ten-year-old boy because we wanted kids to be part of the proceedings. As a result of negotiations, all agreed that a Gordon Human Relations Council would be created in which both the Indian and non-Indian communities of Gordon would be equally represented.

One of our priorities was dealing with police brutality. We offered proof of constant harassment of Indians by law enforcement officers that was routinely ignored or dismissed without investigation. For example, several Indian women accused a police officer named John Paul of raping Native girls. One of the women stated, "He waits outside the cafe for any Indian woman, follows her for about a block, forces her into his police car, and takes her two or three miles out of town. Then he abuses her." Marvin Ghost Bear spoke of one incident where an Indian girl was brought into jail by officer John Paul, who tried to fondle her. When she resisted his advances, John Paul took her into a cell where Marvin could hear her crying and screaming for help. He could do nothing because he was locked up himself. As a result of pressure from AIM, the mayor and the chief of police agreed to fire this man.

For Indians, conditions in local jails and hospitals were atrocious. Schools were bad also. As boys grew their hair long and braided it, teachers beat and harassed them. We elicited a long list of complaints. State and local officials listened to us, agreeing to put things right. We got a promise that Indian teenagers who were charged only with misdemeanors would not be placed in jail with adult criminals. We set up a phone chain, enabling us to keep track of offenses against Indians and take prompt action when needed. An agreement was signed whereby a federal grand jury would thoroughly investigate Raymond Yellow Thunder's murder.

I felt that we had won a victory. Whites and Lakotas celebrated the beginning of a new era of understanding between us in the Gordon auditorium. Severt Young Bear came with his Porcupine Singers. He brought the drum and his singers to the center of the dance floor. Among the songs was one that grabbed me and made my heart beat faster. It had no words and did not need any. Severt told me that nobody knew exactly who had first performed the song, but he was sure it was a young Oglala boy in his mid-teens. Later that song became our famous AIM song. Crow Dog said, "The sacred power of the eagle is in this song. Thunder power resides in the drum. It represents the sacred hoop."

The trial for the murder of Raymong Yellow Thunder was held at Alliance, Nebraska. Leslie Hare was sentenced to six years in jail, and his brother, Melvin, got two years, both on a charge of manslaughter. The Hare brothers should have received the ten-year sentence prescribed by law for their crime. Still, without AIM they would have gone free without serving a single day. All across the country AIM was given credit for fighting for the rights of Indians everywhere when no one else had the courage to do so.

The march on Gordon changed things for Lakota people, for AIM, for American Indians everywhere. It issued a warning to racists in the whiskey towns surrounding the reservation that if they killed an Indian, they would be tried and jailed. AIM would make sure of that. And so we were elated. Among the Lakota people, many felt that Gordon was a turning point, that Indians didn't have to take the abuse anymore. Hundreds of them joined AIM. As Mary Crow Dog put it, "Gordon was flint striking flint, lighting a spark that grew into a flame at which we could warm ourselves after a long, cold winter."

We had to bury Raymong Yellow Thunder in a ceremonial way. We talked to his sisters. They said, "We don't want him to be buried by a white man." We all agreed that he should be put to rest in Porcupine, a place he loved and where he had made his home for a long time. Leonard Crow Dog, as AIM's spiritual leader, was the right man to bury Raymond in a traditional manner. Crow Dog said:

> I'll help you. This must be done in the ancient Lakota way. I'll bury him here so that he stays with us and his soul will help us in the way of the spirits. In the old days we put our dead in the crotch of a sacred cottonwood tree to let the wind and the rain take care of them. We can't do that anymore. Raymond will turn to dust. He will always watch over us. We will sing together for his soul, and we will put a plate of spirit food out so that he should not go hungry on his way to another world.

More than a thousand people came to witness Raymond Yellow Thunder's last rites. Clyde Bellecourt, Russell Means, Herb Powless, and I were the pall bearers. Crow Dog planted a feathered staff with an eagle plume in front of the open grave. He anointed Yellow Thunder's face with sacred red paint and prayed to the sacred four directions. Four times he blew the eaglebone whistle. Then we smoked the pipe and its smoke rose up to the sky—Great Spirit's Breath.

On a hill east of Porcupine, we gave Raymond Yellow Thunder back to the earth. George Eagle Elk, a Lakota medicine man, chanted the honoring song. All those who were Lakotas joined in, just as the sun went down. It was AIM's first traditional burial.

It was during the Yellow Thunder protests that I met the love of my life, the woman who became my companion during the days when our lives hung in the balance, when we often did not know whether we would see another sunrise. Her name is Darlene Nichols, but everyone calls her Kamook, a nickname her mother gave her that is actually the name of a famous Japanese sumo wrestler. She became my wife and gave me four daughters and a son. Kamook is a Lakota from Pine Ridge. I was thirty-two and she a girl of seventeen still in high school when we met.

When my AIM companions and I had first arrived in Pine Ridge, nearly a week before the caravan left for Gordon, Nebraska, we were invited for a big feed by Kamook's aunt, Lou Bean, a wonderful, feisty Oglala woman who became an outstanding AIM member. Lou served up a big meal of turkey and a lot of fry bread. She told us we could stay at her house until we left for Gordon, so I spent four days at her place. That evening some of Lou's relatives, including Kamook and her sister, Bernice, came over with a lot of pies. I thought the two were among the most beautiful girls I had ever seen. Kamook and I talked to each other about high school, AIM, our lives. I was not making a move on her but there was a subconscious stirring, a spark, some awareness or awakening within me. I dropped her off at her home that evening. I told her I was going to Gordon but would be back. She asked me, "Will you really come back?"

I said, "Yes, definitely."

I saw her a few times before and after Gordon. She asked questions, wanting to know about AIM, about our struggles. We held hands as we talked. Kamook graduated from high school, and I went back to Pine Ridge to see her. I kissed her then for the first time and I knew this was the woman I wanted to be with. Kamook, too, had fallen in love, not so much with me as with a speech I had made at the Billy Mills Hall at Pine Ridge. She told me that she had been hungry for that kind of words—words that she had never heard before. She was a tower of strength for me, sharing the good as well as the bad and taking incredible risks during the years we were together. She would have died for our cause. She almost did.

Kamook joined me and my AIM friends, taking long trips with us. It became apparent that she and I were teaming up. We decided that we had to be up front about our relationship, so we told her dad and mom. At first her mother was not very happy about it. She told Kamook, "Why are you going out with an older man? It's not going to work." In the end they gave us their blessing. I became part of Kamook's extended family, the kind of family I had never before known.

CHAPTER 10

Fishing in Troubled Waters

The whites stole the whole country. Sure as hell they did. They stole the air, the grass, whatever they could get their hands on. Why should we go on licking their damn butts? I'm getting old and cranky, so I say anything that runs through my mind.

—Martha Grass, Ponca

In May 1970, at Cass Lake on my own reservation, a confrontation took place between us and the whites living on our land that almost turned into a shooting war. The conflict had simmered for more than a year before it finally exploded. The state of Minnesota had always acted against our people and in favor of whites who had bought land on our reservation—vacation-home owners, storekeepers, tourists, and the so-called sportsmen, deer hunters and anglers. The state enforced rules and regulations that destroyed our people's livelihood by forcing us to take out hunting and fishing licenses and deciding for us how much game and fish we should be allowed to take.

Our tribal council finally challenged the state in court and won the case. A U.S. district court judge ruled that we had retained our "aboriginal rights" and should be entitled to hunt, fish, and gather wild rice without any regulations from the state of Minnesota. He also ruled that the tribe had the right to control non-Indian hunting and fishing on the reservation.

This caused an uproar among whites in and around the rez. White homeowners, storekeepers, and restaurant workers began arming themselves in "defense of their interests." They twisted the governor's arm, making him appeal the federal court's decision. Cass County joined his appeal, and white bureaucrats resumed trampling on our rights. The appeal meant that they would bring in deputies and sheriffs who would patrol the lakes to insure that no Indian would be allowed to fish without a license issued by the Department of Natural Resources. We maintained that, according to federal law, we didn't need a license, but Cass County said, "You do need one, and we'll arrest anyone who comes to the lake without it."

In April I got a call from Dave Munnel, our tribal chairman. He said, "Dennis, in about a month from now the fishing season will open, and we're going to have some trouble with these white people up here. It's going to be real bad this time. We need some help."

We were talking on the phone, so I said, "Dave, we need to meet privately," because I was afraid that my line might be tapped. We did meet—Dave, Clyde Bellecourt, and I. We agreed that AIM would come up and make sure that Indians got on those lakes to fish without a license. We would be the security for the fishermen of the tribe. I issued a call to our chapters to come to Cass Lake. We had a huge gathering there a week before the start of the fishing season.

A very nasty deputy by the nickname of Big Red, who used to beat up on Indian people, had just become sheriff. As a deputy he had used his long stick to push Indian people around. He would poke old people in the chest with his nightstick. At the gathering, I warned our people that we would face him, his deputies, and probably also a bunch of vigilantes who would try to keep us from going to the lakes. As many as three hundred armed AIM members came to Cass Lake from Minnesota, Wisconsin, Michigan, and the Dakotas. We held a press conference, where we announced that we would not allow our people to be prevented from going on with their traditional fishing. After the press conference we showed off our weapons, demonstrating to everybody that we meant business and that we would be out there marching.

The sheriff immediately asked for a meeting with Dave Munnel. Afterward, Dave came out to our camp. He told me, "Dennis, the sheriff said that they're going to arrest your people if you come to town, if you are driving around, or if you are armed." I told our people what the sheriff of Cass County intended to do. We thanked Dave and he left. We did not want him to participate in our planning. He knew that as a tribal official he should stand aside from what we would do. He could not risk being involved with AIM. After he was gone, I told everybody that we were going to march the next morning to Cass Lake, that we would have our arms with us for all to see, and that we would give the press something to write about.

The next morning an assistant of the governor came to see us and asked us not to march on Cass Lake with arms. He wanted to know if there was some way we would call off our plans. I told him we would call things off if the state would back away from its position. He said they could not do that. I said, "Then we are going to walk." All afternoon we had negotiations with the governor over the phone. The sheriff tried to butt in, insisting that he should have a part in the negotiations. I said that there was nothing this sheriff could ever negotiate with us and that we would never deal with him. Finally the governor suggested that the Minnesota Chippewa Tribes should meet with him that afternoon to see what could be done.

In the evening, Dave came out to our camp to tell us the news—AIM had not been invited to the governor's meeting. Dave said the state of Minnesota had agreed that Indians could fish without a license within the boundaries of the Leech Lake reservation. I said, "Well, we didn't gain anything. That was ours from the beginning. They tried to take it away from us, but there are still other violations of our rights that have to be addressed. So tomorrow morning we still are going to walk."

In the meantime the white resort owners tried to get into the act. They sent a representative to tell Dave Munnel, "What you Indians are doing is spreading fear among our community."

Dave answered, "We have always lived in fear for the past four hundred years."

At the same time they published pamphlets, saying, "Radicals, leftist activists, and ex-convicts using communist tactics are working among American Indians to promote serious trouble in Minnesota. They are using the same kind of tactics pioneered by Martin Luther King and other racist agitators." We replied that we were proud to be compared with Dr. King. Then they threatened us, saying that they were also armed and would resist us with force if we marched to Cass Lake.

I called their bluff and announced that eviction notices were being issued to four thousand non-Indians on the Leech Lake reservation. All businessmen and property owners would be asked to vacate their property on the reservation within sixty days. No leases would be renewed. We also blocked all access roads to Cass Lake. I was pretty sure the resort owners would not dare face us in a showdown.

March we did, the following morning. We marched down to the lake, about three hundred strong, everybody carrying a rifle. We walked right through the town, turned around, and walked back the way we had come to our camp. Nobody dared stop us. No one was arrested. The harassment of our people stopped that day. In the end we made an agreement—the whites would be subject to state game laws, but the tribe would enforce its own laws among its own people.

The worst problem I saw, however, was not the clash between white and red but the clashes among ourselves. I was worried about the lack of self-discipline and the tendency toward self-indulgence in our own ranks. I said that we must behave in a serious way if we wanted others to take us seriously, and that anyone using alcohol or drugs should be removed from AIM leadership. I insisted that the continuous partying had to stop, that junkies, winos, groupies, and Saturday-night warriors had to go. I thought I would have overwhelming support on this, but I was wrong. I was outvoted. I did not want to believe it.

One of our members in a high leadership position told me, "Who are you to tell me what I can put in my mouth or what I can swallow? That's white man's shit." Another accused me of wanting to indiscriminately purge the Movement. Even Clyde told me:

Dennis, you've made a tactical mistake. AIM is an organization of young people. In their white man's schools and foster homes they were told endlessly how to behave themselves—be sober, comb your hair, save your money, don't give it away, wear a necktie, don't sleep around, that's a sin, and so on and on. They were forced to live according to the white man's standard of behavior. AIM came and liberated them from all that bullshit, taught them to be wild, free, and unafraid. Then here you come telling them, "Behave yourselves!"

We were both right, but my speech created a big controversy and a temporary split among the AIM leadership. I was so angry that I thought of leaving AIM and founding another organization. I am now glad my friends persuaded me not to leave. The split did not last long. Our struggles were just beginning. New challenges awaited us and soon we were united again in a common cause. AIM was turning into an Indian rights fire brigade. Wherever Native people were in trouble, AIM was called in to help. One AIM member complained, "All these tribes and groups are using us."

I replied, "That is as it should be. It's our job to be used. That's what we're here for."

CHAPTER 11

One Hell of a Smoke Signal

We will not leave this building of injustice. We are prepared to die right here. Our women and children have taken this risk for 482 years. They are used to it. The police are waiting to storm the building. They are listening to our drums. They are welcome.

—Floyd Young Horse, Lakota

The idea was born on a beautiful sunlit day at Crow Dog's Paradise on the Rosebud Sioux reservation. It was August 17, 1972, shortly after the annual Sun Dance, the most sacred of all Plains Indian ceremonies. A few of us, Lakotas and AIM members, were sitting under the pine-branch-covered arbor of the dance circle. Some of us had pierced our chests in giving flesh offerings to the Creator; our wounds were still fresh. We talked about our lack of power, our inability to run our own lives, and about how the Bureau of Indian Affairs in Washington, D.C., still ruled over our tribes and treated us as wards of the government. We felt that something had to be done, something big, to get us out from under the heel of the government.

And so the idea of a great Indian march to Washington was born. It is said that Robert Burnette, ex-marine and twice chairman of the Rosebud Tribe, first thought of it. But in a medicine way, the idea of such a march had been stirring in the minds of a half-dozen American Indian leaders. As I remember it, it was Bob Burnette who gave the march its name, "The Trail of Broken Treaties."

Presidential elections were coming up in November. We hoped that after we arrived in Washington, we could persuade both presidential candidates to make a commitment to American Indian independence. The caravan would be the biggest undertaking that Indians had ever made. It would require the cooperation of many tribes, organizations, and persons in leadership positions. We decided to have a large meeting soon in Denver, Colorado, with as many participants as possible to make the idea born at Crow Dog's Paradise a reality.

During the second half of September, a number of involved persons came together at the New Albany Hotel in Denver to carry our plan a step further. Our meeting happened at just the right time and the right place. A number of other Indian groups were already in town having their own meetings and conventions—the National Indian Brotherhood from Canada, the National Indian Lutheran Board, the National Indian Committee on Alcohol and Drug Abuse, and others. Bob Burnette, Reuben Snake, Vernon and Clyde Bellecourt, Russell Means, George Mitchell, and I were there. Many American Indians who had come to discuss issues of Indian people both on and off the reservation were staying at the New Albany Hotel. We had three hundred people upstairs to help decide how to organize this march.

I felt that three hundred were too many to agree on anything, so I gathered a smaller group of some thirty people downstairs for a strategy session on the ways and means. We had to decide on the main purpose of our march. The group resolved to present the government with a number of demands to meet our basic, most important grievances.

We also had to name the people who would be in charge. We elected two cochairmen—Bob Burnette and Reuben Snake, who was a Winnebago from Nebraska, an AIM member, and director of National Indian Leadership Training. Anita Collins, a Paiute-Shoshone from Nevada who was AIM's national news editor, was elected secretary, and LaVonna Weller, a Caddo lady from Oklahoma and first woman president of the National Indian Youth Council, became treasurer.

Finally the question of how the march was to be organized had to be settled. I suggested a caravan starting from the west coast, winding its way across the country, and ending up in Washington, D.C. In the end we had three large caravans starting from different points to join up in Minneapolis for a last-minute strategy session, which was to last four days. Then the caravan would begin the final leg of its trip to Washington. Clyde Bellecourt was appointed to handle the logistics for the caravans as they entered Minneapolis.

One caravan led by Sid Mills, a young Yakima Indian and decorated veteran who had been badly wounded in Vietnam, was to start out from Seattle, Washington. Sid had previous experience from organizing a fight for Indian fishing rights at Frank's Landing near Puget Sound. Another leader of this caravan was Hank Adams, an Assiniboine and founder of the Survival of American Indians Association. He had been shot and almost killed by white racists the previous year while he helped Indians in their fishing rights struggle on the Nisqually River. Russ Means was the third leader of this caravan. Once their caravan reached South Dakota, it would join a caravan from San Francisco, California, led by me.

A third trail from Los Angeles, California, would be led by my old friend Bill Sargent, an Ojibwa, and by Rod Skenandore, an Oneida. Their group would come through reservations in the Southwest, all the way to Oklahoma, then join the other two caravans at St. Paul, Minnesota. I insisted that all caravans stop at as many reservations as possible, picking up people who would join the Trail. We later found that we had stopped at no less than thirty-three reservations. The trail people also visited sacred or historic sites such as Wounded Knee.

At the end of that planning session in Denver, I emphasized the spiritual aspect the Trail must have. Each caravan should be led by a medicine man carrying the sacred pipe and drum. Drums would beat night and day to remind America of the 372 treaties that had been broken.

After the planning meeting, I drove with a friend to San Francisco to organize things there. We had to find our own funding to get things started. On our way we stopped at various towns and told people that we would be passing through again with the caravan. We asked, "Can you give us some help? Can you put us up overnight? Can you feed us?" We made contacts along the way wherever we could. I planned to come with a drum so that we could sing some songs and have blanket dances along the way to raise gas money.

When we reached San Francisco, we headed directly to the Indian Center. There I met Dave Chief and Gail Running Crane, seventeen, from Montana. They asked if they could join the caravan. I said, "You are too young. You have to get your parents' permission." Many other young people at the center were determined to join the caravan. A number of these teenage activists proved their enthusiasm for our cause by getting permission from their parents to make the cross-country trip. Meanwhile, I kept in touch with Russ Means in Seattle and Bill Sargent in Los Angeles to see how they were doing.

We left San Francisco on October 6 in a caravan of five cars crammed with people, many of them young and traveling with their parents' blessings. I felt like a mother hen as I tried to keep our little caravan together and moving without losing a car. Our first stop was Dekanawida-Quetzalcoatl University at Davis, California. They made us feel welcome and held a big dance, where we took up a collection. We were soon on our way to Reno, Nevada, where we talked with a lot of Indian people and picked up a few more cars for our caravan. Then we continued to Winnemucca, Nevada, to Stanley Snake's place and had a sweat and pipe ceremony there. By that time we had ten cars in our caravan.

Each time we stopped, I would check with Russ and Bill to see where they were. Bill was off to a slow start, but Russ was moving along. My caravan arrived in Salt Lake City, Utah, to a large welcoming crowd of students, among them fifty or so Indians. One was a striking Navajo girl named Angie Begay. Later on, she and I would form a relationship from which would be born a beautiful daughter, Ariel.

We went to the Mormon Church and made an unsuccessful plea for a good-sized amount of money to support the Trail. Our delegation was denied admission and locked out of the Mormon Tabernacle. Such treatment was not surprising considering that for centuries, Mormonism had defined the indigenous people of North America as "godless savages." Many Mormons thought Indians were unfit to bring up their own kids and, for decades, these people ripped Indian children from the arms of their parents to be brought up properly by "good Mormon, God-fearing parents." For this reason, in some tribes Mormons are called "child stealers." AIM demanded money from the Mormon Church as reparation for the suffering it had inflicted on Indians.

At about the same time that we were asking the Mormon Church for some help, the National Park Service was refusing the request of Russ and his people to erect a cast-iron plaque honoring the Lakota and Cheyenne warriors who died during the Battle of the Little Bighorn on the Custer Battlefield in Montana.

As my group left Salt Lake City, we picked up some more cars and then we all drove south to the Ute reservation. There more people joined us, increasing our caravan to twenty cars. Our growing caravan wound its way to Denver, where a big powwow was held for us, then headed north into Wyoming. From there we drove on to Pine Ridge where Dicky Wilson, the tribal chairman, had declared "open season on all AIM members daring to set foot on" *his* reservation. We, of course, drove into Pine Ridge anyway, and we picked up more people. While we were there, we heard that the northern group had already come all the way up to Pine Ridge and would meet us over at Wounded Knee. We had stopped on the side of the road when somebody at the tail end of our caravan started hollering and waving his arms around—he had seen Russell's wagon train coming. We all converged at Wounded Knee in forty-five vehicles of all kinds.

A woman came up to me and pointed down toward the ravine where in 1890 so many helpless Lakota women and children had been massacred by the Seventh Cavalry, Custer's old outfit. "If you go there at night," she told me, "you can hear the ghosts of those murdered people wailing." I believed her.

More and more Lakota people arrived at Wounded Knee— Leonard Crow Dog, AIM's spiritual leader, came in from Rosebud with about a dozen people. Frank Fools Crow, the oldest and most respected among the Lakota medicine men, arrived from Kyle on the Pine Ridge reservation. Chief Red Cloud also came in from Pine Ridge, while Leonard Peltier joined us from Turtle Mountain in North Dakota. From the little hamlet of He Dog came seventeen-year-old Mary Ellen Moore, who later at Wounded Knee would give birth to a baby boy. Old grandfathers and grandmothers came; young women with small children came.

The Trail of Broken Treaties had snowballed beyond our wildest expectations. By the time we left Wounded Knee, our caravan had grown to eighty-five cars with more than three hundred people straggling over miles of highway. We didn't know then that four months later we would be back at the Knee under very different circumstances.

When we got close to Minneapolis, the Oklahoma column merged with ours. On our way through Minneapolis, all the different caravans finally came together. We had a big meeting in St. Paul chaired by Reuben Snake. One hundred and fifty tribes were represented. We put together a number of working groups to write position papers. Out of these we formulated our final demands—the famous Twenty Points, which we intended to deliver to President Nixon.

During the four days we were in Minneapolis, we held a half-hour drumming and singing rally that blocked all traffic on Fifth Avenue. There was a big building under construction in the vicinity. There were cheers and laughter from our group when we saw a crane operator put up a large sign on the twentieth floor. It read, "CUSTER HAD IT COMING."

We chose Bob Burnette, George Mitchell, and Anita Collins to precede us in order to make arrangements for food and shelter, as well as to enlist support among civil rights groups, church organizations, and especially among politicians and government officials. Russ, Clyde, and I were supposed to keep the caravans moving and prevent straggling, which was not an easy task.

Our four-mile-long caravan made its entry into Washington, D.C., during the pre-dawn hours of November 2, 1972. We had asked for a police escort but did not get it. We decided that, before doing anything else, we would make a "wake-up call" at the White House. We drove through downtown Washington with about sixty cars, honking and tooting as loudly as we could. We got to the White House around 6:00 A.M. and circled it. We put out a six-man drum and raised our voices in a war song, letting Nixon know that we had arrived, then drove into the capitol city still blowing our horns. We got our police escort in a hurry.

We were all dog-tired. Most of us had driven all night. I had not slept in twenty-four hours and could hardly keep my eyes open. We just had to get a few hours sleep. We had been promised good accommodations and plenty of food, but things went wrong. Somebody led us to a church. Before we entered, Leonard Peltier pointed at something at our feet—a dead, run-over rat. Some welcome mat! We were told to go down into the basement, where we spread our bedrolls in the dark. I had hardly relaxed when I felt something crawling over me. At first I thought it was a cat, then I saw that it was a *rat*—the biggest I had ever seen. They were all over the room. "There are *rats* down here!" One woman screamed that a rat had bitten her baby on the arm. A young girl yelled, "There not only are a lot of rats down here, but thousands of cockroaches too!" An elderly Ojibwa lady complained to me that the toilets were broken.

We had people in wheelchairs and on crutches with us, and there was no place comfortable for them to rest. Martha Grass, a feisty Ponca woman from Oklahoma, mother of eleven and grandmother of fifteen, came to me with a young boy she had brought along. They were shivering. She said, "Here it is November, and there is no heat. Over at the BIA, those bureaucrats are warming their asses on soft upholstered chairs. They have beautiful offices where they sit comfortably behind big, shiny desks and never do a damn thing for us." She went on, "They want us to starve to death or freeze. I'm tired of being kicked around. To hell with it!"

Clyde said, "This is worse than the worst slum in St. Paul."

Bob Burnette was angry as hell. He said that he had gotten so many promises of help and good accommodations from organizations and individuals, but they had all reneged on their word. He knew it was because of pressure from the government.

Clyde said, "Enough of this bullshit! Let's get out of here! Let's go have a talk with the BIA!"

The Bureau of Indian Affairs building was the logical place to go. It seemed as though all of us automatically drifted to that place. The building itself was a large, four-story chunk of white marble in the so-called "federal style," like most government buildings in Washington. Broad stairs led up to an imposing, triple-entrance portal. It stood on Constitution Avenue at Nineteenth Street, just a few blocks away from the White House. Across the avenue, the needle-like Washington Monument rose from a large grassy area.

Slowly more and more Indians drifted into the BIA building as if drawn by a magnet. They came in by ones and twos, or in groups. At that time, we had no intention of occupying the BIA. We simply had no other place to go. By dawn six or seven hundred Indian people were lounging in hallways, lying sprawled on sofas, falling asleep in chairs, or standing around a big statue of a chief, arguing and not knowing what to do. A few people who had food with them improvised some breakfast.

We finally met up with Bob Burnette, George Mitchell, and Anita Collins, who had been sent ahead to set up interviews. They had been in D.C. and New York City for almost three weeks. I had told them to arrange meetings with the Interior Department, the Department of Labor, Department of Commerce, and all other offices involved with Indian affairs. Anita told us, "We have set up all these meetings as planned, and now all doors are closed to us. I don't know what's going on. They are holding out on us."

Bob Burnette started ticking off all the meetings he had lined up that had subsequently been canceled. He told me, "There is something strange going on here. A week ago I had confirmation that we were going to meet with all of these people, and now they act as if they don't know us. Something is wrong. The persons we had appointments with seem to have backed out under some kind of threat from the administration."

Our people started to get impatient. They were tired and stressed-out from the long journey. They needed to have food and water and a good rest. They were getting more and more riled up. Martha Grass yelled, "Let's get those BIA people down here. Let's find out why they are not meeting with us!"

Finally around 11:00 A.M., some minor official came down to see us—or maybe he was only an aide to some minor official. I told him, "We are supposed to have a meeting here at the auditorium."

He said, "You Indians are not even supposed to be here!" Another "low man on the totem pole" bureaucrat joined in. He answered all of our questions with, "I don't know." We called people we knew, such as Senator Edward Kennedy, Hubert Humphrey, and Walter Mondale, but nobody was willing to meet with us.

At noon I went out to see what was happening on the street. I found the entire avenue in front of the building filled with additional Trail arrivals. There were cars and school buses from Sisseton, South Dakota, and more from Oklahoma, a big group from North Carolina, Native people from Whiterocks, Utah, and every kind of vehicle from all over the country. I said to Clyde, "Man, this thing is getting bigger by the minute!" Some young men had set up a drum in the auditorium. The drumbeat and singing began to reverberate throughout the building.

At about 2:00 P.M., some BIA people came down from the second floor and announced, "It's official. The government agencies don't want to meet with you at all." That's when people got really angry and started yelling and cursing. Martha Grass began shouting again, saying "Get the commissioner down here. Get the commissioner!" At about 3:00 P.M., Louis Bruce, the Commissioner of Indian Affairs, came down in person.

Louis Bruce is a fine and decent man. He is half Sioux and half Mohawk. He sympathized with us, but he had no power. The government had tied his hands. When he read to us the memo from his superior, Assistant Secretary of the Interior Harrison Loesch, which forbade him to give us any assistance, there was complete chaos. People began yelling and screaming, not at Bruce, but at what he represented—the federal government. The memo stated that he was to give "no direct or indirect assistance to the American Indian Movement demonstration in Washington." Loesch emphasized, "This is to give you very specific instructions that the Bureau is not to provide any assistance or funding, either directly or indirectly." We definitely were not welcome in Washington.

Bruce had no part in the government's position with us, and he was willing to help us. He said, "I cannot support the decision of the government. I just can't defend it." About thirty of us went upstairs to Bruce's office—including Bob Burnette, Martha Grass, Russ, Vernon, Clyde, and Carter. Bob told Bruce, "Harrison Loesch, Assistant Secretary of the Interior, assured me that the government would give us local support."

Bruce phoned Loesch, who said he did not recall any such promise. After the call, Bob shouted, "Loesch is lying through his teeth!" At that moment, Loesch phoned Bruce back and ordered him to clear the building of Indians and close it down. Bruce looked sad and angry. He told us that he would not follow orders, that he was the Commissioner of Indian Affairs, and that his job was to help the Indian people—not to throw them out. He told the people assembled in the auditorium, "This building will remain open to all Indians."

There was a huge roar of applause. Bruce said he would keep the building open all night. Loesch and others phoned repeatedly, ordering him to leave the building. Each time he refused. Finally, he was told that he was relieved of his position as commissioner. He said that it did not matter, that he would stay.

Russ and I had a meeting outside the BIA building with a man who was reported to be from "Housing." I said, "Where are we to stay? We will not go back to that rat-infested church."

He said, "Well, that's your problem. We didn't invite you. We didn't tell you to come here. We're not in the housing business."

Meanwhile, someone had made some calls and said that we could stay in some armory. He gave us an address. This time a few of our people checked the place out first.

They came back in no time, saying, "That place is just as bad as the church. It's like a tomb. It's like being in a freezer. It has no cooking facilities, no shower, and the toilet facilities are totally inadequate for our crowd."

Much was going on simultaneously in different parts of the building; people had begun to spread out. A few women discovered a cafeteria in the basement and started brewing coffee. Small tribal groups settled down in empty offices. By then it was past 5:00 P.M. Most BIA employees had left—many ahead of quitting time because they were afraid. In the auditorium, Russ made a speech, Carter made a speech, and other people made speeches too. But it was Martha Grass who made the point that, "this is the BIA building. This is an Indian building. This is our building, and we're going to stay right here!" So the decision was made that we would stay the night.

Up to that time, the building had not been taken over. It was crammed full of Indians because they had no other place to go. They were simply waiting for a resolution to negotiations. All of this changed instantly when a scuffle broke out between Henry Wahwassuck from Kansas and a lieutenant from the Metropolitan Police. Wahwassuck had been speaking with black civil rights leader Stokely Carmichael, who had come to offer his help, when Metropolitan Police officers tried to enter the building. Wahwassuck would not let them inside.

The lieutenant had got it into his head to clear the ground floor of Indians despite Wahwassuck's refusal, and so he called in a platoon of heavily armed guards with helmets and billy clubs. They forced their way in, clubbing down everyone who tried to resist. People had blood running down their faces from the beatings. Some of our people tore the legs from chairs and tables in order to defend themselves. Outside, riot police—looking like men from Mars with their helmets and face shields—began to surround the building as reinforcements for the guards battling us inside. Pretty soon word reached the group upstairs that the police were storming the building.

I looked at Russ and Clyde and said, "Seal off the building!"

Russ shouted, "Close all the doors!" We ran down the stairs to the main floor, into the middle of the fight.

Our people were driving the guards out of the building. Some of the police panicked and jumped out of windows. Others were trapped inside, and some of their fellow policemen clubbed their way inside again in order to rescue those left behind. There was some hard fighting going on. At last we kicked their butts out. Once the building was clear, I urged our people to barricade all doors with whatever was available—desks, chairs, tables, photocopy machines, lockers, and file cabinets. Soon we had the whole building sealed off. Meanwhile, the police outside had cordoned off the whole area, letting no one get near. We were masters of the building.

The occupation of the BIA building entirely changed the spirit of the Trail. At first the Interior Department was in charge, telling us what to do. Then suddenly we were in charge. We were no longer there by default. We had become *occupiers!* Those of us who had been meeting in Bruce's office joined the people downstairs, where I announced, "This is a takeover, and we are going to stay here until we get some answers." The people vowed that they would defend the building. It was *ours* then. By then the reporters had begun arriving. They wanted to talk to Clyde Bellecourt, to Russell Means, and to Dennis Banks. The takeover became big news worldwide.

That first night, I went downstairs to see how Henry Wahwassuck was doing. He had a cut on top of his head and his knuckles were raw and hurting. We talked and visited, then found an empty room and made our space in there. I didn't have a sleeping bag, but I had a blanket and I found a pillow somewhere. I told those who had come with my caravan to settle down wherever they could find a place to plant themselves. Some of our men and women saw themselves on the eleven o'clock news that night as they watched coverage about the takeover. I settled down and went to sleep, wondering how long this occupation would last, wondering what would come of all this. About midnight word came in that we could stay one night but we would have to vacate the building in the morning—they would use force if we didn't leave then. From then on, we would have two moments of crisis every day— about nine in the morning and six in the evening, when police would arrive threatening to eject us by force.

The next day we got up early and had some coffee. Support started to come in from the black community. They brought in sandwiches, hot dogs, cold drinks, and all kinds of supplies, saying, "This is going to be a long haul." On this second day of the occupation, November third, we put up a big sign over the entrance—the BIA building became the "AMERICAN INDIAN EMBASSY." We also set up a tipi on the lawn in front of the building. We hoisted an upside-down American flag up the flagpole. A row of young security guards stood in a line across the pathway leading to the entrance, controlling who could come in and who could not. Strangely enough, the police did not interfere with people going in or out of the building, nor did they stop the various demonstrations taking place outside—some in support and some in opposition to us.

At about ten o'clock on that second morning, we let the press in. We appealed to the media to let the country know the reasons for the takeover and what our demands were. We made speeches to them from the stage of the auditorium and gave interviews on the steps outside. If necessary, we used a bullhorn. And we dressed up for the occasion. Russ wore a red shirt with a beaded medallion over his chest. An eagle feather dangled from one of his braids. Clyde wore a black, wide-brimmed Uncle Joe hat and a bone choker around his neck; I draped a colorful Pendleton blanket over my shoulders.

The one in our group most interviewed by the press was Floyd Young Horse, a Minneconjou from Eagle Butte, South Dakota, because of his classic, full-blood face, his red-wrapped braids, and his fine sense of humor. He told reporters he had come in an "Indian car" with so many things wrong with it that it shouldn't be up and running at all, but somehow "its spirit was keeping it going."

On the second day, more people joined us. John Trudell, a Santee Sioux and AIM leader, arrived; as did LaDonna Harris, Kiowa-Comanche, who was president of Americans for Indian Opportunity and wife of U.S. Senator Fred Harris; Carla Blakey from the Saulteaux people and her daughter, Chery; and Chief Oren Lyons with a delegation of Six Nation People. Many non-Indian supporters also came. Black power advocate Stokely Carmichael was the first; then black activist Marion Berry, who later became the mayor of Washington, D.C.; Jim Williams, a spokesman for the Black Panthers; Dr. Benjamin Spock, who wrote what some folks call the "bible of child-raising"; and Wavy Gravy, the Merry Prankster in his psychedelic bus, arrived with people from the Hog Farm in New Mexico. He wore an earring the size of a small egg dangling from his left lobe.

Richard Erdoes came down from New York City with his wife, Jean, and two teenage sons, who were toting a tiny kitten they had rescued from the highway on their way down. Erdoes said it was just his style to take over a building with a purring kitten in his arms.

On that second day of the occupation, tensions multiplied, soon becoming almost unbearable. A man in a fancy uniform appeared, waving a paper at us. It was Chief U.S. Marshal Wayne Colburn, with whom we would have to deal a few months later at Wounded Knee. He had a court order requiring us to vacate the building by midnight. Colburn was scared. We could see the fear in his eyes when he confronted our young men homemade spears and clubs in their hands and their faces painted for war. He was actually trembling. He cried, "I come in peace! I have no choice but to carry out the court order!" But he did not carry out his threats.

Attitudes hardened on both sides. Negotiations got nowhere. Things got worse and worse. The government offered us the large auditorium in the General Services Administration building a few blocks away. There we would have comfortable quarters with all the facilities we needed. We accepted the offer and sent some people to check it out. They found the doors locked. A government spokesperson explained that the doors would be opened after "a complete and peaceful evacuation" of the BIA building. We didn't fall for it. We felt sure that once we left our present quarters, the auditorium would remain locked while the BIA would move to reoccupy its building, leaving us with nowhere to go. Our anger burned red-hot.

Excitement and the fear of bloodshed were in the air—increasing numbers of police in a solid mass five ranks deep stood ready to attack us. Another marshal appeared with one more order to clear out "or else." We had about seven hundred people in the building. Many had armed themselves with homemade weapons—rebar and fishing rods with knives tied to the tops, clubs made from chair legs, some bows and arrows found in a closet, golf clubs, and whatnot. Some people piled up as many as sixty typewriters on the roof and upper window ledges. They had also gathered loose roof tiles and filled trash cans with boiling water to hurl down on the heads of police if they dared to try evicting us. We taped the windows so they would not be shattered by tear gas canisters.

Many girls and young women stood ready to fight alongside the men. Seventeen-year-old Mary Ellen Moore tied a letter opener to a broom handle. "What do you suppose you can do with that?" one of our young security guards asked her.

"Get them in the balls before they get me," was her answer.

The drum was beating. Crow Dog blessed the warriors with sage and then he fanned them off, using an eagle wing to fan smoke from the burning sage toward the men to bless them. A number of our men had painted their faces for war, with lipstick if they could find nothing else. I knew that the police outside—with their helmets and flak vests—realized they were not facing a bunch of flower children or student anti-war protesters. We were dead serious.

During the second day, some Oklahoma people requested a private meeting with some of the leadership, so we went up to the second floor to find out what they wanted. They told us, "We uncovered some information. We have been sitting in this office all night long, going through the files in those metal cabinets, and we discovered how they have been ripping us off—stealing reservation oil and natural gas out of Oklahoma and also Wyoming."

I told them, "Start making copies of everything, and let's take it out of here. Anything you can find that might be incriminating evidence, make copies of it. Let's take it with us." Pretty soon we had boxes and boxes full of documentation.

Before dawn on our third day inside the BIA building, I told the government negotiators, "We will not leave. We will fight. We will die here if we have to." We weren't leaving until someone in the government—other than an aide or intern—was willing to sit down and talk with us and hear us out.

"We have now declared war on the United States of America," said Clyde Bellecourt. "We are ready for battle!"

We held a quick leadership meeting and decided that the elders and children must be protected. We sought to have the oldest and most infirm as well as the youngest children seek safety outside the building. Between midnight and 4:00 A.M., government officials made three offers to provide for these people, but most of them decided to stay. Only a very small handful left to find shelter at the YMCA. The night passed uneventfully. As dawn came, many of our young men finally flopped down wherever they could find a little space and tried to get some sleep. The now-former Commissioner of Indian Affairs, Louis Bruce, was staying with us. He said, "I cannot defend the bureaucracy of this country any longer. I am staying with my people."

I remember November 4 as the day on which strange things happened. Once again the marshal appeared with a new restraining order. Government officials declared that we were going to be ousted by force. Secretary of the Interior Roger Morton issued a statement calling us a "splinter group of militants." He said, "It is obvious to me that the seizure and continued occupation of the building are nothing more than a form of blackmail by a small group which seeks to achieve, through violent means, objectives which are not supported by a majority of reservation Indians."

Outside on Constitution Avenue, a group of marchers had come to show support. They formed the weirdest support group we ever had. It was led by the Reverend Carl McEntyre, a right-wing nut, who shouted, "Hallelujah! We have a message for our Indian friends. All right, you Indians, we want you to have your rights as long as you're not Commies. Support the war in Vietnam!" They chanted "Onward Christian Soldiers" and began to shout repeatedly, "Free Morton! Free Morton! Morton, come down; we want you freed!" It was not clear whether they thought we held the Interior Secretary hostage, or whether they had confused Morton with Louis Bruce.

Clyde shrugged his shoulders and said, "Just another demented freak."

Also on this day we finally got a call from the White House. Leonard Garment, Nixon's advisor on minorities, wanted to meet with Bob Burnette, who they thought would be easier to handle than guys like Russ, Clyde, and me. At the same time, Brad Patterson, another Nixon aide, met with George Mitchell, Anita Collins, and Hank Adams. These talks led nowhere. I realized that we might not be able to stay much longer and that I should concern myself with the documents we had discovered. In the end we ran out of copy paper and took the originals. The evidence filled a good-sized room. During the night we backed a U-Haul van right up to a rear doorway and started loading it up. When we were done, we parked the van near the edge of the BIA building's parking lot, where we hoped it would escape attention and be available to be moved out on a moment's notice.

November 5 was a stalemate. We demanded to see President Nixon and John Ehrlichman, Nixon's top domestic affairs advisor, but they sent the usual low-level flunkies. We wanted to discuss our twenty points. They offered to let us use the auditorium "during reasonable hours," take showers, and do our cooking in the cafeteria. This was comical as we were in full charge of the building. I told Clyde that things would end in a battle because both we and the government had boxed ourselves in. "We cannot afford to give an inch now, and they won't either," I said.

November 6, we were hanging by a hair. Judge Pratt said we had to leave the building by 6:00 P.M. After that, marshals would arrest all Indians who remained inside. We had fire hoses ready at the windows. There was a rumor that we had the building wired for destruction. It said we had enough dynamite from the Black Panthers to blow the whole place sky-high. Later asked whether this was true, Vern told a reporter that "smoking had been restricted to the basement!"

Outside, the building was ringed by police wearing not only their helmets and flak vests but also tear-gas masks. A lawyer acting on our behalf appealed the court's decision, warning of the dreadful possibility of bloodshed. Margaret Millen, an elderly Indian lady who was the only BIA employee who had continued to work throughout our siege of the building, appeared with a machete, ready to fight on *our* side. Secretary Morton told the press, "The Indian militants have done things their way. Now we will do things our way. Everybody involved in that building will be prosecuted!"

Anger and frustration were rising to a fever pitch. Our people were tired of hoaxes and tricks and broken promises. The atmosphere inside became chaotic and beyond control. Some of the younger people started trashing the building, smashing the BIA's expensive, elegent furnishings and ripping up the posh leather couches. Frustrated activists covered the walls with slogans. One read, "BIA, I AM NOT YOUR INDIAN ANYMORE."

There was a serious discussion about whether we should burn down the building. Mary Ellen Moore said to me, "I am willing to fight for what I believe in. I am willing to burn this building down, if that will change the ripping off that the BIA is doing."

Clyde was against burning it down. I said, "The government would be happy if we torched the building with all the incriminating papers proving how our land had been stolen and how we were cheated. They would be glad to have more excuses to persecute us. On the other hand, if the police made a final, all-out attack against us, then whatever happens, let it happen."

Russ said, "If we go, there's going to be one helluva smoke signal! This building is not going to be here anymore." Those of us who were against intentionally burning down the BIA won out.

For awhile it looked as though we would have to fight for our lives. A large army of vehicles drove up and parked in various places around the building. Police cars with flashing lights drove back and forth past the building as if waging psychological warfare. I shouted to observers on the other side of the avenue, "I invite all of you to stay and witness the massacre about to happen!" At 5:00 P.M. it seemed the government still was determined to make a full-scale assault. However, at the last moment the deadline for leaving the building was extended another forty-eight hours. It was, after all, the night before presidential elections. A few dozen dead Indians wouldn't have looked too good on that occasion.

Sometime afterward, a young Indian woman from New York wrote in a letter to AIM, "During the time we waited for the pigs to come, we sang and danced. . . . We were waiting for the moment we would die if necessary. At 5:00 P.M. we had what we called our Last Supper. I thought, 'At least we won't die with our stomachs empty—like so many of us had while we were alive.' I had to go to the bathroom, but no one was allowed to leave our battle stations. Some of us were stationed outdoors. I went around where there were some bushes. It was just like home anyway, to go to the bathroom in those bushes." The police never came. She added, "Finally, our leaders decided we could all go back in the building. Tired and relieved, we went to sleep."

The administration finally sent some top-level officials to negotiate with us. Fred Carlucci, head of the Office of Management and Budget, Leonard Garment, Nixon's advisor on minorities, and Secretary of the Interior Roger Morton, whom we called "Secretary of His Limousine," came to the BIA.

At last we hammered out an agreement. Under it the White House would set up a task force to seriously consider our twenty demands. The task force, headed by Frank Carlucci and Leonard Garment, would sit for six months and review every aspect of Indian policy. It would be made up of officials of all government agencies dealing with American Indians and would consult with our representatives every step of the way. Also, we explained, we would need sixty-six thousand dollars for travel expenses to get all of our people home. I don't remember who came up with this sum, but the government paid it to us in cash.

Of course, the government later reneged on their promises. They rejected our demands as "impracticable." They publicly reviled us for our radicalism and for the damage done to the building, though the extent of the damage they cited was beyond any damage we had done. We suspect the building was further damaged after we left to make us look worse—by whom we don't know. The government also convinced a number of tribal chairmen, Uncle Tomahawks and Hang-around-the-Fort types who depended entirely on government handouts for their livelihood, to condemn us as a splinter group that did not represent Indian people in general.

In spite of all this, members of over two hundred tribes and two dozen Indian organizations had come together in unity to try to make a change and to break the Bureau's power over us. The Trail of Broken Treaties was the biggest show of strength by our people in a hundred years.

Before we left the BIA building, one of us had taken a crayon and had written in bold letters on the large movie screen in the auditorium, "We do not apologize for the so-called destruction of this mausoleum, for in building anew, one must first destroy what is rotten! When history recalls our efforts here, our descendants will stand proud." So it was the sixth day and time to go home.

The government bribed us to leave with promises that were broken almost as soon as they were made. They promised to "seriously" consider our twenty demands but soon "officially and formally" rejected all of them. They promised not to prosecute Trail members for actions taken during the occupation, but broke this promise too, claiming their agreement did not cover the "theft of government property," the documents we had seized. The Trail of Broken Treaties ended as a trail of broken promises. The racist and ultra-conservative press called the action a "failure," saying that AIM and the Trail people had lost face and the sympathy of the public when the building was trashed. They also called the occupation "a defeat for the radicals who achieved nothing." We did not see it that way. For everyone who had taken part in the Trail of Broken Treaties, the takeover had been a victory. For the first time ever, members of some two hundred tribes had acted together for a common cause. I was proud to have been a part of this. If nothing else, we had sent up one hell of a smoke signal.

CHAPTER 12

The Town with the Gunsmoke Flavor

You're seeing that we have a group of AIMers here and a group of my supporters here. They're going to clash one of these days and it's probably pretty soon. And that scene is going to be the end of my supporters or the end of the American Indian Movement—one or the other.

—Dick Wilson, Tribal Chairman,
Pine Ridge reservation

After the BIA takeover, our attention turned to South Dakota, the state we felt was the most racist toward Indians. Pine Ridge reservation, home to some twelve thousand Oglala Sioux Indians, was a scandalous exhibit of economic racism. In early 1973 Pine Ridge was a scene of desolation. Most people lived in tarpaper shacks without running water, electricity, or indoor plumbing. Some lived in small, ancient log cabins with dirt floors. One family's "home" was a tiny, ramshackle 1920s trailer. Its owner, with typical Oglala humor, told me his floor space was the size of a "white man's throw rug." At least three-quarters of the people were in desperate need of decent housing. The average yearly income on the rez was $1,500. Shannon County, which the reservation is part of, was then and is to this day the poorest of all the more than three thousand counties in America.

At that time on the rez, about 70 percent of the working-age people were unemployed. The rez had no bank, no general store, no movie theater, no hotel or motel. It had, however, a brand new airstrip long enough to accomodate jet planes. Unfortunately, no one on the rez owned a plane and no airline serviced this area. The BIA maintained that it had not financed this tribal "asset." The airstrip had been contracted by the tribe's own politicians and paid for by tribal funds, which proved to many people on the rez that not all crooks are white.

There was one area of Pine Ridge that the Oglalas with their *heyoka* sense of humor called "the industrial park." Its single building was a warehouse in which the government stored commodities for welfare recipients; without that food the people would have starved. It housed years-old white flour, powdered milk, powdered eggs, processed cheese, lard, beans, and other starchy stuff. Pine Ridge was a place of despair.

The situation on other reservations in South Dakota wasn't much better. But not everybody on Pine Ridge was poor. A very few did quite well. Among them was a pudgy, short-haired mixed-blood named "Dicky" Wilson, Pine Ridge's tribal president. Wilson maintained a private army of about eighty heavily armed thugs, paid by government money that was meant for other, more positive programs. The government even supplied them with armor-piercing bullets. They did not hesitate to fire-bomb, maim, or murder Wilson's opponents..

People on the rez called these hoodlums "the goons." Wilson took pride in that name. He boasted, "These are *my* goons! G-O-O-Ns, Guardians of the Oglala Nation." Reporters from the *Shannon County News* regularly called Wilson "that famous Indian fighter, the Bureau's goofball, raised on a diet of dumb pills." But there was nothing funny about Wilson. Under his rule, Pine Ridge was a killing field. Between 1972 and 1976, more than sixty full-bloods were killed by the goons he paid for with federal funds.

The U.S. government pumped twenty million dollars into Pine Ridge while Wilson was tribal president. This gave him the power of patronage. He handed out cushy jobs to family members, friends, and supporters. He publicly declared, "There is nothing wrong with nepotism. I take care of my own."

Wilson "took care of his own" by giving away eighty thousand acres of Pine Ridge land to the United States, land that became part of the Bandlands National Monument. Land is at the very core of the traditional Lakotas' soul. Many Lakotas have never forgotten nor forgiven Wilson's theft of their sacred Black Hills.

In return for Wilson's "gift," the government gave Wilson full support against his opponents, among whom were his own vice president, Vern Long, his tribal judge, Hobart Keith, and members of OSCRO, the Oglala Sioux Civil Rights Organization. Investigations of fraud involving Wilson's election were put on the back burner. The government also furnished weapons to Wilson's goon squads, ignoring that he used funds earmarked for health and education to pay his private army.

The goings-on at Pine Ridge were a national scandal. Aided and abetted by the BIA, Wilson stayed in power by open, unabashed election fraud. At last, the Oglalas began to fight back. They asked AIM for help. As opposition developed, repression increased. You could feel it coming—the very air trembled with the force of the impending explosion. The fuse had been lit. It would take only time—a short time—until the flame reached the powder.

Pine Ridge was a big concern, but it was not our only concern. South Dakota was the most racist state in the country, and Rapid City was the most racist town in South Dakota. Rapid City—Rapid, for short—is the gateway to the Black Hills. On the east the town is flanked by grain elevators. Toward the west rise a series of hills, from which a monolithic cement dinosaur overshadows the town. In between sprawls the downtown business district with its streets full of saloons and shops—western clothing stores, curio shops, jewelry stores featuring "Black Hills gold," pawn shops, and gun shops. In the middle is the historic Alex Johnson Hotel with its lobby of beamed ceilings covered with Indian designs, a place where wealthy visitors can get a gourmet dinner. Rapid City is a tourist center as well as a typical cowboy town.

We came to Rapid to do something about discrimination against Indians—to encourage local businessmen to hire Indians, to get better medical treatment for Indian veterans, and to sensitize the white citizen in general. Of special concern was an Indian ghetto called Sioux Addition, a kind of Indian Soweto, three miles out of town. The Indian people who lived there had come to Rapid seeking work, but were rejected by white landlords and employers—by white establishment, in general. They could not afford Rapid City rents and soon found themselves on a dead-end street with no public services, no schools, no garbage collection or street lights. The city police and fire department ignored Sioux Addition as if it didn't exist.

We felt the city owed AIM some consideration in addition to the basic respect it owed Indian people in general. We had helped the town at a time when Indians and whites were in need. During June 1972, a great flood had devastated the town. Rapid Creek had ripped right through the center of town, swallowing up houses and killing two hundred thirty people. AIM jumped right in to help. We worked to recover bodies, find shelter for people who were suddenly homeless, and deliver food supplies and blankets, giving help to all who needed it—Indian and white alike.

Our help was not appreciated. This was John Wayne country, where an Indian took his life in his hands if he entered a white bar, and where American Indians were treated like blacks in apartheid South Africa. When Rapid Creek flooded, a call was sent to all AIM people to come to Rapid to help local Indians reclaim their rights. We all stayed at Mother Butler Center a two-story building with a dormitory. During January 1973 there were about two hundred AIM people there, plus many local and reservation Lakotas. The Jesuit priest in charge of the Mother Butler Center made us welcome, but he was almost the only white who showed any gratitude for the help we gave the town during the flood.

Tensions were running high in Rapid in late 1972. We discovered that here had been an acceleration of racist ugliness involving crude sexual harassments of Indian women as well as a number of incidents in which older American Indians had been abused and subjected to discrimination. I declared a freeze on the city. I announced that we would shut down the whole business district because of the maltreatment inflicted daily upon Indian people there.

We had first tried to wake up the white officials and businessmen in a peaceful, non-confrontational way. We invited government officials to an AIM conference—men from the BIA, from the Justice Department, and from the Office for Economic Opportunity—but they did not take our complaints seriously. We wanted to set up a mediation board where both whites and Indians could honestly talk about our respective problems, work to lessen the tensions between us, and to have a show of good will. But we got nowhere. We felt pushed into confrontation; we had little choice but to confront Rapid's problems.

Rapid's white citizens looked upon us as terrorists. They locked themselves into their homes and drove around in their pick-up trucks with loaded rifles and shotguns in the gun racks.

We followed through with our threats to shut down the business district. Our people picketed in front of establishments such as Northwestern Bell Telephone, Black Hills Power and Light, Kmart, Piggly Wiggly, Dunkin' Donuts, First National Bank, Safeway, the Coca Cola bottling plant, Ellsworth Air Force Base, and the local BIA office. In other words, we shut down every single commercial and government establishment of any size in Rapid City.

Resentment, so long suppressed against the way we had always been treated, finally boiled over. Fights started in the Frontier Bar, the Stockmen's Bar, and other places where Indians had often been beaten up or abused. In the Bronco Bar, which had a sign in the the window warning, "INDIANS ENTER AT THEIR OWN RISK," a white rancher flung a glass of whiskey into the face of an Indian. Pandemonium broke out. Some of our young women had exhanged their buckskin mocassins for "shit-kickers"—boots with steel-tipped toes—and used them on the shins of white opponents. Fights were breaking out everywhere, inside saloons and outside in the street. Police went amok, busting heads with their nightsticks, looking for anyone who looked like an Indian. Mary Ellen Moore, in the ninth month of pregnancy, was beaten to the floor inside the Frontier Bar and defended herself with a broken ashtray.

About two hundred AIM people were arrested and carted off to the old, vermin-infested Pennington County jail. There weren't enough paddy wagons to transport them all, so the mayor ordered a fire truck and an old Greyhound bus to take the overflow. Crow Dog led a large group of Indians who joined hands and danced in a line snaking around the jail all the while singing war songs to the beat of the drum.

When the clashes between whites and Indians started to get out of hand, Russ and I set up a "demilitarized zone." We were fighting and negotiating at the same time with the town's most prominent citizens, and we were actually getting some of our demands addressed. A racist city official, however, countered by passing inflammatory resolutions against the Indian "disturbers of the peace." At Pine Ridge, Dicky

Wilson panicked and asked the government for reinforcements when he heard about what was going on in Rapid City. He got them—eighty U.S. marshals with .50-caliber machine guns, which were as yet kept out of sight. All in all, our actions at that time improved the situation for the Indians of Rapid. Tension in nearby towns, however, was reaching the breaking point.

We were immediately faced by a new challenge. There was a town named Buffalo Gap in the eastern foothills of the Black Hills. It got its name from its location in an opening in the hills—in the old days, buffalo herds made a trail through this gap to reach the open prairie. Buffalo Gap was not much of a town—a bank, a liquor store, a post office, a tiny church, and two saloons. That's about all. The place looked like scenery from a cheap western movie. On weekends the bars were crowded with white ranchers and cowhands from Hermosa, Custer, and Hot Springs. Buffalo Gap was White Man's Country.

On Saturday, January 20, 1974, one of the two saloons, Bill's Bar, was crammed with customers. Among them were Wesley Bad Heart Bull, an Oglala, his mother, Sarah, Sarah's friend Robert High Eagle, and a white gas station attendant, named Darald Schmitz. On several occasions Schmitz had proclaimed loudly, "One day I'll get myself an injun!"

Wesley had been warned by the owner of the bar not to come any more. "You are not welcome here!" he had been told, but he came anyway. Wesley was not easily intimidated. He was tough. Schmitz, drunk as usual, cursed Wesley. They had words.

Schmitz finally left, shouting, "I'll kill that son of a bitch!" The next day, Wesley Bad Heart Bull was found dying in front of Bill's Bar with a knife stuck in his chest. Schmitz had stabbed him seven times.

Wesley died on the way to the hospital in Hot Springs. There were witnesses to the stabbing—even the bartender said Schmitz had attacked Wesley without provocation. Sarah and High Eagle had seen Schmitz leave the bar with the knife in his hand. Schmitz, who admitted killing Bad Heart Bull, was arrested and taken to Custer, the county seat. He was charged with second-degree manslaughter, the lowest charge possible in a case of homicide. He was released immediately on bail and never spent a single hour in jail.

While our people were still "putting the freeze" on the white businesses of Rapid, I was in Salt Lake City as field director of AIM, organizing an anti-alcoholism program. On January 24, Ron Petite, who had gone up to Rapid City to do some investigating, called and told me what he knew about the Wesley Bad Heart Bull case. He said that this was a case AIM should become involved in.

I immediately flew to Rapid City and joined Ron and Herb Powless to see what we could do. I also got Ramon Roubideaux, our Indian lawyer, to come. Ramon went to Bill's Bar to talk to the bartender and two other witnesses. They all were willing to testify that they had heard Schmitz say he would "get that red son of a bitch." It really shook me up to see the same old bullshit—a charge of second-degree manslaughter when it should have been a murder in the first degree charge. We knew from experience that on the lesser charge Schmitz would not do any time at all. We asked Wesley's mother, Sarah, whether we should continue to pursue the case. She gave us her permission. I asked Ramon to talk to the county attorney, the South Dakota version of a district attorney. Ramon wanted to file a charge of murder against Schmitz, but County Attorney Hobart Gates flatly refused to change the indictment. We knew it would take a confrontation to possibly change his mind.

There were other matters to be dealt with at the same time. Even before Wesley Bad Heart Bull was stabbed, a date had been set for further hearings on civil rights violations in Rapid City, Pennington County, and the State of South Dakota. These hearings had been set for February 3, 4, and 5. Many Indians from several states came to testify.

As soon as these hearings were over, we decided to go to Custer, where Darald Schmitz would be arraigned. We notified the court, the town's officials, and the police that we were coming so as not to take them by surprise. I told the mayor, the state attorney, and the sheriff that about four or five carloads of Indians would arrive on February 6. They agreed to meet with us on that date at 9:00 A.M. inside the old courthouse. Custer officials, however, said they would admit only five of us. The group chose to send Leonard Crow Dog, Russell Means, Ramon Roubideaux, Sarah Bad Heart Bull, and me. We told the people who had participated in the civil rights hearings, "Tomorrow we are going to Custer to have Schmitz charged with murder and to show support for the Bad Heart Bull family. If any of you want to come along as a gesture of solidarity, then join us."

On the morning of February 6, we gathered at the Mother Butler Center. I had thought that a few cars and at most fifty or sixty people would come. Waiting for us instead were more than thirty cars and over two hundred people. In the early morning, we formed a wide circle. Crow Dog began smudging everybody with sage and fanning them off. I knew we had to be prepared for any eventuality. Rumors were flying about a swat team waiting to attack our people. In Custer there would be fear and paranoia on both sides of the fence. I told everybody there was a good chance we would be met with armed resistance, but just from looking at them, I knew they were ready. I sensed a real strength in our eager young people and felt good about them. They were like young colts hard to rein in.

On the way to Custer we ran into a blizzard that made driving hazardous. We set out in two caravans of fifteen cars each, one led by Russ and the other by me. I could hear the honking behind me, "Let's go!" I was waving cars on, sometimes getting out of one and into another, guiding them through the snow and making sure everybody was safe on the fifty-mile journey from Rapid to Custer.

We finally arrived in Custer at about 1:30 P.M., a few hours late due to the terrible weather. Custer is a cowtown with some two thousand inhabitants. During the summer it is a tourist trap swarming with thousands of visitors en route to the Black Hills. Visitors entering the town are greeted by a large billboard with the words, "WELCOME TO CUSTER— THE TOWN WITH THE GUNSMOKE FLAVOR." Another sign proclaims: "CUSTER, HOME OF THE FLINTSTONES."

Main street is lined with motels, bars, cheap eateries advertising "buffalo burgers," boutiques, Indian curio shops selling fake tomahawks made in Hong Kong, rock shops with phony "ancient arrowheads," and models of Mt. Rushmore in a dozen sizes.

We went at once to the courthouse, an old building of red brick with a white wooden porch. When we got there, our meeting with County Attorney Gates was a disaster. He greeted us with an angry, "You're late! You were supposed to be here at nine!" He seemed to be unaware of the blizzard and poor visibility that had slowed us to a crawl. At first he refused to let any of us into the courthouse.

Finally, he agreed to let only four of us in besides Ramon Roubideaux, our lawyer—Leonard Crow Dog, our medicine man; Russell

Means; Dave Hill; and me. He refused to allow Sarah Bad Heart Bull, the mother of the murdered man, to enter. She had to stay outside on the porch steps in spite of the snow. Our efforts to change Gates's mind about Sarah failed. We asked him if the rest of our people could come in. There was a hearing room large enough to hold over a hundred people. He said no. Ramon pleaded, "There are women and children outside in the cold. It's snowing *hard!*" Gates still refused. He ordered Sheriff Ernest Pepin and Deputy Bill Rice to guard the double door against any Indians trying to enter.

We told Gates that we wanted the charge against Schmitz changed to an indictment for murder. Gates told us, "I will prosecute this manslaughter case to the fullest extent."

I said, "You know it was murder."

He replied, "I do not." Ramon tried to show Gates evidence he had gathered from eye witnesses to the killing.

Gates said, "I already have all the evidence I need. It was just a barroom brawl."

I told him, "In a barroom brawl, you get a bloody nose, but here you have a dead body. That's *murder*."

"No," he kept insisting, "it was just a brawl."

I argued with him. Russ argued with him. We got nowhere.

We were unable to contain our anger. There was a lot of hollering and yelling on both sides. Totally frustrated, Russ stormed out of the room and went outside. In a few words he informed the crowd what was going on inside. The people responded with a deep, angry growl. Russ motioned Sarah to come with him into the building. They were refused entry by the state police. The crowd rushed up the porch steps and tried to break the door down. They succeeded, but were met by fifty state troopers in full riot gear with helmets and face visors. Every trooper carried a gun and an extra-long nightstick. Fighting broke out immediately, both inside and outside the building, on the porch in front of the courthouse, on the steps, and out on Mt. Rushmore Road. There were pitched battles going on all over the place.

Sarah Bad Heart Bull, who still persisted in her efforts to enter the building, was thrown down the steps. A trooper came from behind her and put a nightstick across her throat. Using full force with both of his hands, he almost choked her to death. Inside the courthouse, I had to defend myself against a trooper coming at me with a three-foot club aimed at my head. I hit him on the arm, breaking his wristwatch, but not the bone. Suddenly a tear-gas canister came flying through the air. In no time the whole building was a cloud of tear gas. The state police were hurling the canisters at us to drive us out of the building. They chucked the canisters at the crowd in front of the building, but our people just threw them back into the courthouse.

There was pandemonium in the hallways; the situation was totally out of control. Nightsticks clashed with chair legs and whatever our people could get their hands on. Tear-gas canisters were met by rocks and loose bricks. The air inside the courthouse became unbearable. It was nearly impossible to breathe or see. My eyes were pouring water and my face and lungs seemed to be on fire. I tried to open a window that was stuck, then grabbed a chair and smashed it through the glass. I stuck my head out the window and gulped the fresh, cold air. Crow Dog was the first to leap out the window. It was about a six-foot drop. I came out after him. People later told me I was grinning, shouting, "I follow my spiritual leader!"

Fighting continued on the street for the rest of the afternoon. The state police were no longer armed with only handguns and nightsticks. As if by magic, they appeared carrying rifles and shotguns. Reinforcements were coming in at a steady pace. Firemen, men from the Department of Game, Fish, and Parks, rangers from Custer State Park, and some ordinary white citizens were deputized to help the state troopers subdue us.

One young Oglala ran up the steps of the court house with two big, heavy cans of gasoline he had taken from Dave's Texaco station opposite the courthouse. He sloshed the gas all over the steps and the porch. There were puddles of gasoline everywhere. Another young man ran up with a box of matches and tried to ignite the gas.

The crowd roared, "Do it! Do it! Do it, AIM! Do it!" Some women and girls made the spine-tingling, high-pitched brave-heart cry, which sent chills through the crowd.

One of the state troopers pointed his gun at the young man with the matches, screaming, "If you try to set fire to this, I'll shoot! I'll shoot to kill!" He paid the trooper no mind. Again and again he tried to light a match, but the wind blew them all out. The trooper kept screaming, "I'll shoot to kill, so help me God!"

A girl ran up onto the porch holding a flickering candle, shielded from the wind by her hand. The state troopers pointed their guns at her, too, but that did not deter her. The snowstorm blew out her candle as well. Finally, another young man ran up with two burning flares, the kind you set out on the road as a warning after an accident. I guess he got them from the gas station. Again the crowd shouted in unison, "Do it! Do it! Do it, man, do it! AIM! AIM! AIM!" He threw the first flare, but it fell short. He got closer and threw the second flare. It landed in the middle of the biggest puddle of gasoline and in a fraction of a second the whole front of the courthouse—porch, steps, and wooden fence—became a sea of flames.

A huge war cry went up from the crowd. The sign, "WELCOME TO CUSTER, THE TOWN WITH THE GUNSMOKE FLAVOR," was ablaze. The log-house chamber of commerce building was soon torched. As it burned, it sent up a huge shower of glowing red sparks that obliterated everything else from sight. A fire truck arrived to try to save the chamber of commerce building. Indians threw rocks, pop bottles, beer cans, and whatever else they could find at the firemen, who backed off. In no time there was nothing left of the wooden structure but a heap of black ashes mingling with the falling snow. One of our women got too close to the flames of the courthouse porch and her clothes caught fire. Friends rolled her in the snow to put out the fire. Two police cars were torched and gutted. Somebody tried to set fire to Dave's Texaco station but, luckily, did not succeed.

The fighting continued. Police were clubbing down Indians right and left. There was blood in the snow. Russ had been beaten to the ground and was sitting, dazed, on the lowest of the courthouse steps, handcuffed, with one of his arms badly hurt. He was guarded by the smirking sheriff in his cowboy hat. Troopers dragged a beautiful young girl by her feet throught the snow and, in the process, ripped her blouse off so that above the waist she wore nothing except her bra. Indians were lying facedown in the snow, held there by two or three troopers searching and handcuffing each of them.

Out of nowhere, a big tanker truck full of gasoline appeared, perhaps on its way to Dave's Texaco. The driver had driven almost to the courthouse, then stopped when he suddenly realized that he had landed in the middle of a riot surrounded by flames. He panicked. He just sat there bug-eyed and paralyzed. I thought, "Oh, no. If that truck catches fire, it will blow up and everyone will be burned to death!"

Indians screamed at the driver, "*Move*! Get your ass out of here!" I ran to the truck to tell the driver to leave.

He only stammered, "What's going on? What's happening?" I jumped on the driver's side of the truck, pushed him over, and grabbed the wheel.

I asked him, "How do you operate this thing?" but I could get no answer out of him. I finally got the truck into gear. For a moment I thought of driving the truck close to the courthouse to set the whole building on fire, but I got hold of myself. I backed the truck out of the danger area. I could see that two Indians still stood, waving a red AIM banner and a four-direction flag of the four sacred colors.

Twenty-two people were arrested that day—nineteen Indians, two whites, and one black. Among those taken to jail were Sarah Bad Heart Bull, the mother of the murdered man, and Russell Means. I was arrested and charged later. A deputy told Russ, "We were waiting for you sons of bitches! You were looking for trouble and you got it!" Russ told him, "If we had wanted a riot, we would not have brought our women and children."

Sarah Bad Heart Bull was tried for "riot with arson." She was sentenced to one to five years and actually served five months in prison. Her son's murderer was acquitted by an all-white jury and he did not serve a single day in jail.

CHAPTER 13

A Place Called Wounded Knee

Before AIM our young people lived in despair. They drank themselves to death. They were ashamed to be Indians. Some committed suicide. At Wounded Knee they became warriors again and began to feel good about themselves. They began to feel good about being Sioux, Cheyenne, or Ojibway. They put on red face paint, let their hair grow long, and proudly wore their ribbon shirts. Under fire they learned to respect themselves once more, and after almost one hundred years, they were ghost dancing again.

—Dennis Banks, Ojibwa

The days after the disastrous confrontation at Custer were for me days of soul searching and deep thinking: "Who is Dennis Banks? What is AIM? What is that person called an Indian?" There were so many questions to answer.

About February 15, 1973, I was in Pierre, South Dakota, the state capital, addressing the state legislature at the invitation of Governor Kneip about racism in South Dakota. I told them that I felt the situation at Pine Ridge had gotten out of hand. We wanted to get along. We wanted race relations to improve, but if Custer was a foretaste of things to come, I warned, there could be serious confrontations ahead.

Pierre is in the northernmost part of the state, and we were still up there on February 19 or 20. We decided to camp near Eagle Butte at Red Scaffold, where some relatives of Madonna Gilbert, one of our bravest women, lived. We went there to relax for a few days with no thought that great events were about to unfold. Alex Charging Hawk was host to the fifteen or twenty of us. We bought a lot of groceries— flour, rice, potatoes, and *pejuta sapa*, or "black medicine," a Lakota name for coffee. Somebody donated a cow and we had a big cookout. We just were taking it easy.

We were unaware that at Pine Ridge, things had gone from bad to worse. Dicky Wilson managed to defeat his impeachment for corruption and voting fraud by more voting fraud. His vice president, Vern Long, resigned in disgust. The goons shot out windows in his home and killed his horses. Wilson installed two .50-caliber machine guns on the roof of the tribal council building, which was promptly renamed Fort Wilson. The U.S. government's favorite Indian also had the building sandbagged. Hallways contained shotguns and rifles stacked against the walls, ready for use. Canisters of tear gas stood in rows wherever there was room. During elections, Wilson gave Pine Ridge citizens wine, whiskey, and money to vote him in.

Pine Ridge was swarming with FBI agents and U.S. marshals in blue jumpsuits. Already the first APCs—some carrying machine guns— were arriving to protect the government's darling against big, bad AIM. Wilson abolished all constitutional rights. Fear was spreading all across the rez. No AIM member was allowed to set foot on Pine Ridge, not even Russell Means, who was a member of the tribe and whose family lived on the rez.

About 3:00 A.M. on February 27, I was awakened by a loud pounding on the door. I was asleep inside the house. Ron Petite, who had been sleeping outside in a tent, came in to say that someone from Pine Ridge had arrived with a tape from Russ. We sat down immediately and listened to it. Russell's voice said, "Dennis, we need you to come down here to Calico as fast as you can make it. We're having a big meeting there tomorrow, and we think it will be a matter of great importance. We need you. Bring as many people as you can. Don't come through Pine Ridge. You might get stopped or even hurt." Calico, South Dakota, was just a tiny settlement consisting of about a dozen houses, but it contained a wooden building that served as a community center and meeting hall. The town was some five miles west of Pine Ridge.

By then it was four o'clock in the morning. We made some coffee. Ron said, "What now?"

I told him, "Well, wake up everybody and tell them where we are going. Tell them we are leaving for Pine Ridge today." Ron woke everybody up. There were some people camped pretty far away from us, way down by the river, so we had to wait until the sun came up in order to account for everybody. Alex's wife, Vicki, fixed a great big breakfast for us. Then I told everyone, "The Oglala people have invited AIM to help them. Things could become serious." I asked whether somebody knew a back way to Calico that would allow us to avoid Pine Ridge. Somebody did. I said, "Let's round everybody up and get going!"

It took our eight cars two or three hours to get on the road. Ours were typical "Indian cars." Three of them had flat tires and no spares, and it took time to fix them. Finally, we hit the road. I was in the lead car with Ron driving.

We arrived at Calico Hall Community Center at 3:15 P.M. There were about two hundred and fifty people milling around outside because the building was so full of people that no more could squeeze in. The debate took place in the basement of the Calico church, where tribal leaders sat at the several long tables near the back of the room. I mingled with the people, quietly shaking hands. Russ was there, as well as Carter Camp and Clyde Bellecourt. All of the people we needed were in Calico.

As far as I remember, Russ and I were the only representatives of AIM in the church, listening to what was said and witnessing what was taking place. We felt that we were guests, that the speeches and decisions should be made by the traditional Oglala Sioux alone. Chief Frank Fools Crow, Pine Ridge's oldest and most respected medicine man, was speaking in Lakota. Pedro Bissonette translated everything he said. Pedro was the founder of OSCRO, the Oglala Sioux Civil Rights Organization, and one of the staunchest opponents of the Wilson regime.

Fools Crow said that he had followed the ways of the pipe all his life—in peace—but that there comes a time when one must fight for survival of the Oglala Nation, for its spirit. This was the time for the tribe's young men to go ahead and take care of things. Fools Crow said that if that's what we had to do, then now was the time to do it. I needed no translation to feel the passion, the desperation in his words, which gripped the hearts of all who were in that church. Pedro Bissonette spoke after Fools Crow. So did Severt Young Bear and Chief Tom Bad Cob. Many stood up to speak and it seemed that by doing so, they freed themselves of a great burden that had weighed heavily on them.

However, it was the women—Ellen Moves Camp, Gladys Bissonette, Lou Bean, and Hildegard Catches—who dominated the discussion. They were losing patience and wanted to take action. They shamed us men by their power and daring for making decisions. Ellen Moves Camp made a great impression upon me. I had seen her earlier at the Yellow Thunder demonstrations in Gordon and at Custer, but listening to her impassioned words at Calico was when I first felt close to her. She pointed a finger at me saying, "Dennis Banks, what are *you* going to do?" She didn't expect me to respond; it was a rhetorical question. All the same, her words stung me. I felt as though I had been stabbed with a knife.

Ellen continued, "Ever since we came here, we have been surrounded by marshals, goons, and spies. They have been watching us every minute. They're reporting every step we make. They could come in here right now to arrest us for exercising our constitutional rights. Dicky Wilson has forbidden any meetings, speechmaking, or traditional dancing on the reservation. But this is our land, Lakota land. It belongs to us, not to him and his goons. The goons are only minutes away, armed to the teeth, trying to frighten us. They come in here staggering drunk, saying filthy words to us, shaking their fists in our faces. Dennis Banks, what are you going to do about it?"

Gladys Bissonette, Pedro's aunt, also pointed her finger at me, making an even stronger appeal, "You AIM people, what are you going to do? You are supposed to be warriors. What are you going to do? If you men can't do it, then we women will. Even as I speak, the FBI and marshals are taking over our schools, hospitals, and sacred places." Then she said the same thing in Lakota with such feeling and anger that many in the room began to weep. Finally she added, "We must take action today, not tomorrow."

One of the men said that most of the people present wanted to storm the tribal council building and retake what was rightfully theirs. "But," he said, "that would be playing Wilson's game. That's what the goons expect us to do. There are just waiting for us with their machine guns, waiting to mow us down."

Lou Bean said, "Then let's not go to Pine Ridge. We'll fool them. Instead, let's go to Wounded Knee and make our stand there."

Her words shot through the crowd like an electric shock. I felt chills running down my spine. Gladys Bissonette spoke to the men again, saying, "Let's go to Wounded Knee right now!" The women were showing us the way. Leonard Crow Dog stood up and said that Wounded Knee was the most sacred place for the Lakota and the best place to make a stand. Severt Young Bear stood up then and said that in going to Wounded Knee we would bring a good spirit to the ghosts of our people who were massacred there in 1890.

Russ and I stood up to give a last word. This was the only time we spoke during the meeting. I said that we would commit the American Indian Movement, body and soul, to the struggle, however long it might last. And if necessary, we would die in this struggle. Fools Crow ended the debate by saying, "Then we'll go to Wounded Knee. The AIM warriors will lead us."

My heart was racing. My adrenaline surged at the thought of what we were about to do. I knew the drum was calling us and we were heeding the call. Carter Camp said, "Let's secure Wounded Knee now. We have some three hundred warriors ready to go. If we're going to do it, let's do it right now."

I said, "Let's organize the caravan." We had fifty-four cars. I rode in the lead car with Chief Fools Crow. We had a leader in almost every car.

This time we did not avoid Pine Ridge. We made a show of defiance by driving through the cold night, right past Wilson's headquarters with our lights blazing, car horns honking, and AIM flags fluttering from our car antennas. The goons and marshals came running with guns in hand, trembling at the thought of an impending attack. We drove right past them—they stood there open-mouthed and uncomprehending. I saw people running back and forth on the roof of the tribal council building like ants out of an ant heap stirred with a stick. It must have been about six o'clock in the morning; it was just barely beginning to get light. Our caravan seemed miles long. There were cars and cars and more cars. The miracle was that, with so many old clunkers, not a single vehicle broke down. It seemed as if the spirit of the people had inspired the spirits of our old wrecks.

After we had arrived at Wounded Knee and secured the area, the first thing we did was hold a prayer meeting at the long ditch—the mass grave of our slaughtered people. Meanwhile, some of our men were going through Gildersleeve's Trading Post, stripping it bare, taking firearms, ammunition, and food—all items we really needed. I looked for Pedro Bissonette and found him grinning, wearing a big war bonnet somebody had hocked years before at the trading post. I told the people standing around the trading post not to take anything and not to make a mess of things because it would reflect badly on us.

The Gildersleeves had a long history of exploiting Indians. Since beginning their operation in the early 1900s, they had expanded the trading post into a cafeteria, a pawn shop, and a curio shop as well. There were stories—many stories—of the Gildersleeves opening local Indians' mail and endorsing and cashing the enclosed government checks. The Gildersleeves said it was to cover debts that were owed to them. So cleaning out the trading post was a little payback that some of our people felt was justified.

It did not take the government long to react after we reached the Knee. Within an hour the little hamlet was surrounded by roughly one hundred marshals in combat boots and flak vests. A lone FBI agent in an expensive-looking business suit stood on a knoll surveying the scene. Two armed personnel carriers came down an incline, the drivers' heads comically sticking out the side windows. Two helicopters hovered overhead. Later, we were buzzed by low-flying planes.

Wounded Knee is situated inside a small valley surrounded by the rolling prairie of low hills covered with Gamma and buffalo grass. Vegetation is sparse, though here and there stand clusters of evergreens. The site is dominated by the hill on which the Sacred Heart church stood; twenty-five years later, only the foundations of the church remained. Downhill below the church flows the creek in which so many victims of the 1890 massacre perished.

We set up a defense perimeter and command post around the small, white Sacred Heart Catholic church on the hill next to the mass grave. The perimeter was a low wall, maybe four feet high, made of sandbags and cinder blocks. A child could have jumped over it. We hung a large four-direction flag from the church steeple. We established a sort of no-man's land, a strip about five hundred yards wide between us and the nearest Feds. We called it the DMZ after the demilitarized zone in Vietnam. In the middle of the zone we put up a tipi for any negotiations that would take place between us and the government.

We took stock of the situation. Including what was taken from the trading post, we had roughly thirty-five firearms, mostly .22s and hunting rifles. One of our men, Bobby Onco, a Kiowa from Oklahoma, had an AK-47 with a banana clip, a souvenir from Vietnam. I don't think he had any ammo for it; he used it to impress the media and the marshals. Later during the siege, we set up a stovepipe, which caused a panic among the Feds. "Oh my God, those Indians have a rocket launcher!" We certainly didn't have any rockets and had almost no ammunition. What little we had usually did not fit the strange assortment of arms we carried, and we doubted that much of it could reach the Feds five hundred yards away. It was a puny force that faced the mightiest government in the world with its huge arsenal of deadly weapons! We also had very little food. Most of our people thought we would occupy the Knee for no more than two or three days. Our leadership knew better.

Everybody went over to the church. It was small, but it was the biggest building we had. The church's Jesuit priest, Father Paul Manhart, was sitting in the basement, frightened. I went down to see him because I did not want him to have the wrong idea of why we occupied the church. I said, "Father Manhart, you can have anything you want upstairs—food, coffee, whatever."

He said, "Please, for God's sake, don't harm me."

I told him, "Father, we're not here to hurt you. You can walk around and talk to whomever you want. You can find out why we're here. Nobody will hurt you."

He did not want to believe me. He looked at us as if we were redskins from some old movie come there to scalp him. He kept repeating, "Please don't harm me."

A car full of goons raced up the hill, snapped off two shots at us, then took off as fast as they could. It was not a big thing, but it was an indication of what was to come. We put the grandmothers and small children in the church basement to keep them out of harm's way.

Upstairs, the church was crowded. In fact, it was packed. People kept coming in and we couldn't find space for them. Some eventually settled down in the trading post, which slowly was transformed into a boarding house. I told our Oglala people, "If anybody wants to go home and get a change of clothing or a blanket, you should do that now because at any moment the Feds will set up road blocks and you won't be able to return. We don't know what's coming down on us."

During the first twenty-four hours of occupation, Wounded Knee was a beehive of frantic activity. It was up to Clyde and me to find people on the outside we could count on for support. We called AIM chapters, churches, and organizations that had helped us in the past, telling people to come up and help us with food and supplies. The phones were open and had not yet been interfered with, so we could call anybody we wanted throughout the world. The response to our call for help was immediate. Support for us began to come in from around the country. Demonstrations for Wounded Knee were held in many cities. People even walked to the village under the cover of night, bringing backpacks full of food and supplies. Everybody present was trying to volunteer for a variety of tasks. I had never seen so many people totally committed to a single cause.

There were occasional shots fired throughout the night. Some of our young men shot out the street lights on the main drive so that we could move about in the darkness without becoming easy targets for our enemies. I began to wonder about the consequences of our actions there at the Knee, hoping and praying that nobody would be shot or killed. It had always been my main concern over the many years I had been with AIM—that somebody would get trigger-happy and provoke a deadly incident. I did not want a brother or sister to suffer because of an error on my part or someone else's or because of somebody's uncontrolled emotions. We could not allow single individuals to develop their own agenda. The entire leadership made it clear to everyone what should be done and what should not. There would be no firing except in self defense, and—even then—only if sanctioned by our leaders.

We felt everything had to have some kind of approval by the leadership because our actions and the possible consequences—were more serious than they were at the BIA takeover or the Custer action. Wounded Knee was an event that would bring the world's attention to our struggle. One of the things I had learned was that the possibility of negotiation must always be there. We had to be willing to negotiate with even our most stubborn opponents, even in the midst of a fight.

Among us were people from many tribes: Navajo, Ojibwa, Sac and Fox, Potawatomi, Iroquois, Lumbee, Shinnecock, Pueblo, Kiowa, Comanche, Ponca, and several more, including tribes from the northwest. About 65 percent of the people present were local Lakotas from the Pine Ridge, Rosebud, Cheyenne River, and Standing Rock reservations. Even some non-Indians had come to help us—Chicano brothers, young white men and women from the '60s counterculture, and a white doctor with a few nurses. We welcomed them all.

People came and went. During the first two days, some of our elders, such as Pete Catches and Frank Fools Crow, left for home at night and came back in the morning. Although we had already put up our roadblocks, the Feds had not yet established theirs. Even after the marshals and FBI agents had closed ranks around us, they were never able to seal us off completely. Supporters always trickled through. From the beginning until the end, we were able to maintain two-way traffic in spite of everything the Feds would do to prevent that. The Feds had their tripwire flares, their snipers with night scopes, and their attack dogs. Oscar Bear Runner and Severt Young Bear were our specialists in getting through. They always seemed to know how to avoid the Feds' patrols and dogs. I think we Indians were just naturally better at this kind of night work because we lived so close to the earth.

We had gathered up eleven white people and were holding them in one of the buildings near the trading post. Father Manhart, the Gildersleeves, and the couple with an unpronounceable Polish name who had been hired to run the trading post were among them. We put our guards around them, not to prevent them from escaping, but to prevent them from being harassed by any impetuous young guys. We let them go after the first two days. They were the strangest "hostages" you ever saw. They refused to leave, saying they were afraid of the goons and the trigger-happy marshals. They told us they felt a lot safer with us.

Once it became clear we were going to be at Wounded Knee for a while, we realized we had to decide who was in charge of what. Leonard

Crow Dog and Wallace Black Elk were, as usual, our spiritual leaders. Stan Holder, a Wichita from Oklahoma, was appointed head of security. Lorelei DeCora from Iowa took charge of our "hospital." She later married Ted Means, Russ's brother. Russ became our spokesman because he had charisma and "a good mouth." Carter Camp was to gather support and sometimes take charge of the warriors. Matt King, Jr., was our official interpreter, and I became one of the principle spokespersons for AIM.

Kamook was with me at Wounded Knee. We slept that first night in a car. Around two or three o'clock in the morning I kissed her and said, "Please, please, don't get yourself hurt. What is happening here is a major, major event in the history of our people. It will affect their lives and our own lives. It is a privilege for us to be here at this time. I don't know how long we'll be here or how it will end. Out there the Feds have heavy weapons and enough ammunition to kill every Indian in South Dakota ten times over. People might get wounded or killed. I pray with all my heart that this won't happen. I love you. Please, please, don't get hurt!" And though the cold night was full of threats, Kamook and I were snug, warm, and full of hope for the future.

CHAPTER 14

The Siege

*This is not an AIM action. It is an all-Indian action. They can't do any-
thing worse than kill us. Be prepared to defend this position with your
life! The Feds will be coming soon. What is at stake here at Wounded
Knee is not the lives of a few hundred Indian people, but our whole
Indian way of life.*

—Dennis Banks, Ojibwa

On our second day at the Knee, I woke up early in the morning, about
5:00 A.M. I sat up in the car and realized how strange it was to wake up
knowing this was a decisive moment in my life, that this morning was
only the beginning. I wanted to be part of this movement with all of my
body and heart, as a negotiator or as a combatant. I did not care which.
I realized that the takeover could last ten days or even longer. As I sat
there in the car, I realized that we had to take a definite plan of action.

That day began as an armed stand-off. Shots had been fired. Both
we and the Feds had roadblocks up. Joseph Trimbach, head of the FBI
in South Dakota, was already at the federal roadblock, arresting any of
our people who tried to leave. We had to develop a game plan immediately. We had to act as an organized group and insure that we would be
seen in the right light. It was important that the American people and
the people of the rest of the world understood why we occupied this
place and why it was so sacred to us.

There was a knock at my car window at around 7:30 A.M. It was
Clyde. He said, "Dennis, we'd better call the leadership together."

Inside the trading post, some people who had a huge pot of coffee bubbling called out, "Come in, come in, have some hot java!" so we decided to hold our meeting inside the museum there. That museum was an obscenity. The signs read, "WOUNDED KNEE MASSACRE HISTORIC SITE. SEE THE MASS BURIAL GRAVE, CURIOS FOR SALE. MASSACRE PHOTOGRAPHS AND POSTCARDS. EDUCATIONAL."

Items that had been taken from our slaughtered people were displayed in glass cases. They had large photographs on the walls, almost poster-sized, showing our frozen dead, their bodies grotesquely twisted as death overtook them. The photos showed dead mothers with their murdered babies and Chief Big Foot, lying stiffly in a half-raised position as though he were still trying to stand up. They showed soldiers grinning among the heaps of slain victims, of bodies stacked like firewood, ready to be dumped in a common ditch. Little personal objects like beaded buckskin dolls taken from the hands of the dead children were also on display. The museum even sold offensive poems about Uncle Sam not taking any "guff" from ghost-dancing Injuns, "cause he ain't built that way."

Amidst all this repulsive stuff, we held our meeting. First we decided the Oglala elders would be the main negotiators. They would be at the center of everything we did. AIM would take a supporting role. Our AIM men and even some of our bravest women would be in the front lines defending the perimeter. Then we further defined the roles individuals would play. Russ would assume the role of spokesman for the Oglalas, while Clyde and I would act as spokesmen for the American Indian Movement.

We had already written up our demands and sent them to the Feds with a man from the Justice Department's Community Relations Service. We told him, "Communicate this to whoever is in charge." He handed our demands to Trimbach. We demanded that we personally be allowed to discuss various issues with presidential aide John Ehrlichman and Senators Kennedy, Abourezk, and Fullbright. The letter ended with:

The only options open to the United States government are:
1. They wipe out the old people, women, children and men by shooting and attacking us.
2. They negotiate our demands.

Before noon on the second day at Wounded Knee, Trimbach arrived in a car with a white flag attached to the antenna. He stopped at the FBI roadblock, got out of the car, and started walking toward us. Carter met him in no-man's land. It was there, between their roadblock and ours, that discussions began. Carter wanted their assurance that the Feds would not advance any further. Trimbach said he would not and could not assure us of that, and that the only thing he could guarantee us was safe conduct to Pine Ridge, which of course would mean our arrest. He returned to his roadblock, saying he would be back in the afternoon.

Later in the day when Trimbach came back, he was met by Russ. He told Russ that our only option was to surrender. Russ, of course, laughed at this. Trimbach repeatedly accused us of forcibly occupying the village. Russ responded that this was our land and that the FBI and marshals were the trespassers. The discussion became heated as Trimbach insisted over and over again, "Your only hope is to surrender." Trimbach wrote in his report, "It soon became apparent that Means was getting more excited, and that I was getting more nervous; and I, therefore decided to leave without engaging in any further conversations with him." According to Russ, Trimbach was scared shitless and made off as fast as he could. So then it was war.

We situated our defenses among the four roads that intersect at Wounded Knee. On the northwest side, we dug out our Last Stand bunker near a small housing project to block the road from Manderson. On the northeast side, our Little Bighorn bunker blocked Big Foot Trail where it crossed Wounded Knee Creek on its way to Porcupine. As the Big Foot Trail led southwest to Pine Ridge, we blocked it with our Star bunker. The nearby unpaved Denby road headed southeast from Wounded Knee. Where it crossed the creek, we placed the Lil' California bunker on one side and the Denby bunker on the other. South of the Knee between the Star and Lil' California bunkers is where we situated the Crow's Nest bunker. To the north between our Last Stand and Little Bighorn bunkers was the Hawk Eye bunker. West of the church, we set up another bunker called Black Elk. Our bunkers were nothing more than covered holes in the ground. The government's field command post was a luxurious Winnebago motor home with a two-way radio, located on top of a hill along our eastern perimeter. It was called "Red Arrow."

Originally our perimeter enclosed "downtown" Wounded Knee and the Sacred Heart church on what some people called Fry Bread Hill. The hill dominated the landscape of open, rolling prairie. The church housed some of our people and was always jam-packed. It had an altar and plaster-cast figurines of Jesus, Mary, and Joseph flanked by vases of paper flowers. We took so much fire from the Feds that the statues had bullet holes in them. We turned the church basement into a kitchen. Behind the church lay the cemetery—a rectangular mass grave in which the victims of the 1890 massacre at Wounded Knee were buried.

Downslope, south of the church, stood the Peace, or Negotiation, Tipi and two sweat lodges. Further south and across the Big Foot Trail was the trading post, which served as housing. The museum area of the trading post compound became our security headquarters. Below the trading post and across Denby Road stood a row of four houses; the one with heat and water became our clinic. To the east were two small churches, the Tipi Church and the White Church, the latter of which was made into another kitchen. Below the Tipi Church stood Lansbury House, the comfortable living quarters for the Church of God missionaries.

We set ourselves up in these structures that constituted the interior of our perimeter—some ten buildings and about a square mile of rolling prairie of withered buffalo grass dotted with snow patches. The land around Wounded Knee was open, with few trees and almost no cover. Whatever ground cover had existed outside our perimiter had been burned off by Feds in an attempt to eliminate hiding places, and the fires had made the surrounding country acrid with dense clouds of whitish smoke. The Feds could do nothing, however, about the little gullies and arroyos that made it possible for us to sneak in and out of Wounded Knee.

Already by the second day, the media had arrived. We were thankful for their attention. As long as the press were there, we could not be attacked. Carter Camp told one reporter, "I tell you, if it were not for you people, this government would have slaughtered us as it did in 1890."

The number of Feds steadily increased—two hundred on the first day, two hundred fifty on the second, three hundred on the third, and so on. In the end their number had swollen to almost five hundred, including ranchers and vigilantes of all kinds who were eager to "bag themselves one of them red savages." Wayne Colburn, Chief U.S. Marshal and our old adversary during the BIA takeover, arrived. The army was there too, even though the use of the army in domestic conflicts is expressly forbidden by the United States Constitution.

Almost as soon as we occupied the Knee, army advisors and observers from the Pentagon made plans to drive us out of the village. They supplied the federal agents at Wounded Knee with an unbelievable amount of military hardware, enough to kill the whole Oglala tribe. There were fifteen armored cars—APCs—one hundred thousand rounds of M-16 ammo, eleven hundred parachute illumination flares, twenty sniper rifles with night-vision scopes, powerful searchlights, submachine guns, bulletproof vests, gas masks, C rations, ponchos, blankets, and helmets. Low-flying army planes performed photo reconnaissance missions, which frightened some of the older women. They thought we were about to be bombed. After the planes left, we "liberated" a nearby rancher's steer for food. One woman remarked, "If they accuse us of killing this steer, I'm going to tell them those planes just scared it to death!"

A top-secret plan called Garden Plot was developed by the Pentagon to deal with us. Army activity was coordinated by the Directorate of Military Support, an undercover Pentagon unit that was in charge of the army's assistance to law enforcement agencies. Col. Volney Warner, Chief of Staff of the 82nd Airborne Division, was ordered to Wounded Knee on February 29. He was told to wear civilian clothes, presumably to hide the fact that the army was illegally involved in a domestic conflict. One of the first things Warner did—to which we probably owe our lives—was to refuse a request by the FBI to commit two thousand regular army troops to overrun Wounded Knee. The Feds would have followed the soldiers to arrest any survivors. Warner rejected the idea of repeating the 1890 massacre.

We found out what went on behind the scenes years later when certain memos and orders were declassified under 1975 amendments to the Freedom of Information Act after the Watergate scandal. In one of those declassified memos, Warner had written, "The aim of the game is not to kill or wound Indians. An army involvement resulting in loss of life and injury would reflect badly on the army. Time is of no essence. The object of the exercise is not to create martyrs." He removed the Garden Plot plan's references to "using deadly force" and persuaded the FBI to change their usual "shoot to kill" rules to "shoot to wound only in cases of self-defense."

He had asked FBI agents if they were still "shooting to kill." One agent answered, "Rifles are for that purpose." Warner pointed out that a second Wounded Knee massacre would be disastrous. He made fun of the Feds for being afraid of "Indians armed with women and children." If not for him, I might be dead now.

Of course, Warner's views were not popular with the administration. An option paper prepared by one of the president's aides suggested that Nixon authorize "massive force," then calculated how much the operation would cost and how many Indians and soldiers were likely to be killed. Nixon's advisors presented him with two choices: to take Wounded Knee by force—regardless of casualties—or to withdraw all federal forces and let AIM and Wilson's goons battle it out among themselves, which would be "much less expensive." These men played at deciding our fates without our knowledge.

Before long I realized that we were in for a long haul. I knew the Feds would try to starve and freeze us out. But this was our kind of war—we have been fighting hunger and cold all our lives.

Tensions continually increased. On March 1, two APCs with .50-caliber machine guns mounted on the fronts came within five hundred yards of our perimeter. The clinic had its first patient that day—one of our young men accidentally shot himself in the hand. On the same day, someone fire-bombed the Pine Ridge home of AIM's communications director, Byron DeSersa. No one ever doubted that Wilson's goons were responsible. They had made obscene phone calls to the house before throwing Molotov cocktails through a window. The explosions and shattered glass seriously injured Byron's wife. Byron had told the press earlier, "Wounded Knee is sacred to us in the way that something becomes sacred through pain, grief, and loss."

On that same day, both of South Dakota's U.S. senators, James Abourezk and George McGovern, arrived and tried to mediate between us and the government. Abourezk was sympathetic, but McGovern in his fashionable polyester suit was less so. They achieved nothing.

On March 2, an additional group of marshals arrived to reinforce those already there. With them came fifteen local ranchers who volunteered to help the Feds. In a nearby Nebraska cowtown, several hundred more ranchers had discussed the events and made a resolution that "those fucking Indians [had] raised more than enough Cain," and that "a company of red, white, and blue he-men should be formed to make an end of the AIM nuisance."

That day I happened to talk to one of our young people who worked security at the Black Elk bunker west of the church. He showed me his .22-caliber rifle; the broken stock was held together with duct tape. He told me with a grin, "I have only one bullet for this." He was better off than the guy who had a World War I Italian rifle—not a single bullet would fit it.

We still had some food left for the warriors who had been on watch all night. Some of our women served them a breakfast of hard-boiled eggs, cereal, powdered orange juice, and coffee. Lizzy Fast Horse, a grandmother several times over, was in charge of the cooking. She soon ran out of eggs, as the Feds had started to prevent people from bringing us food. Obtaining a steady stream of supplies for us was not easy. Once, I made light of the situation by announcing, "That was not beef you ate today, but an old horse, a nag!" Clyde Bellecourt replied, "We will eat our horses, dogs, cats, rats, and even dirt before we will submit."

Again and again, the government's negotiator, Ralph Erickson, gave us the same ultimatum. "The U.S. offers to let the Indians go free to leave Wounded Knee without threat of mass arrest. . . . But Indians will have to surrender their weapons and all males must identify themselves. There is no intent to punish persons unknowingly involved, but even if we wished to do it, we could not close our eyes to the criminal violations that have occurred." He added, "There is no question of amnesty or that charges won't be filed against the Indians if violations of the law are found. . . . The use of force to retake the village has not been eliminated as an alternative. You must leave by 6:00 P.M. or face immediate arrest. We want you to leave during daylight hours so that we can be sure that you are all out." He went on, "We have to be firm. We can't be wishy-washy or you guys would be there forever."

On March 3, Dicky Wilson issued his own local call to arms:

FELLOW OGLALAS, FELLOW PATRIOTS

What has happened at Wounded Knee is all part of a long range plan of the Communist party. First, they divide the people, get them to fight among themselves . . . disrupt the normal function of society, and demand the removal of officials, including myself.

To combat this unpleasant nuisance we are confronted with, we are organizing an all-volunteer army of patriots. We need all able-bodied men over eighteen years of age. We are requesting General Chesty Puller, U.S. Marine Corps, retired, to take command.

There is no doubt that Wounded Knee is a major Communist thrust. They have established a beach head. Now it is up to us to get them out. We will organize while the federal government is negotiating. And when the federal government has yielded, conceded, appeased, and just plain surrendered, we will march into Wounded Knee and kill Tokas, Wasichus, Hasapas, Spiolas, and hippies. They want to be martyrs? Let's accommodate them. Since the American Indian Movement is supported by non-Indians, we are enlisting the help of all non-Indians on the Pine Ridge Reservation. Let's get this show on the road.

Translated from the Sioux language, "Tokas, Wasichus, Hasapas, and Spiolas" meant Indians from other tribes, white people, black people, and Hispanics. In other words, Wilson called upon his followers and anyone else with a racist agenda to join a killing party. However, his eight- or nine-hundred-man army never showed up, nor did General Puller show much interest in taking command of Wilson's goons.

As early as February 28, the marshals circulated the order, "Do not let newspaper personnel into the area." Beginning March 3, reporters were denied access to the hamlet. On March 4, our telephone lines were cut. The phone had been our only way of communicating with the outside world, except for sneaking out and making our way to Porcupine, nine miles distant, through a cordon of marshals with sniper rifles. Always they put the pressure on, "You have to give yourselves up or we're coming in!"

On March 4, the Feds began to measure the quantity of gasoline in the gas tank of every car that, for one reason or another, was allowed to go into the perimeter. They wanted to make sure no one could secretly donate some gas to us.

Amidst the distrust that surrounded Wounded Knee, Indians from dozens of tribes achieved a degree of unity never before dreamed of. Most decisions were made by unanimous consent. On rare occasions we had differing views on things, but we were able to come to a consensus.

We were not without problems, however. Our engineer, Craig Camp, one day became angry and confronted the leaders. He said, "Things have gone to your head. Your noses are stuck in the air. You want only to talk to the media. You guys better get your act together. Spend some hours a day with the people doing bunker duty digging slit trenches. Collect garbage. We're *all* Indians here. There's no such thing as higher-class Indians for the media, and lower-class Indians doing all the shit work." With that he resigned. I begged him to reconsider but could not persuade him. I felt that he was right, and that I, as a member of the leadership, was partly to blame. We then made our medicine man, Leonard Crow Dog, chief engineer in addition to his duties as our spiritual leader.

Wounded Knee was becoming more dangerous overall. Almost every day we were fired upon—sometimes only a few rounds, at other times a heavy barrage. We never knew what would set it off. In between, there were negotiations. Most of the time we could communicate through a two-way radio with Red Arrow, the Feds' command hub, often trading jokes or insults. We had many cease-fires and truces, which were always broken by the Feds. On March 4 at about 8:00 P.M., an APC drove right up to our entrenchments and fired upon us. They also set off a tear-gas canister. We shot back and a firefight ensued in front of the Sacred Heart church. Bullets whizzed all around us, past us, over our heads, burying themselves in the earth next to our feet. It was a miracle that nobody got hit.

On March 5, we were pleased to hear that Bill Kunstler, a famous civil rights lawyer from New York, was joining our defense team. He joined the people already working on our behalf—our own Indian attorney, Ramon Roubideaux, Beverly Axelrod, Kenneth Tilsen, and Mark Lane. They set up headquarters in Rapid City and founded WKLDOC, the Wounded Knee Legal Defense-Offense Committee. The Feds allowed our lawyers access to us most of the time.

Finally on March 6, the government issued its ultimatum. Erickson declared, "Negotiations cannot be made at gunpoint." He advised us, "The situation has become extremely grave. Evacuate your women and children before it is too late. You are given until nightfall on the eighth to evacuate Wounded Knee." The hostile faction of the press called Wounded Knee a "guerrilla theater," but this was no theater. This was war in the truest sense. I warned the government, "The Massacre of

1890 started when one shot was fired. Now, one shot could start a great new Indian war right here!"

We had to be prepared for the worst. Some of our young men burned the wooden bridge over Wounded Knee Creek to prevent APCs from overrunning us from the south. Black smoke rose from the slowly smoldering ruins. We soon realized that Crow Dog was a wizard at devising creative means of defense. Under his direction, we strengthened our bunkers, making them five feet deep. Women made sandbags from pillow cases and old clothes. Crow Dog taught the men who had no firearms to make their own zip guns. Then he filled Coke bottles and lightbulbs with gasoline. He put fifteen hundred of these on one fuse, strung them all the way around our central positions and connected them to a battery so that we could set off the whole system simply by touching the wires together. We pounded charcoal to make gunpowder for use only as a last resort. We planted several round metal 16-mm film canisters, each about the size of a medium pizza. We pretended they were teller mines. We made stove pipes look like recoilless rifles. We used every trick in the book to create an impression of strength.

We were so out-gunned, so much weaker than the Feds. We naturally wanted to avoid an armed conflict, but we knew the government could force the issue. Early on, I sent out a call to arms to all our Indian and non-Indian supporters. They came—some with guns, some without. One day, no less than forty walked in at one time. We had by then established our system of gullies, which allowed hidden access to our perimeter. The Feds could never close them because they could never find them. They called them "AIM's Ho Chi Minh road." On March 7, the first airborne help arrived. A small plane obtained by Rocky Madrid and Owen Luck was able to land within our perimeter. It carried food supplies donated by sympathizers. The Feds fired hundreds of rounds at the plane but, luckily for us, did not hit it.

Until March 8, we had led a charmed life. In spite of the Feds opening up on us whenever they had the slightest excuse—or no excuse at all—no one had been hit. But on that day we suffered our first two hits from government fire. We decided that Crow Dog as our medicine man was most qualified to handle whatever surgery was needed. Our white doctors, medics, and nurses were treating upper respiratory problems and even pneumonia, but had not expected to be handling bullet wounds. Milo Goings had been shot in the knee. Crow Dog first used his special medicine, which he called "redwood," to make Milo's knee numb. After the medicine had taken effect, Crow Dog dug the bullet out with a small pocketknife. He disinfected the wound with a special herb and used deer sinew to sew up the wound. Milo said that he "didn't feel a thing." He healed in a very short time.

The other victim was a young kid who got an M-16 bullet in the wrist. Crow Dog again applied his redwood medicine, then he cut a slit in the wrist and pulled the bullet out with a pair of tweezers. Then he cleaned the wound with his disinfectant herb. The young man could use his wrist again within two weeks. A few days later, a man called Two Shots was hit in the ball of the foot. Crow Dog's operation techniques were again successful.

The hospital we set up at Wounded Knee was a simple two-room, one-story building across from the trading post. One room was the surgery and dispensary; the other room was the living quarters of Lorelei DeCora and Madonna Gilbert, the two women who ran the clinic. Lorelei was AIM's state director for Iowa. After Wounded Knee, she became a nurse for the tribal hospital at Rosebud. As I write this, she is trying to establish a diabetes clinic at Porcupine. Madonna was always a brave woman who could hold her own in any fight. Lorelei and Madonna used both Western and Indian medicine in treating their patients. They had no antibiotics, painkillers, or even bandages. Outside Wounded Knee the donated medical supplies were piling up, but these supplies were stopped by the Feds or the goons. So we did without. On one wall Lorelei had scrawled in large letters: "BLEEDING ALWAYS STOPS IF YOU PRESS HARD ENOUGH ON IT." Good advice! A number of us took that advice once fighting started in earnest—the hospital was under fire almost every night.

Every week the Feds allowed in a team of a doctor or two and several medics. The Feds always searched them carefully, going through all of their medical supplies and equipment piece by piece. Pat Kelly, a white physician who had come from Seattle with a small medical team, told us, "I'm a Vietnam veteran, and the things I have seen here—the tracers, the flares, the government burning off of all cover down to the last shrub, the APCs—it's what I experienced in Vietnam. It's like a flashback to Da Nang."

Lorelei and Madonna risked their lives bringing the wounded in from bunkers and trenches. They were concerned for the people living in flimsy homes and tarpaper shacks who had slugs coming right through their walls, concerned about the women chatting and joking in front of our improvised outhouses while bullets whizzed past them.

Taking care of sanitation was also a part of the medical team's duties. They dug the latrines and buried waste in lime pits. Carla Blakey, a Saulteaux Indian from Canada, transformed an old garage into a four-stall women's toilet. When, after a heavy exchange of fire, one of the medics making the rounds, yelled inside, "Everybody alright? Anybody need tranquilizers?" Carla laughed and said, "Imagine a place where you gotta have tranquilizers just to go to the can!" In spite of the primitive conditions, our clinic was better managed than the BIA hospital at Rosebud.

The people the Feds called "friendlies"—the goons and vigilantes—caused a lot of trouble. Both had set up their own roadblocks. The Feds ordered them to remove the obstructions, but without much success. Whenever things were quiet or the government and our people seemed close to an agreement, either the goons or the vigilantes began firing, trying to imply that we were shooting at the Feds and that the Feds were shooting at us. We knew they intentionally stirred up trouble and provoked firefights.

On March 7, the government's ultimatum was still in force—"Get out or else!" Our warriors put on face paint. Crow Dog daubed red circles on their foreheads and blessed each man. Then for the first time we heard an ominous sound—the Feds opened up with a .50-caliber machine gun. The .50-caliber was a fearful weapon; a few rounds could knock a wall down. Firefights broke out all through the day, but suddenly, late in the day, we called a new cease-fire. It was quickly broken when shooting began again.

On March 9, a woman was hurt by flying glass when rapid fire caused havoc in the part of the trading post where she was staying. The Feds began shooting tear gas into some of the bunkers. As one of the Feds boasted to a newsman, "We want to flush them out in order to make them into better targets." By that time, the ranks of the Feds had swollen to four hundred.

On March 10, John Adams, a sympathetic Methodist clergyman connected with the National Council of Churches informed me that he had brokered an agreement. The roadblocks would be coming down, and the media and whoever else wanted to could simply walk in. As we watched through our binoculars, it seemed as though the Feds were giving up their positions. A government spokesman announced, "We will not move on Wounded Knee tonight. The Justice Department will make every effort to arrive at a peaceful conclusion to the tense and dangerous situation." I should have been tipped off by the fact that he added, "but we must enforce the law and that we *will* do." I was happy. I was fooled, however. I thought we had won and so I declared victory. I thought, from what the Methodist clergyman had told me, that Washington was going to accept our demands.

There was drumming, singing, and cheering. More than a hundred of our people left and went home, while many new warriors, including chiefs and elders, joined us. But victory did not go smoothly. During the night vigilantes snuck in and set fire to the trading post. The fire was discovered and quickly extinguished. Just as it was now easy for friends to come in, it was also easy for enemies. We were forced to send out patrols and to put our roadblocks back up again.

The Oglala chiefs and headmen talked things over in the Peace Tipi and declared that, from that moment on, they would negotiate with the United States as one nation to another nation. They issued a proclamation:

LET IT BE KNOWN, MARCH 11, 1973, THAT THE OGLALA PEOPLE
WILL REVIVE THE TREATY OF 1868, AND THAT
IT WILL BE THE BASIS FOR ALL NEGOTIATIONS.

Let the declaration be made that we are a sovereign nation by the Treaty of 1868. We intend to send a delegation to the United Nations.

We want to abolish the Tribal Government under the Indian Reorganization Act. Wounded Knee will be a corporate state under the Independent Oglala Nation.

In proclaiming the Independent Oglala Nation, the first nation to be called for support is the Six Nation Confederacy (The Iroquois League). We request that the Confederacy send emissaries to this newly proclaimed nation.

Sovereignty! That had been in the back of our minds all along. That's what we had dreamed about for so many years—to be out from under the white man's rule, to govern ourselves again, to be truly independent. Now it had happened, but it meant the war was not over. It had barely begun.

CHAPTER 15

A Nation Reborn

We are going to Ghost Dance for the people buried here in that ditch.
There won't be no coffee break.

—Leonard Crow Dog, Lakota

It was now a whole new ball game. All previous negotiations were meaningless. The Oglalas became what they had been before the white man took their sovereignty away—an independent nation. The Oglalas demanded the same recognition the United States accorded countries such as France or Italy, and they asked the same from the United Nations. In this request, the Oglalas faced the greatest confrontation yet—if we ultimately succeeded, then other Indian nations would also become independent. The whole system under which the United States had ruled us—a system so carefully built over two hundred years—would simply collapse.

Official acknowledgment of the Treaty of 1868 would mean not only that our Sacred Black Hills, but all of the Dakotas, much of Montana, Wyoming, and Minnesota with all their natural treasures—coal, oil, uranium, gold, and silver—would revert to us. White America would never give that up. It would fight for the land tooth and nail. The odds against us were astronomical. I had no illusions. Still I would fight for Indian sovereignty no matter the cost, if only to establish the principle for future generations.

At Wounded Knee, we formed a new warrior society with brothers and sisters from many tribes. A warrior is not the same as a white soldier who gets paid, gets a pension, and who kills because he is ordered to. To us, being a warrior is not about killing. A warrior should be the first to go hungry and the last to eat. He or she should be the first to give away one's own moccasins and the last to get new ones. That is what being a warrior is all about.

When the chiefs, holy men, and elders took council in the Peace Tipi, we all agreed that AIM people should be excluded from the meeting. We felt that the Oglala people should make all decisions regarding their future without outside influence. The traditional leaders emerged from an all-day council inside the tipi and told the crowd that they had chosen to declare their nation's sovereignty. They had voted to send delegates to the United Nations and to inform the White House in Washington, D.C. that the Oglalas were going to be independent from now on. AIM was eager to help them. We assisted them in setting up a provisional government and then everyone present began strengthening our positions at Wounded Knee—we planned to be ready to repel any invaders.

We made the Pine Ridge reservation, onto which the Oglalas had been driven by force, a land base. We had this land, we had a government, and we had the support of Indian people on the Pine Ridge reservation. We even had the support of the majority of white America. In the Harris poll, two-thirds of the Americans informed of events at Wounded Knee sided with us. What was at stake was not merely the lives of a few hundred people, but a way of life and our right to live it.

To make it perfectly clear that the United States was now a foreign country and that the Oglala Nation now had borders like other nations— borders that included Wounded Knee—Russell Means made a statement: "If any foreign official representing a foreign power, specifically the United States, comes in here without permission, that will be treated as an act of war and dealt with accordingly." He added that spies would be shot by a firing squad. The last bit was a typical piece of Russell rhetoric.

Oddly enough, the guys sent by the government to spy on us were four postal inspectors guided by two vigilante ranchers. Of course, it wasn't about inspecting the mail. Postal inspectors are federal agents with the same powers as the FBI. They can make arrests. The four postal inspectors carried guns and wore badges when they came to our border. Our security stopped them at the checkpoint, disarmed them, and arrested them. They were made to stand in a row with their hands on their heads, shivering. They were photographed, and their pictures appeared in local newspapers, which must have been embarrassing for them. Once caught, the "postal inspectors" immediately identified themselves as federal agents and said, "We are armed. We have handcuffs," trying to forestall our security from discovering their identity and roughing them up. They said they had come to "check out mail tampering." We thought this was more than a little strange—four federal agents concerned with mail fraud during a major confrontation with daily firefights!

The postal inspectors were brought into the museum, which served as our security headquarters. They were told to sit down and wait. Their guns, handcuffs, and badges were piled on a table. One of the inspectors was so scared that he pissed in his pants. The urine ran down his leg, forming a puddle on the floor. When Leonard Crow Dog came in, one of our security guards asked him, "What do we do with these characters?" Leonard told him that it was early in the morning, that it was cold, and that they probably needed some coffee. They were provided with coffee and scrambled eggs although our food supplies were low. For the better part of an hour, Crow Dog explained to them what the situation was at Pine Ridge and why we had occupied Wounded Knee. Then he had the agents politely escorted out of the perimeter.

Later, after our stand at Wounded Knee was over, Leonard Crow Dog, Stan Holder, and Carter Camp were tried and convicted on charges of armed robbery and interfering with federal officers in the performance of their duties. They faced the armed robbery charge because they had come into the room while the guns were lying on the table. They had not been present when the guns and cuffs were taken away from the "postal inspectors," but their presence in the same room made them guilty in the eyes of the law. The courts did not go after the security guys who actually disarmed the inspectors because they were only interested in nailing the leadership. The second charge was brought against them because they had interfered with the agents' attempt to spy on us.

Even before we dealt with the U.S. spies, we were further refining the nature of our newfound tribal sovereignty. The newly liberated country was offering citizenship to whomever happened to be within its perimeter. Passports were issued and visas given out to the press and to "foreigners." I said, "This is no longer a perimeter, it is a border." The newly established provisional government formed committees on housing, defense, immigration, internal security, public health, and information. Though he was not officially named as such, Vernon Bellecourt, who was always on the outside doing what he could from a distance, acted as a foreign minister.

The vacant houses of missionaries and business owners who had left on March 6 were taken over for use as kitchens, information centers, sleeping quarters, and so on. The central part of the trading post became an auditorium where people gathered every day to hear the latest news. They listened to speeches by the leadership and elders, voiced complaints about various things we needed to deal with, and sang and prayed together. We had realized that we would have to stay in Wounded Knee for a long time and that security would become all-important. We used a mechanical backhoe to dig deeper bunkers. We put stoves into our bunkers and in some we installed sleeping lofts or bunk beds.

Our new nation created an army that was as unlike the U.S. army as possible. It had no generals or colonels. It was an army of equals. It was made of men and women who respected life and hated killing, because the loss of a life—whether white, red, yellow, or black—is still a loss of life and a victory for death. We had no uniforms, unless you call ribbon shirts uniforms. We had no officers barking orders, but our warriors sang a lot. We had no discipline except self-discipline. Ours was a wonderfully strange army.

At the Knee we had what we called roving patrols. We used cars "borrowed" from local missionaries. We used about five cars, fueled with gas from the trading post pumps, to patrol the hills and keep the marshals and APCs at bay. The first federal roadblocks had been set up about a mile and a half from our lines, and we were able to keep them at that distance. We had our patrols going twenty-four hours a day. The roving patrol squad was made up of men from the northwest—Montana, Washington State, and Northern California. These men were some of our strongest warriors.

One night we heard that the Feds were sniping near the Last Stand bunker on the road to Manderson. They were shooting at some of our people trying to come in. We opened fire on the marshals—not to hit them but to scare them off. It worked. All our men returned safely, and the marshals' fire slackened off on most sections. During that third week it was snowing hard. We rarely initiated firefights, partly because we had so little ammo. There were hardly any firefights during blizzards, but one day the firing got so intense that slugs coming through the walls of the Sacred Heart church carried away the chin of the statue of Jesus Christ, blew a hole in the chest of Joseph, and shot off the hand of the Virgin Mary.

On March 17, the Feds started a firefight that lasted three hours. One of our medics, a Chicano named Rocky Madrid, a really first-class guy, was wounded. He and Owen Luck, a former helicopter medic in Vietnam, ran with their first-aid kits to where our young warriors were under heavy fire. They were clearly identifiable as medics—they wore helmets and armbands marked with big red crosses and carried a white flag—but the marshals opened fire on them with machine guns. The night was illuminated by so many flares that you could have read a newspaper; the Feds must have been aware that they were shooting at medics. For some time the two men were enveloped by tracer bullets buzzing like a cloud of angry bees. Witnesses thought they would literally be blown to bits.

Rocky was hit in the stomach by a bullet that had ricocheted, but he managed to drag himself to the clinic. Crow Dog applied his numbing medicine then used a small pocketknife to dig out the slug, which was stuck in the muscle. He fanned Rocky off with burning sage, using his eagle wing. Rocky said he didn't feel the pain. He was up and going three days later. Owen was not hit. The standoff contiued.

People often forget that AIM is not so much a political organization as it is a spiritual one. Carter Camp and Sid Mills set up a routine in the bunkers so the men could purify themselves by taking sweat baths every evening. Sweat lodge fires were going all the time in the early weeks of Wounded Knee. It didn't matter what race you were. If you were at the Knee, you went through the traditional sweat bath and purification ceremonies. Our ancient Indian religion had found a renewal at Wounded

Knee. It brought us together once again into the Sacred Hoop of our ancient beliefs. We were becoming what we once had been.

It was in this environment at Wounded Knee that our chief medicine man, Leonard Crow Dog, decided to bring the Ghost Dance back, because it was here that in 1890, Chief Big Foot's Ghost Dancers had been massacred by U.S. soldiers. After that massacre, the Ghost Dance was outlawed, as well as all other traditional Indian ceremonies.

Crow Dog told the people:

We're going to Ghost Dance. There are forty of us who want to do it right *here* on that brown, dried-up winter grass and patches of snow. We're Ghost Dancing here where our people were massacred. We'll dance for four days. You'll be tired, but there is no saying, "I'm tired, I've got to rest." There's no rest in the Ghost Dance, no coffee, no lunch break, no cigarettes. There won't be, "I'm a Sioux, I'm a Chippewa, I'm a Mohawk." We'll be dancing as one tribe. And whether it's snowing or freezing, we'll dance.

And maybe somebody among us will get a vision or be in a trance and fall down. Well, you must not be scared of this. We'll not be calling for a medic. The spirit will be the doctor. Just keep going. Don't stop for anything. Hold hands. I'll teach you a song—the voices of the spirits. The drum will be the heartbeat of Mother Earth. The clouds are the dreams—visions of the mind. We will be praying to elevate ourselves from this world to the other world.

The dancers met in a hollow away from the eyes of the Feds an hour before dawn the next morning. It was the same gully where Big Foot's people had been massacred. The dancers moved slowly in a circle in the light flurry of snow flakes. In the center of the dance circle, Crow Dog had planted an evergreen tree—a Tree of Life. Some of the dancers fell down in a trance, some had visions. Four full days the Ghost Dancers danced. Some of those dancing and praying were descendants of the people from Big Foot's band. And we had a sign. A lone eagle circled overhead.

Medicine man Wallace Black Elk told the people, "The Tree of Life withered and seemed to die on that frozen field with the slaughtered bodies of our women and children. But the roots of the Tree are still alive. They are *not* dead. The Sacred Hoop of the people has been made whole again."

During the first days of the occupation we did not have a food problem. We lived off what we found in the trading post—all kinds of frozen and canned goods were stocked for tourists in the little grocery store. We had, on the average, about three hundred supporters living inside the perimeter, besides the local Indian residents who did not take part in the occupation but lived inside the perimeter and had to be fed all the same. Our supplies did not last long. Soon we got down to two skimpy meals a day, mostly rice and pinto beans. At other times the only thing we had to eat was oatmeal. The cooking was originally done in several different areas, but later it was centralized for efficiency. It was necessary to keep all food together so the cooks knew at all times what was available. The food was dispensed in rations according to the number of people in each area. The hospital, however, had priority due to the needs of the sick, the aged, the very young, and the wounded. They came first. And of course, the warriors on the firing line got their meals before the general population because they were putting their lives on the line to protect us.

Acquiring food became a problem. There was plenty of food donated to us by well-wishers, but the Feds would not allow it through. It was piling up in places like Crow Dog's Paradise, and it was up to us to smuggle it in. The government was determined to starve us into submission.

Chief U.S. Marshal Wayne Colburn announced on March 12 that no food for the Indians would be allowed to pass federal roadblocks, saying, "We will establish a tighter perimeter and starve out the occupiers." He added, "I'm sure as hell planning to change their lifestyle. If that means starving, if it means being cold, or not being able to read the evening paper or watch television, or make phone calls, and having no soap to wash themselves or their clothes—well, *good!* They have only themselves to blame!" When the government turned our lights off, we went back to oil lamps and candles. When they turned off the water, we went through the gullies to get creek water. When the Feds turned the heat off in the middle of the Dakota winter, we made a stove out of oil cans and made some heat that way.

It was my job to organize the nightly backpack caravans that traveled through the ravines and arroyos that crisscrossed the area—our underground railroad. The marshals and the FBI knew that supplies were reaching us but didn't know by what route. They did interfere with the few backpackers they could find, but they never could stop them completely. Our underground railroaders were usually guided by someone like Pedro Bissonette or Oscar Bear Runner, who knew the areas well and could make their way to us in dark. They came by starlight or navigated by the light of a distant landmark.

Bringing in food meant a long walk in the night, usually ten to fifteen miles through country teeming with government snipers using infrared night scopes and trained attack dogs. The land was often swept by machine-gun fire and streams of tracer bullets, which Crow Dog said "looked like swarms of lightning bugs." The dogs, at least, we knew how to handle. I think it was Stan Holder and Owen Luck who invented the urine-and-pepper anti-dog defense. A group of men would go along urinating on the ground, laying a trail for the dogs to follow. The trail always ended in a handful of hot chili pepper. Once the their noses connected with the pepper, the dogs were useless for hours.

Our backpacks usually weighed about forty to fifty pounds loaded. Backpacking was exhausting and dangerous. You could get into a crossfire even if agents did not know you were there. If flares illuminated the area, you had to lie down on your belly, often in some ice-covered puddle, and try to make yourself as flat as a flounder.

When passing close to the Feds, backpackers often walked for a considerable time in their stocking feet to avoid making noise. The backpackers who were arrested for their efforts were charged with "crossing state lines with the intent to incite or participate in a riot." By the beginning of April, the Feds had tightened the ring around us so close that hardly a mouse could get through. They finally discovered a particularly well-hidden section of the trail and posted several APCs with mounted machine guns along that path.

By March 30, we were down to two meals a day. A week later it was one meal a day. And then a week after that, we had to get by with one meal every other day with a bowl of thin soup in between. On the day the occupation ended, the only food left was a forty-pound bag of dry pinto beans. The first signs of malnutrition had appeared among the children. They were very thin and had little immunity to infection. A number of people suffered from respiratory illnesses. The elderly and small children were also suffering from intestinal bugs and diarrhea. There was no toilet paper. Most of us used the great outdoors but the toilet in the clinic was backing up. Medical supplies were stopped at the road blocks. Our doctors warned us of the possibility of serious disease. Everyone was coughing. Warriors did bunker duty while running a fever.

Kent Frizzell, the chief government representative at that time, would only let powdered milk and baby food pass into Wounded Knee. He declared, "To my knowledge, the U.S. government has never given food to the enemy to sustain them." We weren't ready to give up yet, so rather than starve, we tried cattle-rustling. A rancher named Coates had a big spread nearby where he ran his cattle. We "liberated" some of these animals, which, according to an old tradition, we called "slow elk." I joked around, saying that many of these cows were straying into our perimeter, which made them illegal aliens or even agents disguised as cows.

Some of our young warriors who hunted the slow elk were from the city. They didn't quite know how to go about it. Once they led in a cow that none of them knew how to kill or butcher. A white reporter shot and skinned it for them. Another time they came in with an ancient stringy bull whose meat was likely to break our teeth. I put up a poster showing the rear end of a bull with big balls and a cow with an udder. I jokingly wrote underneath, "This is a bull. This is a cow." It was the backpackers who kept us alive.

Part of my job was keeping morale up. When people are hungry and freezing, they need a morale booster. That was me. There was a mimeograph machine in the trading post, and we had a lot of paper—as much as two thousand sheets—so I started a daily newsletter to all the people at the Knee. My news service became really important after the telephone line was cut. I would get up before dawn and type out the day's message. Every day the backpackers came in with tidbits of information. They also brought us newspapers. Sharing the news connected all of us with one another. I told the people about our supporters all across the country. It was my job to boost their spirits. Every night I handed out news bulletins and distributed mail that had been smuggled in by our runners. Many times I played psychiatrist to people with troubled minds. I also arranged for people on the inside to get word to their families and friends on the outside via our underground railroad.

Before the phone lines were cut, I would read to the people messages we received from hundreds of well-wishers. Letters, telegrams, and phone calls came from every part of the world. Once we got a call from a group of skins in Vietnam, telling us they wished they were with us at the Knee, that the real war was happening in America, not in Southeast Asia. During one meeting, I read aloud no less than seventy telegrams from supporters. These telegrams were prayers for our survival and for victory in our struggles. Russ also had a job to do in getting word out to the press, telling the world that the Oglalas themselves occupied Wounded Knee, not some white commies and hippies as Dick Wilson had told the press.

On April 5, after days of wrangling, a solemn agreement was signed between us and Kent Frizzell, which seemed to finally end the siege. In the name of the government, Frizzell accepted six of the ten demands representing the conditions under which we would disarm. Under this agreement we would get congressional hearings on the continuing validity of the 1868 Treaty of Fort Laramie, and a meeting at the White House. The agreement was signed in front of the media. On the same day, our delegation of Leonard Crow Dog, Russell Means, Tom Bad Cob, and Ramon Roubideaux left for Washington, D.C., to finalize the agreement.

We had won a further concession—the phone lines were opened once again so that those of us staying at Wounded Knee could communicate with the delegation and discuss their progress. In the meantime, I experienced some of my happiest days inside our encircled little village. It was a time when Kamook and I could begin to breathe again. She had shared so much with me, often going out to the firing line with the first-aid crew, taking food to the warriors, and being pinned down by fire during intense exchanges. I felt relief that she was safe.

On April 11, eighteen-year-old Mary Ellen Moore gave birth to a healthy baby boy. I remember thanking the Creator for giving us a new life. To me the event was the symbolic rebirth of something good and beautiful that had died in the snow of 1890. The day before we had heard a recurrence of ghostly crying from the grave of the 1890 massacre. Even some of the marshals heard it from their sandbags. We were told later that some of the Feds couldn't stand the sounds and broke down. I felt, as many others did, that our ancestor spirits were with us, moving about at the time of this baby's arrival.

The birth took place inside a trailer during a firefight. Josette Wahwassuck acted as the chief midwife. She was seventy-two years old, and we called her "Grandma AIM." She had delivered thirteen babies before this one, so she knew what she was doing. Josette was assisted by Annie Mae Pictou, Vernona Kills Right, and Ellen Moves Camp. It was not an easy birth. Mary was in labor a long time. The little newborn was called "Pedro" in honor of Pedro Bissonette, who was a friend of Mary's. The naming of a baby always has a special significance, but even more so this time—Pedro was later murdered by BIA police. Through Mary and her son, his memory and name live on.

We informed Red Arrow, the Feds' communications center, of Mary's birthing and the possibility that she might need to be moved out of the perimeter. The Feds had seen a lot of our people braving the exposure to danger, milling around the trailer, drumming and singing in spite of the bullets. They wondered what could be going on over there. Just as soon as little Pedro gave his first cry, I went into the trailer with a few others to hug Mary, and I wept openly. She was not even done with the birth yet, as the afterbirth had yet to be taken care of. The people neither minded that nor did they pay attention to the marshals' bullets whizzing by. Everybody was just eager to see the baby, hug Mary, and thank her for the great thing she had done for us. The baby's natural father was not at the Knee and was never in partnership with Mary after that, but she had a circle of family here all around her. After awhile, little Pedro was dressed. Josette held him up briefly through the trailer window for all the people to see. A cheer and a brave-heart cry rose up when the crowd saw him.

By then the prairie around us was on fire. The Feds were still burning off all the underbrush to deprive our backpackers of cover. Vernona told me, "They're making a smoke signal to announce the birth of our little Wounded Knee warrior." That night there was a ceremony among the people. The AIM song was sung for little Pedro, and I remember talking to the Great Spirit in the sweat lodge, giving thanks for this new life.

The next day another event occurred that gladdened me. There took place a wedding between Nogeeshik Aquash, an Ojibwa, and

Anna Mae Pictou, a young Micmac woman from Nova Scotia. Around the second week in March they had come in with a group of four or five other people from the east. Nogeeshik was a thin, rather elegant-looking man who wore a stylish, flat-brimmed hat. Annie Mae was a small woman, barely five feet tall, but—as I was glad to find out—she had the heart of a lion.

Usually Stan Holder would bring newcomers over to us leaders late in the afternoon. I remember that March day when he brought the couple and their companions to the trading post so we could talk to them. I spoke to both of them and asked Nogeeshik and Annie Mae what they wanted to do. I told them, "You can be on the firing line, you can help with the cooking, you can go out and hunt, you can bring food in for the warriors, you can be on security, and there are other duties to perform."

They looked at each other and Annie Mae said, "We'll both take the firing line."

And I said, "Alright." I assigned them back to Stan, who took them to the Crow's Nest bunker. When I saw Nogeeshik and Annie Mae about two or three days later, they were digging in. They had found a place to dig themselves a big foxhole. I thought to myself, "These two are going to stay here for the duration." I saw Annie Mae cooking, digging latrines, and helping out at the first-aid station, but mostly she and Nogeeshik stayed close to their foxhole on the firing line.

One night in early April, Nogeeshik came up to me and said that he and Annie Mae wanted to get married at the Knee. This idea thrilled me. I told him, "Maybe you should see Wallace Black Elk and, together with your request, give him an offering of tobacco." Normally Crow Dog would have performed the marriage, but he was still in Washington, D.C., with our delegation.

Though we had sent a delegation to Washington, D.C., to negotiate peace, there were still firefights every night. I was usually absorbed by the raging battle, but I would sometimes get a glimpse of Nogeeshik and Annie Mae. She sometimes had a handgun strapped to her waist but more often carried a rifle. She always seemed busy—I never saw her idle. She was one person who never was a burden. In fact, she lightened the burdens of everybody else. That's how I remember her inside Wounded Knee.

Wallace had told me about their wedding plans and wanted to know what he should do. There was still the possibility that Crow Dog might come back in time to perform the ceremony. We were waiting for word from Russ. He, Crow Dog, and the other delegates were supposed to negotiate with the White House people, then they were to call us to say whether the administration, which we hoped would including the president, would meet with us to end the occupation. But the call never came.

Finally, Russ called me from his room in the Washington, D.C., hotel where he was staying. He said the White House people still had him on hold, that at any moment a meeting might take place, and that they had told him to stand by. On April 8, Russ was reported to say, "We are at an impasse. We've abided by the agreement, and we're still waiting. There are over two hundred men, women, and children whose lives are on the line at Wounded Knee, and we're sitting here in this goddamn bourgeois hotel that we can't afford, getting fucked over by the White House."

It didn't seem that either Russ or Crow Dog would be attending the wedding. Nogeeshik and Annie Mae were growing impatient and wanted to be married with the pipe in the big hall of the trading post, where we had set up command. Wallace asked me, "When should we do it then?"

I said, "Well, as soon as possible. Within a week."

He said, "Well, set a date."

"Alright. We'll have it on April twelfth." I said this on impulse and then remembered that date was my birthday. That was just fine with me. It would be a memorable day.

Four male elders gathered on that same evening that Mary had given birth and advised Nogeeshik on the meaning and duties of an Indian marriage. Four women elders did the same with Annie Mae. Afterward, the four men and four women made flesh offerings for the couple. Tiny squares of skin were cut from their forearms as a sacrifice to ensure a good life for those about to be wed. Then we held a sweat lodge ceremony. I felt good. Here we had a birth, and right after it a wedding was about to take place. I took that as a sign of life continuing for us. I felt there would always be Indians, that our history was not about to end, and I thought, "Tomorrow there will be a joining of two people together as man and wife. Children are being born. This is no longer an occupational force; this is a community coming alive here at Wounded Knee." So we prepared for the next day.

On the morning of April 12, we began the ceremony. Nogeeshik treated us to a small give-away—very small under the circumstances—but the spirit was generous. We were still hoping Crow Dog would arrive, but we proceeded with the wedding ritual. Wallace Black Elk performed the ritual, and it was beautiful. He put the blanket over their shoulders—two radiant people sheltered by one blanket, four hands joined in holding the pipe. I introduced Nogeeshik and Annie Mae to the people. Most of them already knew the groom and bride, but every day new people came to the Knee. The big room was packed with about three hundred people, a joyful gathering after so many weeks of stress. I took my place at the drum, and we began singing songs the way Wallace instructed us. Of course, we sang the AIM song, all five verses of it. Martina White Bear, a young Winnebago woman, did the cedaring and fanning off. She said to me, "That's the way I want to be married someday."

Wallace spoke, "My brothers and sisters, this is a great happening—the first marriage ever performed at Wounded Knee under the Independent Oglala Nation. And I want to thank you—*you* who have come to aid the Oglala Sioux in this time of trouble and uncertainty. And now you are part of our family. We are really proud of you, and may the joy of the Great Spirit be your strength. That is my prayer."

We smoked the pipe, first the newlyweds, then the four men and four women elders who had come to be part of the ceremony, then the inner circle, and then the drum group. We all shook hands. I went up to Nogeeshik to shake his hand. I looked down on Annie Mae, and she gave me that shining, big, beautiful smile. I said to her, "Today is a good day."

She nodded yes.

I said, "By the way, Annie Mae, April twelfth is my birthday. So your wedding was a birthday gift to me."

She smiled again and said, "Thank you, thank you, thank you."

The two of them were very proud as they returned to stand on the firing line together. It was a fine example for the other warriors to see these two together under fire in the face of such odds, standing up to the greatest military force on earth. That to me was showing America that we were going to go on. We were not just about foxhole duties and fighting the Feds. We were continuing with our lives. We knew the government could and would put us in jail, could even kill us, but nothing could stop our movement. We had a destiny and we were going to survive!

CHAPTER 16

The Stand Down

My mind is crowded with thoughts of those warriors who fought and died for us. They were brave men and brave women. I shall not eulogize their deaths. Instead I shall draw on their life memories and be strengthened.

—Dennis Banks, Ojibwa

At Wounded Knee we were starving. Shelves were bare. We had run out of food. The Feds had tightened the noose around us. It became harder and harder for our backpackers to get the needed supplies to us. We were always hungry now. One night, a small plane suddenly landed on the road in front of the trading post. Owen Luck and Rocky Madrid had gotten a plane, a pilot, and four hundred pounds of food for us. We were surprised and delighted. The Feds were also surprised but less happy. Although it may sound like a lot of food, when you consider that we had to feed an average of three hundred and fifty people every day, it is easy to see that four hundred pounds of food would not last long.

We had received garbled messages that other friends on the outside were organizing an airdrop with even more food for us. We yearned for it like a man stranded in the desert yearns for water. But we waited in vain. Then early one morning, we heard the sound of engines overhead. People were shouting, "Our planes are coming!" But it was only two Phantom jets screaming over us, breaking the sound barrier and temporarily deafening all of us. They were taking aerial photographs of our positions for the benefit of the marshals. It was not what we had hoped for. I began to doubt that the airdrop was real; I resigned myself to the likelihood that it was not going to happen.

On April 17 at about five o'clock in the morning, I was tapping out my daily newsletter when I heard a humming that sounded like APCs revving up. It got louder and louder until I realized it was a different kind of noise. All of a sudden, Carter Camp came running into my cabin yelling, "Dennis, Dennis, it's happening! Come outside and look!" Kamook and I hurried outside to see three Piper Cherokees coming in very low over the hills to avoid radar detection. The small single-engine planes began circling about five hundred feet above us. Their cargo doors had been removed, so we could see some men kicking out huge duffel bags.

Seven duffels floated down on parachutes that barely had enough time to open before they hit the ground. Only one chute failed to unfold. That bundle broke open when it hit the ground. Two duffels fell so close to the Feds' position that we could not immediately retrieve them but did so later under the cover of night. I don't think the Feds knew what was going on for the first fifteen minutes or so, but when they realized there had been an airdrop, we received sporadic fire from them. Then they began using .30-caliber machine guns and tried to shoot one of our bundles to pieces.

Our people were jumping up and down, yelling, "*Food! Food!*" I thought, "Goddamn! Somebody *cares!* They *care* if we survive or not, and they knew how to deliver this manna from heaven! Plus, the planes were called *Cherokees!*" It was almost too good to be true! The whole airdrop lasted barely five minutes. It had been carefully timed for daybreak when the marshals and FBI would still be snoring in their bunkers.

The lead plane made a second pass to drop one more load at two hundred and fifty feet. Then the Cherokees took off in a big hurry in different directions, bobbing and weaving to prevent the marshals from reading the numbers on the wings. By this time, the Feds were shooting at the planes with machine guns. There was some significant damage to one of the planes, but they all escaped without being crippled.

Months later, I had a chance to meet the organizers, pilots, co-pilots, crews, and even some of the folks who contributed funding for the effort. The man who conceived the idea, Bill Zimmerman, a white friend, also piloted one of the planes. He later wrote a book about the airdrop called *Airlift to Wounded Knee*, which is a long and fascinating story. The other two pilots flying those rented Cherokees were Billy Wright—a black pilot with superb flying credentials and a zeal for helping Indians that made him the perfect flight leader—and Jim Stewart, a white sky-diver who had made over six hundred parachute jumps. Larry Levin was a co-pilot who had raised a lot of money for the airdrop. Numerous others also helped make this miracle happen.

About fifty of our people lost no time dragging the heavy bundles away from the firing line into the security building. We cut them open and began to inspect our gifts. There was a ton of food, including cheese, flour, pinto beans, rice, sugar, coffee, baking powder, salt, lard, powdered milk, peanuts, raisins, ham, oats, chocolate bars, and cartons of cigarettes. There was also a lot of toilet paper, bars of soap, and even packages of Tampax. Our benefactors had thought of everything! We took some of the food immediately to the little white house where we had our kitchen set up. Our happy women were eager to start cooking. Within each of the bundles we found a printed message for all of us. It began:

> To the independent Oglala Nation and their friends at Wounded Knee: Your struggle for freedom and justice is our struggle. Our hearts are with you. . . . This is a fight against an unyielding and brutal government that makes the poor people of the world its victims in its search for power and profit. . . .
>
> One lesson is to realize that the frustration and disillusionment we may at times feel are only the result of a misunderstanding of our real ability to affect the course of this country's policies. Wounded Knee shows us that no matter what the setbacks, just struggles are not stopped by any president or any policy.

I read the message aloud to the people after we all gathered together in a large room inside the trading post. It was very quiet as I read those words. I began to choke up, feeling a tide of emotions rise in me. I finished the page and looked about me. People were crying openly and quietly embracing. I said, "Alright! Let's get to work! Grab all the duffels, make sure that they all are emptied, sort out all the supplies, and *let's start cooking!*" And that's what we did. For us, that food was like the original meaning of Thanksgiving. All the warriors came in from the lines except for a very few who had to stay at their posts. We brought food to those men. Gladys Bissonette and the other cooks prepared a fantastic meal that evening.

We didn't know then that we were heading into one of the saddest days since the siege began. Even though this day began in such a miraculous way, we had reason by the end of it to offer prayers of sorrow along with our prayers of thanks. Frustrated by our unwillingness to give in, the Feds became vicious. About an hour after the airdrop, they sent their helicopter, "Snoopy," into the air over our encampment. A sniper in the copter began taking a bead on individuals—a young kid here, a woman there, a medic, or a dog. Someone else in the copter aimed a handheld M-16 automatic at us.

Eddie Whitewater and a few small children were walking back to their house with a bag of food when bullets riddled the dusty ground around him. He and the kids just stood there transfixed, not knowing which way to run. Our guys opened fire on the helicopter in order to distract attention from Eddie. One of our bullets actually hit Snoopy, which was advised by Red Arrow to leave the area. Our fire gave Eddie and the children a chance to roll into a ditch and hide.

What began as sporadic fire in the early hours after dawn became a full-blown attack of unleashed fury from the Feds. The firefight lasted all day and spilled over into the night. The Feds threw everything at us but the kitchen sink—M-30s, M-60s, .50-caliber machine guns, M-79 grenade launchers, CS gas, aerial illumination flares, a high-powered strobe searchlight on each APC, and, finally, rockets to launch massive gas attacks.

During a typical short exchange, the Feds hit us with anywhere from five thousand to ten thousand rounds, while we answered them with less than fifty rounds. Streams of tracer bullets crisscrossed the village from all directions, raking it from end to end, concentrating on anything that moved. Some areas were littered with empty machine-gun shells. The effect of .50-caliber machine gun bullets was frightful. They simply tore the place apart, knocking entrance holes the size of oranges into the walls and exit holes the size of soccer balls. The seventy to seventy-five warriors manning our bunkers had only about ten small-caliber bullets each to defend us.

Our ranks had increased the night before when a small group of new supporters had somehow hiked in undetected over the hills. Among them was a couple from North Carolina, Frank Clearwater and his pregnant wife, Morning Star. Frank was part Apache and Morning Star was Cherokee. They were not members of AIM but had heard about the trouble we were having and hitchhiked all the way from their North Carolina home, wanting to help us any way they could. He was forty-seven years old and she was ten years younger. Henry Wahwassuck brought them to the command headquarters and introduced them to me. I embraced them, telling them how glad I was that they had come to help us. I asked if they wanted to cook or if they wanted to pull guard duty or patrol.

Frank told me, "I came here to fight. My wife can cook. She can be part of that." Those were the only words I had with Frank. I introduced him to Stan Holder, who asked if they were tired and wanted to rest since they had been walking all night. They went to lie down, he on a cot inside the little Episcopalian chapel north of the Sacred Heart church. Around 9:30 A.M. that morning a burst of fire from the Feds sent a .30-caliber slug through the wall of the church, crashing through the back of Frank's skull.

For over an hour, our medics could not even get to Frank because of the heavy fire the Feds poured in on us. Finally, two brave women medics, Lorelei DeCora and Madonna Gilbert, ran through the curtain of bullets, entered the church, put Frank on a stretcher, and carried him to the hospital. They were helped by three men part of the way. The medics wore helmets and armbands with red crosses and they waved a white flag on a broomstick. Even so, they were continuously shot at by the Fed snipers. The marshals at Roadblock Number Six fired at the stretcher-bearers all the way to the hospital door. It was a miracle they were not all gunned down.

We contacted Red Arrow to request a helicopter to take Clearwater to the hospital, but Chief U.S. Marshal Wayne Colburn gave the order, "No helicopter is to go into Wounded Knee. If they have any wounded, bring them out under a white flag to Roadblock Number One, and they will be flown from there." So we had to do that, and Clearwater was airlifted to the reservation hospital in Pine Ridge. The medics there were horrified when they saw him and said, "We can't handle *this!*"

Clearwater was eventually flown to a hospital in Rapid City. His wife, Morning Star, had been assured that she would be allowed to be with him, but upon her arrival in Pine Ridge she was arrested, dragged weeping from her critically injured husband, and thrown into the overcrowded tribal jail where she, visibly pregnant, had to sleep on the cement floor. They gave her nothing to eat but a bowl of cornmeal mush. She remained incarcerated while Frank underwent surgery. Almost two days went by before Morning Star was allowed to be at her husband's bedside. He never regained consciousness and died eight days after he had been shot.

Morning Star wanted to have her husband buried like a warrior inside the perimeter of Wounded Knee near the spot where he fell. But of course Dick Wilson forbade this, saying that there were tribal laws forbidding a non-Oglala to be buried anywhere on the Pine Ridge reservation. That was bullshit. He lied as usual. There were plenty of non-Oglalas and non-Indians laid to rest on the rez. In the meantime, Crow Dog had come back from the fruitless negotiations in Washington, D.C. He offered to have Clearwater buried on his land. A delegation from Wounded Knee was allowed to accompany Frank Clearwater to his last rest. Both the tribal big shots of Pine Ridge and Rosebud set up roadblocks to stop our funeral caravan. At Pine Ridge, they even opened the coffin to search it for weapons.

In the end we overcame all of these attempts to prevent us from burying Frank in the sacred traditional way. There was a one-day wake held at the home of Chief Frank Fools Crow twenty miles from Wounded Knee, then Crow Dog gave Frank back to Mother Earth on the Crow Dog land, saying prayers in the old Lakota manner. The Feds had begun to deny their actions and to spread a rumor that Frank Clearwater wasn't even an Indian.

Well, he *was* an American Indian brother, and he gave his life supporting his people and our beliefs. He died for us. That is enough for me.

Five others were also wounded on that same sad day that had begun so well, but they all eventually recovered. We mourned Frank Clearwater for four days. On the second day of mourning, the Feds tried to drive our guys out of their bunkers with helicopter-launched CS-2 gas. During one massive wave of tear gas, our people who were stationed in the Little Bighorn bunker ran out through the escape trench and plunged into the freezing creek to wash the tear gas from their faces and clothes. Wounded Knee became more and more dangerous as each day passed. It was impossible to be anywhere out in the open without instantly drawing fire.

People continued to come and go, but more were leaving than arriving. During the last two weeks of April, things were happening rapidly. We knew that we could not hold out indefinitely against the overwhelming strength of the government. Our ammunition was running out. Some warriors had no bullets left. With so many mouths to feed, the food from the airdrop lasted just ten days. The situation was critical. In the back of my mind was the thought that if we finally were overwhelmed, *all* of our leaders should not be caught in the net. Of course, I did not say this aloud. I decided to stay until the last and wanted Carter Camp and Crow Dog to stay also. Russ never did come back from negotiations in Washington. I persuaded Clyde Bellecourt to leave, saying I wanted him to take over our Minneapolis office to run AIM affairs from the outside.

Looking back, I can see that too many of our leaders were at Wounded Knee and that it was foolish to expose them to capture. Not only the AIM leadership was imperiled. Our greatest medicine men were there—Frank Fools Crow, Pete Catches, Wallace Black Elk, Charlie Kills Enemy—and such chiefs as Tom Bad Cob, Matthew King, and Pedro Bissonette. We had too many of our leaders inside the perimeter and not enough on the outside.

Vernon Bellecourt had never been inside the perimeter. He remained outside, acting as a roving ambassador for us. He had a wonderful way with the media. He made speeches, lectured on TV, and arranged for press conferences. He also had a gift for coining catchy, memorable phrases. Ted Means, Russ's brother, was asked to be our general support gatherer, and Pedro Bissonette went on to Rapid City to keep the underground railroad going. He knew the terrain well and could tell the backpackers which way to go and what to look out for. Nogeeshik and Annie Mae had also left by this time. Annie Mae told me she was losing track of her two daughters; she yearned to hold them in her arms again before she continued working for our cause. She did come back after the siege and would later give her life for us.

On April 15, Crow Dog had returned from his failed negotiation in Washington, D.C., to a big welcome. He had been away about ten days. I admired him for returning that late in the game when all signs were pointing to our being overwhelmed by government forces. He didn't have to come back to us; he could have stayed on the outside where he was needed every bit as much as at Wounded Knee. Wallace Black Elk could have provided spiritual guidance inside the Knee, but Crow Dog was the center; his gravitational pull held us together. There was never any doubt in my mind that without Crow Dog, some of our people would have just given up. We were strengthened by his presence. He had that special gift of power.

April 26 was the biggest and fiercest firefight of the siege. It was also the last. It went on for two days. The goons started it by firing in the direction of the Feds to provoke a big shoot-out. The Feds naturally thought we were firing at them and opened up with everything they had. Our warriors returned fire. We tried to tell the Feds over the two-way radio that the goons had started the firefight, but the situation was already out of control. The fight was feeding on itself, growing in intensity from minute to minute. I was up at 5:00 A.M. as usual and Kamook was going out on her assignments with Vernona Kills Right, who was Crow Dog's companion at the time. They were going from bunker to bunker with first-aid kits to see how the guys on the firing line were doing and to give them a morale boost.

The shooting began around 9:30 A.M. that morning. After weeks of firefights you get kind of used to them, but I sensed right away that this one was different. It was terribly intense and it never stopped. All hell had broken loose. There was frantic radio traffic between our bunkers and also between us and the Feds at Red Arrow. The Feds radioed, "Hey, you Indians, if we see one of them dudes jumping out of the bunker with long black pigtails, and if we capture him, first we're going to cut off his hair and then we'll cut off his balls!"

Little Bighorn bunker radioed back, "Go to hell!"

Last Stand bunker reported, "We're being hit hard!"

Denby bunker announced, "We're under heavy fire also, and we're running out of ammo. Hawk Eye, can you get us any back-up? Over."

Hawk Eye bunker radioed to Denby, "Keep your heads down and hold on. Don't waste any ammo. They would like to drive you out of that hole. Don't let them! Over."

Red Arrow radioed Wounded Knee with, "Be advised that if we receive even one single round, we'll hit you with everything we've got!"

Little Bighorn radioed back to Red Arrow, "Fuck you! Over!" And so it went, hour after hour, all day long.

Kamook and Vernona were still making their rounds, bringing coffee to the bunkers. When they hadn't come back in by 2:00 P.M., I began to get very worried. Then Lorelei DeCora came back from her tour of duty and told me, "They are hiding in a gully. They're pinned down, and I think they've gone to sleep." *Gone to sleep?* I couldn't believe it. They had taken refuge in that gully with bullets whizzing over their heads for three hours, and they were *asleep?* But it was true. They were that tired. They had their winter jackets on and were pretty cozy. I was impressed.

The fighting carried over into darkness and through the following day. It just went on and on. In the early afternoon of April 27, I heard somebody yell, "We've got a guy down!" They were trying to reach him where he had fallen near Last Stand bunker. He had been pinned down by a sniper and was hit as he came up to see where the shots were coming from. I ran out of where Kamook and I were staying. Crow Dog was already out there ordering a stretcher to try and bring him in.

The shooting was fierce, but Crow Dog kept urging the stretcher-bearers on, "Keep going, going, going!" We had called Red Arrow to cease firing, that we had a man down, but it took a while for the bullets to stop.

Stan Holder ordered the cease-fire and Carter Camp yelled, "Get that man over here!"

Finally, there was a lull in the shooting. The limp form was brought by stretcher back to the designated first-aid area. It was then I discovered that it was Buddy Lamont, Kamook's uncle and brother to Lou Bean. This came as a tremendous shock to me. Just thirty-one years old, and his life was over. Crow Dog opened Buddy's shirt and took it off. There was a clean wound, a bullet hole right through his heart. He had been shot in the back, and the slug had gone right through and out the front. I had my hand under his head. He was still warm. He looked peaceful, as if he were asleep. Crow Dog bent over Buddy, weeping and saying something to him. He sang a death song as he put sage into Buddy's wound, then he offered a prayer for the fallen warrior.

Kamook came running. She and Buddy had been very close. They loved each other. Kamook cradled Buddy's body in her arms, hugging him and sobbing, "Buddy, Buddy, Buddy!" Kamook cried uncontrollably, screaming at the Feds and calling them killers and murderers. This was the moment I had always feared. One knows that in a struggle like ours, somebody might be hurt or even killed. It's inevitable in a confrontation that turns violent. Nonetheless, you pray that it's not going to happen. A death hurts you so much, and the pain goes very deep.

Buddy had come to me saying, "I want to be with you," putting his life in my hands. When somebody in your care is hurt or killed, you sense the sorrow of the family and feel guilty, thinking that his death is your fault. That is what I felt. That is what Carter and Stan felt.

I watched Kamook and Lou Bean, Buddy's sister, weeping and holding Buddy. The strength of their love shone like a light about them, and I thought, "How beautiful. How strong and brave Kamook and Lou are."

When our side had called for a cease-fire, it had taken a long time for the Feds to quit shooting. Only when we informed Red Arrow that we had a man dead did they finally cease their firing. We requested that they let us bring Buddy out accompanied by the people closest to him. That request was granted. The Feds gave us their word that nothing would happen to those accompanying the stretcher, that nobody would be arrested. So our men lined up in two rows, standing like an honor guard as the body passed the roadblock and the little procession moved slowly down the road. Kamook and her sister, Bernice; Lou Bean and her husband; Mary Ellen Moore carrying her newborn son; and a couple of Buddy's other relatives accompanied the stretcher out of the Wounded Knee perimeter.

As soon as their feet stepped onto Pine Ridge land, they all were arrested and handcuffed. They were taken to jail by Wilson's tribal police and were detained overnight. Some were kept longer. Mary Ellen Moore was separated from her sixteen-day-old baby and transported the next day to the Pennington County Jail in Rapid City where she was fed only crackers and made to sleep on the cement floor. It took her several days to get out. Kamook's mother, Cheyenne, took care of Mary's baby in the interim. When the goons were told by the FBI that they were not supposed to arrest Buddy's family, they shrugged it off, saying, "You're welcome to take them anywhere you want then, but tell them they better not come back to Pine Ridge because something might happen to them." The FBI didn't know quite what to do, so they dropped some of the women at Hildegard Catches's house at Oglala on the rez.

Preparations had to be made for Buddy's funeral. His mother, Agnes, wanted him buried at Wounded Knee. We all wanted this. Of course, Wilson said that Buddy could not possibly be put to rest there, that he would not allow it. The FBI declared that burying Buddy at the Knee was out of the question because it would only stir up trouble. We told them the people were already fasting and involved in sweat lodge ceremonies.

Agnes had gone into Wounded Knee just before Buddy was killed. She was worried about him and had gone in with some food and clean clothes for her son. She had wanted him to come home. Buddy had replied, "No, I've got two nieces in here, Kamook and Bernice, and they are young. And my sister is in here too. I have to stay here for their protection. I'm not going!"

Agnes was afraid for Buddy and for her grandchildren inside the perimeter because of Wilson's threats to go in there with his goons and "wipe everybody out." The food she packed and carried to Buddy during the dark hours before dawn was his last meal. Buddy had told her then, "If anything happens to me, I want to be buried right here at the Knee. Just cover me up in my bunker because I'm here for a good cause. I wouldn't want to be buried at Pine Ridge. If I'm gone, I don't want any of Dicky Wilson's crowd coming around for me—just our people."

So Agnes and Kamook confronted Wilson. Agnes told him, "There's no way that Buddy is going to be prevented from his rightful burial at Wounded Knee." They pointed out that Buddy was tribally enrolled as a member of the Oglala Nation with the right to have his grave anywhere on the Pine Ridge reservation.

Finally, Wilson shook his head and said, "Well, *go on!* Bury him out there."

A few days went by as preparations for Buddy's funeral were made. The weather was cold, rainy, and miserable. One night the trading post caught fire when someone accidentally tipped over a kerosene lamp, which immediately ignited some old curtains. There was a frantic scramble to put the blaze out, but the water had been turned off. People grabbed buckets and ran into the night to the old windmill for water. They slogged back and forth through the mud and cold rain, but it was no use. The fire burned all night. The ammo we had stored in there blew up in the fire. The place was a total loss.

Then the day arrived for Buddy's burial. The Feds tried to impose restrictions on the funeral: only ten close relatives could go into Wounded Knee with Buddy's coffin, the whole ceremony could last no longer than three hours, and so on. But Agnes fought back, saying, "Listen here, I have kids, and then there are the thirty-six grandchildren. And there are wives and husbands to consider." We ignored all the restrictions. In the end, everybody who needed to be there with us got in.

First was the wake at Porcupine that night. All of the chiefs and medicine men and all of the traditional elders were there to honor Buddy. There were hundreds there mourning their dead brother.

Inside the Knee there was talk among the warriors about giving Buddy a ten-gun salute, but I told Carter and Stan, "No, a ten-gun salute is for white soldiers who serve for pay and for a pension. But Buddy was *our* warrior. He deserves a hundred-gun salute." Everything was set for the funeral. We had a cease-fire in place and we were waiting. Finally we saw them coming through the roadblock. Buddy's coffin was in the back of a pick-up that served as a hearse.

We carried him up to his last resting place. All of the chiefs and spiritual leaders walked beside us as well as Agnes, who was flanked by Kamook, Lou Bean, her other five daughters, and the whole family. There were about thirty people in Buddy's immediate family with all of Agnes's kids, grandkids, and great-grandkids. Russell's brother, Bill Means, and all of the AIM people stood over on one side and sang the AIM song. We had one final look at Buddy. The casket was opened at the foot of the mass grave where he was to join the ancestors who had died in 1890. I leaned down to hug him. Someone had fastened a sacred eagle feather to his hair. One by one, men and women from many different nations came forward to pay their respects.

I told security that I wanted a hundred-gun salute—ten men with rifles or shotguns to stand at attention and fire off ten rounds each. So we gave Buddy his hundred-gun salute, and with it we also honored Frank Clearwater and all the other brave men and women who had fought so hard. I happened to look up and see the marshals, FBI, BIA police, and goons standing on their hill, silhouetted against the horizon, watching us. I thought, "Go ahead and watch. Witness our strength and commitment." We put Buddy down at the end of the last song, covering him up as the last flowers were put in place.

Buddy lies now with the spirits of the slain women and children buried in the mass grave. A headstone was later placed over his grave. It bears his army serial number and the name of the unit he served with in Vietnam. It also bears these words, "TWO THOUSAND CAME HERE TO WOUNDED KNEE. ONE STAYED."

Buddy's burial was the end of our struggle. Negotiations went on for a few days more, but we all knew it was over. Talks were almost complete, and it was time to finish them. We hoped the government would keep their promises to hold hearings on the Fort Laramie Treaty of 1868 and to end corruption at Pine Ridge. As of May 5, the only leader remaining at Wounded Knee were Carter Camp and I as well as our spiritual leaders, Leonard Crow Dog and Wallace Black Elk. Carter and I refused to sign the final agreement because we did not want to put our names on a document of surrender.

Meanwhile, Kamook had come back in. She had walked on foot over five miles in the dead of night to join me during the last days. I had felt sad and lonely while she was gone. Now I was happy that she was back. But on May 5 I had to tell her, "The final stand down will be on May eighth. Then the marshals will come in and probably the goons too. So you must leave for your own protection."

Lou Bean said, "Dennis, the police are waiting for you. The FBI is waiting, too."

Kamook added, "An FBI man wanted me to persuade you to give yourself up. He said they would guarantee you safe passage to the nearest jail."

We all laughed and I said, "Thank you, no. I don't want that kind of safe passage." Kamook left in secret sometime before me. We planned that she would meet me on the outside.

We were supposed to stack our arms in the middle of the compound where the Feds could see them. We had a lot of two-by-fours and broomsticks—we painted them black, tied them together, and stacked them out in the compound. From a distance they looked like weapons. It was time for those who wanted to leave the Knee to go for it. We told them to take their rifles and shotguns with them. I would have to go underground. Carter Camp, Leonard Crow Dog, and Wallace Black Elk would submit to arrest the next morning. They wanted the honor of being the last ones out of Wounded Knee, and they deserved it. Lou Bean said, "Dennis, you've got to get out of here, and we don't want you to surrender. We want you to go out tonight."

They picked six guys to go out with me—Henry Wahwassuck, a Potawatomi from Kansas who was my personal bodyguard; Lenny Foster, a Navajo; and four others. That night under cover of darkness, we left Wounded Knee.

The stand down at Wounded Knee took place on Friday, May 8, 1973. On that day, one hundred and forty-six men and women laid down their arms and surrendered. Also surrendered were fifteen inoperable rifles. The Feds lowered our AIM flag and raised their Stars and Stripes while a helicopter hovered overhead. One of the marshals made a victory speech. The marshals and FBI were in full camouflage battle dress, looking for booby traps and hidden enemy holdouts. We had been promised that no goons would be let in, but they were there alright, robbing and destroying whatever they found. Carter Camp and Leonard Crow Dog, in handcuffs, chains, and leg-irons, were put on a helicopter to the jail in Rapid City. All of the others were lined up, searched, and fingerprinted. Wallace Black Elk was manhandled and robbed of his medicine pouch and sacred pipe. Over the loudspeaker a voice proclaimed, "Gentlemen, the village of Wounded Knee is secured."

Today nothing is left of the buildings inside the perimeter of the 1973 siege at Wounded Knee. The government wanted no reminders that Indians once made their stand here, that they fought and died for what they believed in. But it does them no good. What happened there is not forgotten. Wounded Knee was the greatest event in the history of Native America in the twentieth century. It was our shining hour, and I am proud to have been a part of it.

CHAPTER 17

The Waters of Justice
Have Been Polluted

I don't care, and I submit to you that it doesn't make any difference if
conditions on the Pine Ridge Indian Reservation are good or bad.... I
don't care if the 1868 Treaty was violated by the United States.

—Prosecutor R. D. Hurd, U.S. Attorney, South Dakota

There was a manhunt on and I was the prey. The Feds were determined
to get me, not only for Wounded Knee but also for the Custer uprising.
Kamook and I were hiding out with friends in Rapid City, but that was
too close to Pine Ridge, which was swarming with agents and marshals.
We got hold of a car and drove to Utah. For a short while we found
shelter on the Gosiute reservation southwest of the Great Salt Lake.
When it became clear that bail money was not forthcoming, we moved
on to Canada.

There we were joined by Ron Petite and his wife, Cheryl. They
brought with them my nine-year-old son, DJ, a child of my former
marriage to Jeanette. Kamook, DJ, and Cheryl drove across the Canadian border without incident. Ron and I crossed on foot through the
woods, and they picked us up on the other side. From there we drove all
the way to the Northwest Territory, finally arriving at Yellowknife on
the northern edge of the Great Slave Lake.

Even there, we could not stay due to a silly accident. Ron lost his briefcase after leaving it on the roof of the car at a gas station. It fell off into the road. Someone picked it up, found Ron's gun and some AIM papers inside, and took it to the police. The next day there was an article in the local newspaper about the "presence of AIM at Yellowknife." It said that the AIM member was a certain Ron Petite, and that among his possessions was a handgun. So we had to make ourselves scarce.

We took a small float plane that friends had chartered for us to a place at the end of the world called Rae Lakes. It was near the northernmost edge of the continent. The only way you could get there was by plane. We landed on one of the lakes. By then it was autumn and already getting cold. We had brought enough groceries to last us three months—boxes and boxes of provisions. We took a lot of salt to cure meat because we intended to hunt with the rifles we had brought along. We decided to build a log cabin. We had a chain saw and axes—everything we needed.

We settled among thousands of lakes and islands. The lakes were shallow, usually only eight to ten feet deep. The area was supposedly teaming with game, particularly moose. A lot of deer and moose antlers were lying around everywhere, and we often saw hides tacked to the outside walls of local Indian homes. Years before, disgusted with the alcoholism at Yellowknife, the current chief of Rae Lakes had taken a band of about one hundred people up north. They wanted to make a new settlement where there were neither drugs nor alcohol. First they scouted by plane then traveled north up the lake system. Sometimes they were forced to carry their boats across land, but they mostly rowed across water. Eventually they made their settlement at the place they had picked from the air. They built wood-frame houses and log cabins. They had no way of bringing in large supplies of any kind because there were no roads to Rae Lakes.

The people, Northern Dineh, were very hospitable. Chief Rae extended his hospitality to us, and we stayed at his place while we built our log cabin. He told us, "We will help you. All the logs you need are right here. If you build with green logs, you'll have problems next year. They'll start to buckle from the sun. So use only dry wood."

We said, "We'll build it to last only this winter, then we'll see what happens next." As the weather turned sharp, we finished the cabin and moved in.

Next, Chief Rae's men showed us how to fish with nets. The catch out on the lakes was eighty or ninety fish every time the nets were brought in. Our new friends showed us how to hang up the fish in little dugouts, which were covered over with logs to keep bears out. The fish they had already caught would feed the people through the winter, and it was by then cold enough that the fish would not spoil. The settlement was home to a number of dogs, and the people gave each of them a big fish every day. Luckily, there were enough fish for both the people and the dogs.

We also went duck hunting and did well with it. Strangely enough, we didn't see any big game although we knew there had to be some around because of the antlers we saw everywhere.

We were pretty much cut off from the rest of the world. In a way, I liked it—the five of us alone in nature with the nightly concert of wolf and coyote howl.

Just when we had gotten used to our new lifestyle, a message reached us from our AIM friends. It said, "Dennis, we need you back. We have bail money for you. Hurry!"

I told Ron and Cheryl, "I have to go, and I'll take Kamook and DJ with me. The money is there, so after I make bail, I'll return. I've made my decision. I'll leave our stuff here except for some clothes and things we need for the journey."

The three of us flew back to Yellowknife with the person who brought us the message. Some AIM members and sympathizers met us at the airport, then took us to a house where we were fed. I asked the folks who had picked us up if they could provide a plane and pilot for the rest of the trip. We waited for two days, then Doug Durham, a pilot who claimed to be an AIM sympathizer, picked us up in a private plane my AIM friends had hired and flew us back to the States. I hadn't wanted to risk flying on commercial airlines because I would likely be busted by immigration officials. Doug flew us south at treetop level, crossing the border into North Dakota and down into Rapid City. We were almost out of gas when we landed. The needle was resting on E as we touched down. I thanked him for the ride and left him there, but that was not the last I was to see of Doug Durham.

When I was arrested for the first time so long ago for being drunk, my bail was set at something like twenty-five dollars. I had worried back then that I could not make the bail and I thought I would be in jail for a long time. Now with the Wounded Knee indictments, my bail was set at one hundred and fifty thousand dollars, and I thought, "Well, I'll be in the slammer for the rest of my life." In addition to the many counts against me, I was looking at a third felony count commonly called "the bitch"—the Habitual Criminal Act, which carried an automatic life sentence. As far as I was concerned, I should have stayed at Wounded Knee and fought it out to the death. Also, I was facing eighty-five years in prison on charges stemming from the Custer riot alone. Bill Janklow, South Dakota's attorney general, hated AIM and everything it stood for. We heard he had vowed to put all AIM people behind bars for a very long time or, preferably, six feet under. He had publicly said the best thing to do with Dennis Banks was to put a bullet through his head—I was Janklow's favorite man to hate.

At this time the government's strategy seemed to be "Prosecute! Prosecute! Prosecute!" It didn't matter whether a guilty verdict would hold up on appeal, prosecute! It didn't matter if an acquittal was certain, prosecute! Use perjured witnesses if necessary, but prosecute! It didn't matter if the case was weak, or even if it was so trivial as to be absurd, prosecute! Get the leaders, but also get the humblest spear-carrier—prosecute! The idea was to tie up AIM and all of its resources in never-ending court battles.

There were four major trials and a number of minor ones stemming from the events at Wounded Knee. Two of the big ones were the so-called "leadership trials" in which the accused were Russell Means, Leonard Crow Dog, Stan Holder, Carter Camp, Pedro Bissonette, and me. Pedro was already dead when the trials opened, murdered by Wilson's goons. The remaining five of us were originally to be tried as one group, but later we were separated. Russ and I were tried in St. Paul, Minnesota, before Judge Frederick Nichol, while Crow Dog, Carter, and Stan were tried by Judge Edward McManus in Cedar Rapids, Iowa.

The other trials were to take place before Judge Bottum in Sioux Falls, South Dakota. No less than one hundred and twenty-seven of our people were charged in this trial. Nationwide, some one thousand two hundred men and women were arrested because they were AIM members or supporters, anti-Wilson Oglalas, or in some way connected with the occupation of Wounded Knee.

Another trial dealt with the riot at Custer, and I was one of the chief defendants. Naturally with all of this facing us, going back to Rae Lakes was out of the question, so I sent word to Ron and Cheryl Petite to come on home. There was an eleven-count indictment against Russ and me for larceny; burglary; assault; theft; interference with a federal officer; creation of armed roadblocks; arson; possession of destructive devices; aiding, abetting, counseling, commanding, or inducing commission of various crimes; and conspiracy. Even I was impressed.

We managed to get a formidable defense team. Russ was represented by Mark Lane and William Kunstler. My own attorneys were Larry Leventhal, Ken Tilsen, and Doug Hall. Ramon Roubideaux was in charge of general strategy for the whole defense team.

Of these six men, Bill Kunstler was probably the best known. He was brilliant. During his defense of the "Chicago Seven" in 1968, he had become famous. Kunstler was a craggy, handsome man who appeared in court with ruffled hair, rumpled clothes, scuffed shoes, and his necktie out of place. His trademark was a pair of eyeglasses perched high on top of his head instead of on his nose. He had a wonderful way with the jurors. He could play them like an experienced angler plays fish. I sometimes thought he should have been an actor instead of an attorney. I liked him very much, and we became friends.

Kenneth Tilsen was a good man and also became a friend. He was a first-class lawyer, very sharp and able to swoop down like a hawk on any lie or error on the part of the prosecution.

Mark Lane was a great showman and good at sniffing out any misconduct on the part of the prosecution. At times he was wild in his accusations and theories of conspiracies. He wrote a well known book of his own investigations into the assassination of John F. Kennedy. He was flamboyant and sometimes theatrical, making scenes and shouting at the judge.

Ramon Roubideaux, a Lakota who had his practice in Rapid City, was AIM's lawyer. He was a strategist, always keeping his eye fixed on the big picture. Larry Leventhal was an expert in Indian law and a leading figure in many of our trials; Doug Hall was a very capable lawyer from New York City. Jay Shulman, a specialist in jury selection, rounded out our defense team.

Judge Fred Nichol was a decent, no-nonsense kind of person and open to reason. At the beginning of the trial, he believed in the FBI as the protector of the people, fighting crime wherever it existed. He looked upon AIM as a bunch of troublemakers. But still he conducted the trial proceedings in a deliberate, sensitive, and fair manner. Before becoming a judge, Nichol had been a newspaper and radio reporter and had also taught college courses in history and journalism. I believe his background in these fields with their emphasis upon objectivity made him a fair man.

The chief prosecutor was R. D. Hurd, a bored-looking man who, over the course of the trial, would perjure himself, bring in tainted witnesses, and withhold evidence if he thought it would help him to get a conviction. For this, Hurd was awarded a medal by U.S. Attorney General Saxbe and named "prosecutor of the year." Hurd liked loud clothing—checkered jackets and brightly colored pants. He thought that was what important people in New York wore. Hurd was assisted by David Gienapp, an assistant U.S. Attorney from Sioux Falls; by U.S. Attorney William Clayton; and by Earl Kaplan from the Justice Department in Washington, D.C.

For the duration of the trials, the AIM office at Rapid City was split and transferred to St. Paul for the leadership trials and to Sioux Falls for the non-leadership trials. I always wondered why Clyde and Vernon Bellecourt were tried at Sioux Falls; certainly they were leaders just as Russ, Crow Dog, Carter, and I were. My and Russ's trial opened on January 8, 1974. Judge Nichol later called it the "longest and most bizarre political trial of this century."

Originally we did not want Judge Nichol on the trial because we thought he might be biased, as he came from South Dakota. We had made a survey and taken polls that proved we could never get a fair trial in that state, so we filed for a change of venue. The judge granted it, shifting the trial to St. Paul. That made us feel a lot better. Nichol came with us, however. The face-off between prosecution and defense began in the federal courthouse on top of a bluff beside the Mississippi River. It was a cold, dark day with patches of snow on the ground. The temperature hovered around zero. We did not know it then, but the trial would last eight-and-a-half months, of which six months would be consumed by prosecution witnesses. The first month was entirely occupied with jury selection.

The judge wanted to see everyone—Russ, me, the prosecution, and our defense team—in his chambers before the trial opened to lay down the ground rules for how the trial was to proceed. Nichol's manner was reserved—as cold as the weather outside. He said, "Well, gentlemen, as far as the change of venue goes, I can assure you I had good reason to grant you that over two months ago. Even this morning as I was getting on the plane, I met an old friend of mine—at least I had thought of him as an old friend. He said to me, 'You ought to just line them up against a wall.' He meant you, the AIM leadership. If that's what a friend of mine is saying, I can imagine what people who are not my friends are up to. But we will proceed and try to get a fair trial."

We went into the courtroom, where Russ and I made our opening statements. We wore our hair neatly braided and wrapped in strips of red cloth, each of us with an eagle feather dangling from one braid to give us strength. I said, "Ladies and gentlemen, we are having this trial here in Minnesota even though the action took place at Wounded Knee, South Dakota, because we filed for a change of venue. We could not get a fair trial anywhere in South Dakota. Even this morning, the judge told us that a friend from South Dakota told him that they should just line us up and shoot us without a trial."

Nichol shouted, "Mr. Banks! Mr. Banks! What I tell you in my chambers is confidential!"

I continued, "And that's why we are here—because of the prejudice and hatred of people like that with murder in their hearts."

"Mr. Banks! Mr. Banks! Shut up or I'll have you thrown into jail for contempt of court!" I persisted. The marshals stood up, uncertain. They knew they should do something, but *what?* The judge was still yelling at me, "Mr. Banks! That's enough!"

And that's how the trial began. In my opening statement I also said:

> Let the people decide who is guilty of crimes at Wounded
> Knee. When the American people see evidence of poverty, brutal
> conditions, and shotgun murders, they will have no choice but to
> find the U.S. government guilty. On February 27, 1973, members of

the Oglala Sioux Nation began a most historic event that was des-
tined to change the course of Indian history, to change the attitudes
of white America, and to certainly change the policies that were
established by Commissioner of Indian affairs, J. D. Atkins: "The
Indians must be taken out of the reservation through the door of
the General Allotment Act, and he must be imbued with the exalted
egotism of American civilization so that he will say 'I' instead of
'we', and 'this is mine' instead of 'this is ours.'" Wounded Knee represented to the Oglala Sioux and to the Indian people all across the
country a desperate attempt to bring about justice. What is so significant is that Indians and non-Indians alike came together to bring
back our basic human rights.

This is only a small portion of what I said that day. I felt the jury had a
favorable impression of my words. Russ also spoke; he made a brilliant
and stirring speech that had a powerful impact on his listeners.

Then the trial began with tedious allegations and endless charges
that sounded ludicrous. As the days moved into weeks, we saw and heard
the FBI produce "evidence" that we knew was false, misleading, and per-
jurious. There was large-scale and obvious governmental misconduct;
the judge frequently had to remind the prosecution that its "role [was]
not to *win* the case, but to see that justice was done."

Each day as we sat through the testimonies against us, we felt sadness
and anger, but there were also moments of hilarity. One of the funniest
things that happened was when the prosecution put Agnes Gildersleeve
on the witness stand. Agnes was the seventy-two-year-old wife of the
owner of the Wounded Knee trading post. As one of the last witnesses
for the prosecution, she testified to what Russell Means and I had been
doing to her trading empire, how she saw us carrying weapons, and so
on. She said, "Well, Mr. Banks had on a yellow shirt and wore his hair
in red string braids." The judge asked how she could remember all of
this, and she replied, "I have what is called a photographic memory.
Your Honor, I could look at this crowd here today, in the audience, and
I could tell you later that he had red hair wrappings. And twenty years
from now, I'll tell you the same thing."

In cross-examination, Bill Kunstler tried to catch her in some incon-
sistency. She was on the stand for three days, and Bill couldn't shake her

testimony. He told us, "She's just too good. I can't trip her up." So he finally said, "No further questions, your Honor."

Judge Nichol said to Agnes, "Well, you certainly have a good memory, Mrs. Gildersleeve."

She agreed, "That's right, your Honor, I do have a fantastic memory."

When she was excused, she got up, walked to a door, opened it, and left the courtroom. After some time had passed, the same door suddenly opened, and Agnes came out red-faced from the broom closet! The jury saw her mistake and burst out laughing. She was so embarrassed that she had waited for the court to focus its attention on further proceedings before she would come out. She tried to sneak away, but Kunstler saw her and quipped, "Agnes, dear, so much for the photographic memory, eh?"

Kunstler had a knack for finding humor in the testimony of the prosecution's witnesses. At one point he cross-examined an FBI undercover agent named Stanley Keel. Keel was part Indian and had dressed himself like an AIMster, playing the "I am a traditional American Indian" card. Kunstler had some fun with him.

Kunstler: Agent Keel, do you customarily wear your hair long?
Keel: Yes.
Kunstler: Why is that?
Keel: Because I am a traditional Indian.
Kunstler: How long have you worn your hair that way?
Keel: Two-and-a-half years.
Kunstler: And your bone choker, is that traditional also?
Keel: Yes, sir.
Kunstler: And how long have you been an informant for the FBI?
Keel: Two-and-a-half years.

Even the judge cracked up at that one.

Though we sometimes encountered such absurdity, it was the government's audacity that was revealed again and again during the trial. In spite of the prosecution's attempt to cover them up, cases of misconduct were revealed that included the use of false witnesses who testified to criminal activities by Russell Means and me that had never taken place.

Other cases of misconduct included perjury, illegal wiretapping, unconstitutional use of the military in domestic affairs, obstruction of justice, cover-up of serious crimes, failure to furnish relevant information to the judge and the defense, illegally infiltrating an informer into the defense team, violating court order by failing to produce Nixon's Wounded Knee tape, withholding financial records, eavesdropping, interference by the FBI with media coverage, and on and on.

The whole trial was grotesque—a half-sad, half-comical travesty of justice right to the end. To cover the innumerable instances of governmental misconduct here would make this chapter alone the size of the New York City telephone book. For a start, the prosecution trotted out sixteen-year-old Alexander Richards, who swore that he had seen Russ and me commit certain crimes at a time when Richards was actually in jail. It was easy to prove that he perjured himself, and, of course, his testimony was stricken from the record.

The prosecution regularly withheld information the defense was entitled to see. Nichol finally forced the government to hand over its files on us—315,981 documents, some of them up to six hundred pages long. It was a Mt. Everest stack of surveillance. Shaking his head, Nichol remarked, "If this government falls, it won't be because of subversion. It will topple under the weight of its own paperwork."

During the trial, our defense discovered a document in which Joseph Trimbach, Special FBI Agent for Minnesota, North Dakota, and South Dakota, ordered a wiretap at Wounded Knee. The prosecution had stood in the courtroom and denied that such wiretapping had occurred. Nichol commented, "It is my feeling that the prosecution's offering of testimonies that are directly contradicted by a legal document in their possession was inexcusable and is in possible violation of the American Bar Association's standards." He added, "If our system of freedom is to be preserved, the FBI must be servile to our system of justice, not a manipulator of it."

Once, Kunstler noticed that a door behind the bench stood slightly ajar. He tiptoed over and jerked the door open. Two FBI agents toppled into the courtroom, almost falling over each other. They had been eavesdropping on the judge. Nichol was furious.

The most serious instance of governmental misconduct involved the sad case of Louie Moves Camp, the son of Ellen Moves Camp, one of the finest of our women warriors—one I greatly admired. She was one of the women who challenged the chiefs to stand up and fight Wilson, to protect the people from the goons, and to do something about the corruption in the tribal government. She was among those who urged us to make our stand at Wounded Knee, rather than underneath the guns of the Feds and the goons at Pine Ridge. Louie had been on our defense committee in St. Paul, but in all honesty, he was no great help. He did a lot of hell-raising—getting drunk and using drugs. I had to ask him to leave the AIM house. He didn't go very far, however. He was present during the first two months of my trial, then he simply disappeared.

We did not know that he was awaiting his own trial on charges of robbery, assault with a deadly weapon, and assault causing bodily harm, or that he was facing a twenty-year sentence. He disappeared because he went to the FBI to volunteer to testify against us if the charges against him were dropped and if he were paid as well. So Louie and the FBI made a deal.

In August the government suddenly announced that they had a "star witness" who would identify Russell Means and Dennis Banks as conspirators, connecting us to numerous crimes that we would be charged with. The following morning they brought out their surprise witness—and it was Louie Moves Camp. It shook everyone up: "Oh my God, it's *Louie!*" His mother, Ellen, was in the audience. She could be heard asking, "What is he doing? What's he up here for?"

They swore Louie in, and Hurd began to question him:

Hurd: On or about March third, were you at Wounded Knee?"
Moves Camp: Yes.
Hurd: And how long did you stay at Wounded Knee?
Moves Camp: I stayed there for a month and a half.
Hurd: Were you there every day?
Moves Camp: Yes, I was.
Hurd: And did you see Dennis Banks stealing from the trading post?
Moves Camp: I did.

Hurd: And did you see Dennis Banks and Russell Means carrying guns?

Moves Camp: I did.

Hurd: Did you see them arming other people and ordering them to use the weapons?

To all these questions, the predictable reply was "yes," the answer the prosecution needed to link us to the charges against us. After many such questions and answers, Ellen jumped up and cried, "Louie, why are you doing this? You weren't even there. You're lying! You're lying! I don't even know who you are, acting this way. Louie, why?" She was weeping. I felt so sad for her. It was very hard. Finally, the marshals pulled her away and took her outside, where she continued to sob. Here was one of our great women leaders, watching her own son perjure himself—turning against everything she had worked so hard for, lying for the prosecution.

The week was over, so we had two days before we went back to court. Somebody told us that Louie had been in jail just before he appeared in our trial, so Mark Lane went to River Falls, Wisconsin, to investigate the tip. He questioned the local sheriff, who told him that Louie was in a motel under the protection of two FBI agents. Mark discovered that Louie had cut a deal to get himself cleared of the charges against him. The agents had been coaching him on what to say during testimony, but then something happened that the FBI hadn't expected.

One night, after spending the evening drinking with his two protective custody federal agents, Louie raped a young woman he had met in the bar. She called the police and the sheriff had Louie arrested. Then the FBI called the sheriff and told him, "Hey, this is our principal witness in the Banks/Means trial in St. Paul, and we want him released into our custody and not charged. As a matter of fact, we don't want this episode even to be mentioned, because it could ruin our case."

The rape charge was squashed. After Mark heard all this from the River Falls sheriff, he called me early in the morning and said, "Dennis, you have to get over here quick!" We got together with Mark, his associates, and our attorneys. Mark related what he had found out; we all were grinning by the end of his report. I said, "Well, *alright!*"

We spent the whole weekend preparing to cross-examine Louie, which would be Mark Lane and Ken Tilsen's job. Then we got a surprise call from Carol Standing Elk in Oakland, California. Carol told us, "This guy, Louie Moves Camp, was at Stanford University on March seventh giving a speech. We know it because we taped it. The people of Monterey Television Cable Company have him on camera." This was proof that he was in California at a time when he claimed to have been at Wounded Knee.

I said, "Listen, you've got to air-express this to us tonight or, better yet, hand-carry it." Carol got on a plane and arrived in Minneapolis later that same day with the video tape. On the next morning, we watched it. We heard and saw the person doing the interview say:

> Here it is March seventh, and we are here with the people in support of the action by Indians at Wounded Knee. The spokesperson with us today is Louie Moves Camp, who has agreed to talk about the issues involved.

And there was Louie on camera! I said, "Man, oh man, we're going to tear him up!"

It was Monday, August 27; the government's last rebuttal day, as it turned out. Louie was on the stand again. Hurd conducted the questioning, and Louie went on and on like a parrot, giving the kind of answers the prosecution had coached him to give. Our attorneys had decided not to make any objections early on, but to allow him to talk, to trap himself. Finally, Mark Lane thought it was time to end the charade, and he let Louie have it:

> Lane: Mr. Moves Camp, you say you were at Wounded Knee from March seventh until maybe a week before it ended?
> Moves Camp: That's right.
> Lane: So that means every day you were there?
> Moves Camp: Yeah, that's right.
> Lane: That does not mean that you came out and went to Rapid City or Sioux Falls on behalf of the occupants but stayed there all the time?
> Moves Camp: Yes.

Lane: So that means you could not have gone to New York or California to make an appearance on behalf of the Wounded Knee people.

Moves Camp: No, I was there. I never left from March third until a week before it ended.

Lane: You said you saw Mr. Dennis Banks on March eighth and that you observed he and Mr. Russell Means commit the following acts?

Mark went over some of the allegations while Louie answered "yes" to all the related questions. Then Mark asked:

Lane: Mr. Moves Camp, before you came to testify here, where were you staying?

Moves Camp: I was staying at a hotel in Wisconsin this past month.

Lane: Were you arrested in Wisconsin this past month?

Moves Camp: No.

Lane: Do you know a girl named Brenda?

Moves Camp: No.

Lane: Do you know the sheriff of River Falls, Wisconsin?

Moves Camp: No.

Lane: These people mean nothing to you?

Moves Camp: No.

Then Mark stunned the courtroom: "Ladies and gentlemen of the jury, first of all, Mr. Moves Camps says that he never left Wounded Knee after March third. We would like to show you a tape." He darkened the room and put the tape on, and there was Louie giving a speech at Stanford University on March 7. Then Mark said, "Ladies and gentlemen, Mr. Moves Camp says that he was not arrested in Wisconsin, and that he does not know the young woman whose name I mentioned. But I would like to present to you a copy of the sheriff's report on an incident of rape, after which the FBI went over to River Falls and had Louie released into their custody and charges dropped." The courtroom was buzzing.

The judge said, "Will the prosecution and the defense please approach the bench? There will be a fifteen minute recess." We went into Judge Nichol's chambers. The judge was furious—absolutely livid.

He looked at the prosecution with fire in his eyes. "Alright, you better have an explanation for this, a damn good one too, because I am on the verge of dismissing this case due to governmental misconduct. We'll find out about this. If this man, Louie Moves Camp, has been in jail, and these things that I have just heard are true, I'm telling you right now, this case is a hair away from dismissal!"

We all filed back into the courtroom and the questioning proceeded. Williams, one of the FBI agents who had held Moves Camp in custody in Wisconsin, took the stand. He related that on the evening of August 14 (two weeks previous), he, the other agent, and Louie went on a binge, traipsing from bar to bar. According to Williams's own testimony, he downed nine scotch-and-waters while Price, the other agent, contented himself with a mere five. What and how much Louie drank was not mentioned, but he probably swallowed more of the hard stuff than his two drinking buddies combined. Nichol dryly remarked that the two agents had been doing a "fair job of keeping up with Louie."

At 1:00 A.M. when the bars closed, Williams and Price were ready to call it a night, but Louie was coming on to a girl in her late teens named Brenda. Louie told the agents that he wanted to take her back to his room, but they told him that "this type of arrangement was impossible." They left Moves Camp, the girl, and another couple sitting in the bar, and went back to the motel to sleep.

In the morning, the two agents had a rude awakening when Louie called from a place where he was having breakfast. He announced that he was in some trouble, that the girl they had seen him talking with the night before had gone to the police, charging that Louie had raped her. The local sheriff was preparing to have Louie arrested and placed in custody pending further investigation. In court, Lane asked Agent Williams about this:

Lane: Did you get dressed and go down immediately to pick up Louie Moves Camp?
Williams: No, I didn't.
Lane: What did you do?
Williams: I went back to sleep. If you've ever eaten with Louie, you would understand that.

Lane: Why, does it take Louie a long time to eat, generally?
Williams: He usually eats *two* breakfasts.

Testimony revealed that after the agents dragged themselves out of bed that morning, they went down to persuade the River Falls sheriff to drop the charge and release Louie into their custody. On the stand, Williams tried to justify getting Louie released by painting the victim as a slut who enticed Louie to have sex with her and by making it appear that the whole event was just a mutually agreed-upon romp in the hay.

Prosecutor Hurd had known all about the rape charge, but he had told the judge that Louie had been arrested for "public intoxication." In the judge's chambers, Hurd twice denied knowing anything about the rape charge. When it was finally proven that he had lied about it, Hurd tried to squirm out of the accusation by saying that he had been asked whether Louie had been *charged* with rape, and since Louie's charges had been dropped, Hurd claimed his "no" was *not* a lie.

This kind of trickery did not sit well with Judge Nichol. He said to the jury, "Mr. Hurd deceived the court up here at the bench in connection with the Moves Camp incident in Wisconsin. It hurts me deeply, and it is going to take me a long time to forget it. When I finally decided after the hearing behind closed doors in chambers that the sordid story was going to come out after all, Mr. Hurd broke down briefly and cried. I don't know whether it was his conscience or his humiliation."

Hurd replied, "Your Honor, we were not aware, we did not know that Moves Camp was arrested. . . ." Then he reversed himself and stammered, "Your Honor, it appears that the FBI admits the possibility that Moves Camp was in jail for assault." Finally, Hurd was forced to conclude, "Your Honor, we move to have all the testimony of Louie Moves Camp in regard to Wounded Knee stricken from the record." Nichol promptly instructed the jury to ignore what they had heard in Louie's testimonies.

Basically, the trial was over at that point, but there were still a few odds and ends to be taken care of. There was one more witness. Col. Volney Warner of the 82nd Airborne was supposed to be a witness for the prosecution, but as it turned out his testimony was more favorable to the defense by proving that the army had been involved at Wounded

Knee in violation of the Constitution. After hearing his testimony, the judge dismissed five charges against us, saying, "As long as I am a federal judge, the military of this country will never run civilian affairs or have anything to do with the execution of the law. I was a navy commander myself, and I served my country well. But I remember this is a country run by civilian rule, not by military rule. These five charges concerning AIM's confrontation with the army are dismissed."

Special Agent Ron Williams was one of the last on the witness stand. He sputtered so many falsehoods that the judge asked him, "Do you know what perjury is?" When Williams got down off the stand, both Russ and I stood up to place him under a citizen's arrest. A scuffle ensued and Williams ran out of the courtroom with us chasing him down six flights of stairs and out of the building. The St. Paul police were trying to protect him as they ran down the road behind us with their guns drawn. The cops finally managed to put him into a squad car and take off with him. It was a bizarre scene—Russ, me, and a few other people chasing an FBI agent down the road in the middle of winter in St. Paul, Minnesota—like something right out of an old silent Keystone Cop movie.

Finally it was over. The judge was fed up with all of the lies, perjury, and continual misconduct on the part of the prosecution. On September 17, one of the jurors got sick. The prosecution refused to let the remaining eleven jurors decide the case for fear of losing it. The judge blew up and, rather than declare a mistrial, dismissed all the remaining charges.

For over an hour during his final summation, the judge raked Hurd over the coals. "The U.S. Attorney may strike hard blows, but he is not at liberty to strike foul ones. . . . I am forced to conclude that the prosecution acted in bad faith at various times throughout the course of the trial. . . . The fact that incidents of misconduct formed a pattern throughout leads me to believe that this case was not prosecuted in good faith. . . . *The waters of justice have been polluted.* Dismissal is, I believe, the appropriate cure for the pollution in this case." As for the FBI, Nichol concluded, "It is hard for me to believe that the FBI, which I revered for so long, has stooped so low."

It was not only a victory for Russ and me, but a triumph for AIM and every Indian in the country. I also want to give credit to Judge

Nichol. As the trial progressed, Nichol changed his mind completely. We started out as opponents and ended up as friends. That he could overcome his prejudices made me respect him. He grew in stature, day by day. The trial began with the judge yelling at me, and ended in his home with my eating a delicious home-cooked meal served by his wife.

CHAPTER 18

The Symbionese
Liberation Army

*I'm not going to give in to these kidnappers. I'm not going to give them
fifty million dollars. I'm going to give them two million dollars. If they
demand one penny more they can kill her.*

—Randolph Hearst

This was absolutely crazy. On the one hand, the FBI tried to put me
away for life; on the other hand, they wanted my help and even wanted
me to do some undercover work for them. It was crazy.

It happened during the Banks/Means trial at St. Paul. Early in
1974, a group calling itself the Symbionese Liberation Army kidnapped
Patty Hearst, the daughter of Randolph Hearst, owner of a vast newspaper empire and publisher of the *San Francisco Chronicle*. Nobody had
ever heard of the Symbionese Liberation Army. It was led by Donald
DeFreeze, who called himself Fieldmarshal Cinque. The fieldmarshal's
"army" was rather small—composed of only about a dozen people, both
men and women.

The Hearsts were old money. George Hearst had been a U.S. Senator
and the owner of a gold mine. His son, William Randolph, had been the
founder of the Hearst newspaper empire, while his grandson, Randolph,
was the multimillionaire heir. The Hearst newspapers were decidedly

right-wing. Their editorials generally supported the European fascist dictatorships.

Patty's kidnapping created a sensation and a feeding frenzy among the media. When the kidnappers demanded a ransom of fifty million dollars, the police and the FBI initiated a manhunt in an attempt to find the elusive SLA and destroy it. Some people in California zipped up their lips, saying nothing that might expose the SLA in any way. They, in fact, supported the actions of the SLA and tried to hide its members. The sixties and seventies were times when younger Americans challenged the right-wing forces in this country, of which the Hearst empire was an influential part.

In late February, one month into our St. Paul trial, we got a call from George Martin, chairman of the San Francisco, California, AIM chapter. He told us the SLA had issued a cassette tape to be played over KPFA-Pacifica Radio in San Francisco that disclosed their demands to Randolph Hearst in exchange for the release of his daughter. One of their conditions was that the fifty million dollars were to be split among certain organizations that were to distribute the ransom money, or food purchased with the money, to various community groups. Among the organizations listed was AIM, and George Martin wanted to know what he should do.

I told Clyde and Russ, "There is that kidnapping, and the people who abducted this woman want us to be among the distributors of the ransom money to poor people. What should we do about it?"

We agreed not to be involved. Russ called the press, saying, "The SLA are punks. We will have nothing to do with this."

The SLA put out a second tape about two weeks later insisting that AIM must be among the distributors of the ransom money before they would consider releasing Patty Hearst. George Martin called us back. "Dennis, they won't take 'no' for an answer. And the whole town here, absolutely everybody, is warning me that if something happens to that girl we will be responsible for it on account of our refusal."

I asked Clyde and Vernon for their advice. They said, "Yeah, let's see what we can do then. Maybe we could help to bring that girl back safely, because we have so many contacts inside the local communities in San Francisco."

I told them, "Let me think about this. It's Friday. I don't have to be back in court until Monday morning. Maybe I could accomplish something over the weekend."

On Saturday afternoon I spoke to Randolph Hearst over the phone. I told him that I would be willing to help if I could find a way to do that. He said, "I want my daughter back."

I explained to him that I was on trial in St. Paul and had practically no time at all to devote to his problem. He asked, "On trial for what?"

I said, "For the Wounded Knee thing."

He asked, "Who is the judge?"

I told him, "Judge Nichol."

He said, "I'll talk to Nichol on Monday morning early. I want you to be part of this. You have the FBI's blessing."

I explained to the judge on Monday morning that I had talked to Randolph Hearst in San Francisco and that he had asked for my help in the case of his kidnapped daughter. The judge said, "Mr. Banks, if there is a request for you to go out there to help bring that young girl back to her family, I'll consider it."

We went to court that morning, and during the ten o'clock break Judge Nichol called the defense and prosecution into his chambers, saying, "Gentlemen, I just go a call from Mr. Randolph Hearst concerning his daughter, Patricia. He wants Mr. Banks to go to San Francisco to assist in freeing her. He'll call me back. I am going to talk with him so that all of you can listen. I'll put it on the loudspeaker."

When Hearst called back, Nichol told him, "We are in my chambers with the prosecution and defense. Mr. Banks is present."

Hearst said, "We would like to have Mr. Banks excused from this trial in order for him to help us get my daughter released. We have assurances from the SLA that if Mr. Banks does that, they will move forward. Then, hopefully, we will have a good ending to this heart-wrenching stand-off."

Nichol said, "Alright, I'm going to consider this." Nichol paused, then told Hearst, "I've got to get clearance from Washington first. I have to call the Justice Department, which handles the federal trials."

He hung up the phone and asked the prosecution if they had any objection to having a recess for a week. The prosecution said they wouldn't mind if I went to California for a few days, and the defense said they had no objection either. This was the only time in the eight-and-a-half-month-long trial that both sides were in total agreement.

We had just finished discussing the details of the week-long recess when the phone rang again. Nichol switched the speaker phone on and we heard: "This is the U.S. Justice Department, and we are approving that this court be in adjournment for one week in order for Mr. Banks to be able to assist in the Patty Hearst matter."

The judge hung up, looked at his watch, and commented, "It's been only fifteen minutes since Mr. Hearst called here. He certainly has a way of getting fast action from the government. Anybody who can get a federal trial adjournment from them in less than fifteen minutes is pretty powerful."

By that same afternoon Bill Kunstler and I had landed in California. My brother, Mark, had lined the press up at the ready for when we got off the plane in San Francisco. There were some fifty or sixty cameras at that airport waiting for us. The airline people couldn't handle it and tried to find an exit for us without so many reporters. The airline rerouted our plane to another gate, but whatever gate they routed us through was immediately swamped with media. All over the airport, people were running around with cameras, creating a problem for the airlines. So our plane did not stop at a gate, but out on the apron at a distance from the terminal.

To my surprise, they wheeled a moveable ramp up to the door and two men came on board. Then the plane taxied further from the airport. A voice on the speaker said, "Would Mr. Banks raise his hand, please, and notify the stewardess." Kunstler was sitting next to me. He was puzzled, and so was I. After slowly rolling for a while, the plane came to a halt. I raised my hand and was asked to come to the front.

The two men who had come on board approached me, saying, "Mr. Banks, we are from the FBI. We realize that you're on trial, but we've also been informed that you have been excused for a week to assist us. We would like you to cooperate with us in getting Miss Hearst back. We would like to put a wire on you so we can listen in on any meetings you might have with those Symbionese Army people."

I laughed. They were trying to make me into a provisional FBI agent here in San Francisco, while at the same time trying hard to get me behind bars back in St. Paul. It was crazy. I said, "Are you guys out of your minds? How can you be so stupid to think that I would work for you?"

They looked disappointed, saying, "Well, we tried. Only doing our job. Sorry you don't see it our way," and so on.

Finally, we got off the plane and were greeted by tons of media people. We made a few statements and asked them to let us go. I told them, "We don't know any more than you do." They wanted to know why AIM had been selected by the SLA to play a part in the negotiations. I said, "I don't know that either. I only know that we are going to try to get Miss Hearst released." Once Kunstler and I were finally able to leave the airport, we were taken to the sixth floor of the downtown Hilton Hotel. The entire floor was reserved for the Hearst family. There were about fifteen to twenty FBI agents and a large group of law enforcement men standing around. I was feeling very much out of place as I was introduced to all those people. Then at last I met Randolph Hearst.

He addressed those present, saying, "I have asked Mr. Banks to be involved in this case."

I said, "There's a group of community leaders who have also been named by the SLA as ransom distributors. I'll meet with them then let you know what we have decided."

My brother, Mark, my friend Lee Brightman, and I went to meet with the other community groups named the SLA. We settled down to talk. They said that if the SLA was successful in getting the huge ransom, they were not comfortable handling the money, even to distribute it to the poor. What they wanted instead was food—tons of it—to distribute to organizations working with the poor. They said, "Let Hearst buy the food. We'll see to it that it goes to the right places."

I said, "Okay then, let's see how we can make a plan to accomplish this." There were about twenty community leaders there representing the eleven other groups selected by the SLA. AIM was the twelfth group. We met for over five hours, in which we decided to make a joint statement directed toward the SLA.

The next day I got a call from Randolph Hearst saying he wanted to see me. He did not want to meet with the other community leaders. So I met him for lunch at the Hilton. Hearst asked me, "How did it go with the group meeting?"

I replied, "We discussed ways to let the SLA know that we are meeting and to send a message to them through the media not to harm your daughter, Patty. We'll ask them to get in touch with us so that the exchange can take place—I mean, the exchange of ransom for Patty."

He told me, "I'm not going to give in to these kidnappers. I'm not going to give them fifty million dollars. I'm going to give them two million dollars. If they demand one penny more they can kill her."

I was sure he did not mean that literally, but I was shocked.

I told him, "Mr. Hearst, I have children of my own, and if one of them were in your daughter's situation, I'd give everything I own to get her back."

He said, "Well, you are not me. As a matter of fact, why don't you get lost?"

I said, "I am leaving."

I was disgusted with his remarks and felt that I never wanted to see him again. But I also thought we still should try to free Patty. I felt I had an obligation to try, her father and his attitude notwithstanding. So I went back to the committee. I never told them what Hearst had said, but left them with contingency plans. Then I flew back to St. Paul. When I arrived, there was a message from Hearst asking if I would return to San Francisco. Most of my one-week recess from court still remained. So Mark, Kunstler, and I met Hearst once more at the San Francisco Hilton, where he apologized for his behavior.

He said, "You must understand how I feel. Nobody is doing anything to help Patty." The upshot of our talk was that Hearst would give the committee two million dollars to use as they saw fit and see how that would sit with the SLA. We took leave of Hearst that afternoon and went back to the committee. We told them Hearst was offering two million dollars to buy meat and other groceries to be handed out to poor communities. There was an organization called PIN, People in Need, whose executive director came down from Seattle, Washington, to help implement the food distribution. They planned to hire trucks to get the food and deliver it to community groups in the San Francisco and Oakland area.

AIM was not going to be involved in that part. By then I had been in San Francisco all week. I told the committee that AIM had done all we could, that I had to be back in court, but that I would broadcast an appeal over the radio to the SLA on the coming Sunday night. I would be hooked up from a community center in St. Paul to KPFA-Pacifica Radio in the Bay Area, and people would hear me throughout Northern California. A blizzard hit St. Paul on that particular Sunday night and, consequently, our broadcast was delayed because we arrived two hours late. But the people at the community center had waited for us all the same. They knew we would be delivering a message to the SLA.

Our message was broadcast live. I addressed my remarks to the Symbionese Liberation Army and to Patty Hearst. I began by saying that kidnapping was not something that I could endorse as a way to cure social ills. I explained that we, as American Indians, knew what it was to be taken from our ancestral homes, forced into military-style boarding schools, and Christianized and acculturated into a society that only had intentions of using us. I said that this form of kidnapping had left its mark upon all of us but that it had never been the answer to our social problems. I added that birth is an accident and that no one should judge Patty by her parents, just as it is wrong to judge people by their race. I asked the SLA to not harm her or use her as a pawn, but to release her. When we left, it was midnight and the blizzard had grown worse. Some of the people spent the night in the auditorium. In spite of the delays, my message reached San Francisco and was confirmed by KPFA-Pacifica Radio.

As many people know, Patty Hearst was indoctrinated by the SLA and she joined them as a member. She became the lover of the group's leader, Cinque. Armed with an automatic weapon, she helped her new friends rob banks. She denounced her parents as capitalist criminals and stayed underground with the SLA for one and a half years. On May 17, 1974, six SLA members were killed in a shoot-out with the police. Among the dead was their leader, the group's self-styled fieldmarshal. The shoot-out had eliminated half of the SLA membership. Patty remained at large in the company of two SLA members—they had been elsewhere during the shoot-out. Patty was finally captured by the FBI on September 18, 1976. She was tried and convicted on a charge of "bank robbery and felonious use of firearms" and sentenced to seven years.

When I was involved in another trial in 1975 for my role in the Custer incident, I jumped bail and fled to California. In January 1976, I was arrested in San Francisco on federal fugitive charges. Patty was in custody then, but I did not know it. I was being taken with two other prisoners to court on the nineteenth floor of the federal building. We had to stop on the way to pick up women prisoners. Three of us wearing leg irons got out of the elevator. We were all hooked together with me on the end, then the Feds handcuffed me to a white girl. I looked at her and saw that it was Patty. I said, "Hey, you're Patty Hearst."

She said, "Yes."

I told her, "I'm Dennis Banks."

She said, "I know who you are. Listen, my mom told me what you did for me, and we listened to your broadcast that night when you appealed on my behalf to the SLA. If there is anything I can do. . . ."

We went to court. She was arraigned on the bank robbery charges. When we left the court, they handcuffed us again and took us to holding cells. Patty was placed in the cell next to mine. We talked. I said, "Patty, I just want you to know that I'm glad you are all right." I was bailed out shortly afterward.

I saw Randolph Hearst one last time. I was on my way to a meeting in San Francisco and accidentally ran into him in a hallway. He asked me how I was. I said, "Fine."

He told me, "Whatever help you gave me, I still appreciate it very much." We shook hands and that was it. I never saw him again.

John Fire Lame Deer studies a commemorative sign at Wounded Knee, South Dakota, 1971.

A Cheyenne coup stick planted at the headstone of one of Custer's men, Little Big Horn Battlefield, South Dakota, 1971.

Dennis Banks and Russell Means at Wounded Knee, South Dakota, 1973.

Carter Camp, Ponca, at Wounded Knee, 1973.

Dennis Banks *(with binoculars)* sighting federal positions outside Wounded Knee during the takeover, 1973.

Armed Indians atop the roof of the Wounded Knee trading post, 1973.

Armed Indian atop the Gildersleeve and Son Wounded Knee trading post, 1973.

Indian occupiers outside a bunker at Wounded Knee, 1973. Note the upside-down American flag.

Armed fortifications at Wounded Knee, 1973.

Armed Personnel Carrier at Wounded Knee, 1973, manned by FBI agents and U.S. marshals. Photo by Camilla Smith-Kenner.

Dick Wilson, Tribal Chairman of Pine Ridge reservation *(at center in sunglasses)*, and his goons at the Wounded Knee perimeter, 1973.

Dick Wilson *(without hat)*. Photo by Camilla Smith-Kenner.

The offering of the Peace Pipe, Warrior Honor Ceremony at Wounded Knee, 1973. Photo by Owen Luck.

The Wounded Knee sweat lodge with the Sacred Heart church in the background, 1973.

Armored Personnel Carrier near Wounded Knee, Sacred Heart church in the background, 1973.

Leonard Crow Dog at Wounded Knee, 1973.

Wallace Black Elk, Rosebud Sioux medicine man, at Wounded Knee, 1973.

The Iroquois Delegation is greeted by an Armored Personnel Carrier at Wounded Knee, 1973. Photo by Camilla Smith-Kenner.

Chief Oren Lyons *(carrying duffel bag)* heads the Iroquois Delegation's arrival at Wounded Knee, 1973.

Dennis Banks *(in hat)* singing and drumming at Wounded Knee, 1973.

Bury My Heart at Wounded Knee. Sacred Heart church in background.
Wounded Knee, 1973. Photo by Cy Griffin.

Ghost Dance at Crow Dog's Paradise on the Rosebud Sioux reservation, South Dakota, May 1974.

Leonard and Mary Crow Dog, 1975.

Leonard Crow Dog *(center)* during a Peyote Ceremony of the Native American Church, 1975.

(From left to right) Dennis Banks, his daughter Janice, and actor Marlon Brando at a benefit held for Dennis Banks at the St. Francis Hotel in San Francisco, California, on April 2, 1976. Photo by Michelle Vignes.

Dennis Banks at a meeting in Central Park, New York City, New York, 1975.

Clyde Bellecourt.

Oren Lyons, Onondaga.

A demonstration to free Leonard Crow Dog, Richmond, Virginia, 1976.

Mary Crow Dog, Lakota, speaking at demonstration, Richmond, Virginia, 1976.

The "Longest Walk" demonstration, from coast to coast. Marchers entering Washington, D.C., 1978.

Richard Erdoes *(lower front, center)* surrounded by AIM marchers taking a rest along the "Longest Walk," 1978.

(Front row, left to right) Tokala, Tiopa, Tasina, and Tatanka Banks with their parents *(back row, left to right)*, Kamook and Dennis Banks, in 1982. Photo by Michelle Vignes.

Dennis Banks carrying coup stick. Photo from the Banks collection.

Dennis Banks. Photo by Alice Lambert.

Dennis Banks and son Minoh, 1998.

The twenty-fifth anniversary of Wounded Knee on February 27, 1998, was well attended despite a blizzard.

Dennis Banks. Photo from the Banks collection.

CHAPTER 19

The Informer

*AIM plans to carry its terrorism to reservations and towns nationwide . . .
where it will continue its looting and butchery and kidnapping. The
AIM leaders are gangsters.*

—Douglas Durham, FBI informant

At the end of the Banks/Means trial in St. Paul, Judge Nichol gave
voice for over an hour to his outrage about the many cases of misconduct on the part of the prosecution and the FBI. However, he was still
unaware of the worst case. The FBI had sent an informer to infiltrate
our defense team. He was present when defense strategies were discussed between the defendants and their lawyers. The name of this
informant was Douglas Durham. He reported directly to the FBI about
the activities of the American Indian Movement.

After the 1973 Sun Dance at Crow Dog's Paradise I had a meeting
with Bob Burnette, Ted Means, Russ Means, Clyde and Vernon Bellecourt, Lorelei DeCora, and Madonna Gilbert. After we had discussed
South Dakota activities, I said that my friend Ron Petite would like to
make a request, and that I thought he should make it himself.

Ron told our group that he wanted to introduce a man who had
been working in his Des Moines, Iowa, AIM office. There was no
objection, so Douglas Durham came in. He admitted to being a former
policeman who had been busted and since then had been going from

job to job. He said that he liked what AIM was doing and wanted to know if he could help out as a clerk or photographer. He also said that he was a licensed pilot, so it looked like he had some skills that could be useful to the Des Moines office.

Doug Durham was just over six feet tall, roughly one hundred and eighty pounds, well built and rather nice-looking with shiny black hair. I didn't know then that his hair was dyed and that he wore contact lenses to hide the fact that his eyes were gray-blue. He seemed to be about thirty-five or forty years old. He had a very upbeat attitude, wasn't pushy, and accepted the fact that we were in charge and he was to follow orders. He seemed very confident in himself. So we agreed to let him join us. Only Vernon Bellecourt had objected, saying, "Once a pig, always a pig." Everyone else had made statements to the effect that if this guy can help and if we keep an eye on him, then fine, let him work.

My second encounter with Doug Durham was when he piloted a plane to fly me, Kamook, and DJ back from Yellowknife in Canada to the States. In retrospect, I realize that we would have needed some kind of international clearance to cross the border because of the tight aerial security between the United States and Canada in order to nab "criminals" smuggling cigarettes, whiskey, or drugs. I never wondered why we were able to cross the border without any kind of clearance or paperwork. All I knew was that Doug, claiming to be an AIM supporter, had obtained some money, rented the plane somewhere, came for us, and flew us into the States.

After we landed at the Rapid City airport and I turned myself in, Doug asked me, "Do you want me to do anything?"

I said, "Just keep my family advised on the situation and start organizing for my bail." Doug was helpful in the matter of bail, and I got out of jail four or five days later. A large crowd was waiting to welcome me, and Doug was there.

He asked, "What do you want me to do?"

I said, "We've got to deal with the trial situation, but first we've got to get back to Minneapolis and meet with Clyde and Vern. Also, I have to get DJ back to his mom."

Doug said, "Alright, the plane is ready."

During the flight to Minneapolis, Doug and I began to get more acquainted with each other. When he flew me back from Canada with

Kamook, it had been much more formal—strictly business. But on the flight to Minnesota, we began to talk of family and personal matters. After we arrived in Minneapolis, Doug flew the plane back to Des Moines and returned with a van for us to truck around in.

My brother, Mark, was in charge of my defense committee, and he and Doug started working together. Although he does not have a license, Mark is a pilot too and has flown a lot, so he and Doug had something in common. Also, my brother loved comedy, and Doug would exchange one-liners with him. Or they would do take-offs on each other, which they were both very good at. So the two of them got along very well.

But Mark told me one time, "Dennis, I don't know. I have a strange feeling about Doug. He is very good at some of the things he is doing—there is no question about that—but there is just something about him. Sure he's admitted that he was a cop. He's very truthful about that. And I've seen the newspaper clippings about his being busted and taken to court, and all that, but still. . . ." What we did not know was that the stories were all planted, and the clippings were faked.

Doug was very sharp about his manner. It was his job to be clever, to dissemble, and he was damned good at it. He had a way of trapping me into confiding in him. Knowing what to do and what to say and how to get close was the way Douglas Durham infiltrated the American Indian Movement. On a flight over Pierre, the state capital of South Dakota, he remarked casually, "What we ought to do is bomb this place. We could get Janklow right from here with one good bomb." He always made suggestions of that kind.

In the last weeks of October 1973, we started to move AIM's main office, as well as Kamook's and my personal belongings, from Rapid City, South Dakota, to St. Paul, Minnesota. Kamook, who was by then pregnant with our daughter Tash, and I had been living provisionally near Oglala on the Pine Ridge reservation, but we needed to look for a house in St. Paul. We could not find one right away, so we stayed in our St. Paul office, which was in an abandoned school. We made ourselves at home in the auditorium.

People came to us from all over the country. We housed about sixty or seventy people in the school at any given time. Mark was in charge of the office and Vernon was there as well. At about that time, some people in the movement started to become wary of Durham. When

Paula Giese, who worked out of the national AIM office, met Doug, she told me, "Dennis, he's a pig!"

I said, "Come on, everybody tries to tell me that. I know better. Doug's all right."

My feelings of friendship betrayed me. Doug seemed to be very loyal to me. He would do anything I asked him to do. He was a first-class worker who would stay up until all hours doings things that needed to be done. He was a good typist, and he was good at writing letters. He was saving us money by flying me wherever I needed to go. He flew me out to California in a private plane he had rented. We went to Marlon Brando's place and stayed there for three days. Through his association with me, Doug came to meet many important people and found out how they related to AIM.

When December came, everybody took a week off and went home for Christmas. When we returned to St. Paul, the trial was only four days away. All our lawyers, as well as the principal defendants, got together for our first meeting on defense strategy. There were about fifteen or twenty people in all, including Russ, Clyde, Carter Camp, Stan Holder, and Leonard Crow Dog. Among the lawyers were Bill Kunstler, Mark Lane, Ramon Roubideaux, and Ken Tilsen. Also, the people of the Woundeded Knee Legal Defense Committee—WKLDOC—came. By then we had begun pronouncing the abbreviation as "Wickledoc."

Doug set up a tape recorder for us and said, "If you want me to stay and change the tapes, I'll do that. Otherwise, I'll just step outside." By then, Doug had been in and around our defense house and with the movement people, and he had gained a measure of acceptance.

Bill Kunstler thought about Doug's question for a moment then replied, "Maybe the first meetings should be private." Doug complied and left the room.

We held a three-hour meeting that day about the whole defense strategy. When we took a break after several hours, Doug either entered or made it seem as though he had just entered. After a little while, we went back into session. At some point I noticed that Doug was still in the meeting room. I could have said something, but I didn't. We went on for another hour or so, discussing defense matters, then broke up. Everyone left except Doug. He asked me, "What do you want me to do now?" It suddenly occurred to me that I had not actually seen Doug come in during the break, and I wondered whether or not he had quietly sneaked into the meeting without us noticing. Still, I was not alarmed. That would come later.

In October of 1974, William Janklow ran for attorney general of South Dakota against Kermit Sande, the incumbent. Bill Janklow had been the BIA attorney at the Rosebud Sioux reservation. He then became the state attorney. In this position, he tried to prosecute Russ and me, but his underhanded tactics were exposed. Janklow ran on an anti-AIM platform and won even though during the campaign, Sande had strongly accused Janklow of "immorality," alleging that in 1955 Janklow had raped a seventeen-year-old girl in Moody County, South Dakota. Janklow replied that the juvenile delinquency charge against him had been dismissed, and that it had not been a case of rape. "It didn't go that far," he stated publicly, "it was only preliminary to that sort of thing." I found the exchange interesting because on October 16, 1974, I myself publicly accused Janklow of a more recent rape charge.

Janklow and I had never been fond of each other. He had publicly declared that the way to deal with the American Indian Movement is to put a bullet through Dennis Banks's head. Asked by a TV interviewer whether he really had made that statement, he replied, "I never met anybody with a bullet in his head who bothered anybody."

The later rape charge against Janklow was strong. On January 17, 1967, fifteen-year-old Jancita Eagle Deer told her school principal that she had been raped by Bill Janklow. She had been baby-sitting for him and had accepted his offer to drive her home. She said that on the way to her house, he had raped her while holding a gun to her head. The school principal informed a BIA investigator, who then filed a report. In shock by then, the girl was driven to the hospital where an examination was done by a doctor and nurse to determine if indeed she had been sexually violated.

An agent for the BIA, Peter Pichlin, interviewed the doctor and nurse, and determined that the accusation was true. Another agent assigned to the case, John Penrod, reported that it was impossible to determine anything of this sort from a medical exam. Richard Held, a top FBI official, declared that there was insufficient evidence, that the allegations were unfounded, and that they would therefore close the file on the matter.

In 1974, nearly eight years later, I decided to take up this case, not only because I thought it was wrong to allow Janklow to get away with such gross misconduct, but also as a favor to Delphine Eagle Deer, Jancita's stepmother and Leonard Crow Dog's sister, who was very concerned for Jancita. So I became an attorney for the Rosebud tribe. A tribal attorney is not like a regular lawyer who must go to law school and get a degree. All you have to know is the tribal law, which you can learn from a little book. Consequently, I was allowed to practice as an attorney in the Rosebud tribal court.

To open the case I had to have Jancita testify in person, but she was nowhere to be found. The many stories going around about the rape had made her self-conscious. She had wanted to get away to where nobody knew her. At the time we could not find anyone who knew where she was, but I went ahead anyway and filed charges against Janklow in my capacity as tribal attorney.

Then I did a little investigating on my own. I went to the hospital and talked to the nurse who had taken care of Jancita. She described to me how totally traumatized Jancita had been over what had happened to her. I saw the doctor's report. It showed what I believed to be clear evidence that Jancita had been sexually abused. I talked to people who had known Jancita and Janklow at the time of the incident. Different people told me that when Janklow was a lawyer for the tribe he used to get drunk and amuse himself by driving around in his car naked for the "I don't give a shit" effect. He also went around shooting dogs just for the hell of it.

By September, my trial in St. Paul was nearly over. Kamook had given birth to our first-born baby, and I was very proud. Our little girl was called Tashina Wanblee ("Eagle Shawl"). I felt very blessed as I showed my little Tashina off to everybody.

We continued to look for Jancita; I was actively following leads. One day, Annie Mae came to me, saying, "Dennis, we have a lead on Jancita. She is somewhere in Des Moines, Iowa."

I said, "Well, that's where Doug Durham lives. Maybe he should pursue this matter."

She became serious. "Dennis, I would feel safer if I took the assignment and went down there to locate her." I talked it over with my brother, Mark, and told him that Annie Mae didn't trust Doug. Although Mark was always kidding around with Doug, laughing and making terrible puns, he was also uneasy about him.

I asked, "Do you think he's a pig?"

Mark answered, "I don't know, Dennis. If he *is* with the FBI, he sure is clever in hiding it. Maybe Annie Mae ought to be the one to go and see where Jancita is."

I said, "Alright."

We arranged for Annie Mae to catch a flight to Des Moines. She called me the next morning from Des Moines and left a telephone message for me. As it happened, Doug was the one who picked it up and delivered it to me. He noticed the area code of the number Annie Mae had left. As he handed it to me, Doug asked, "Where's Annie Mae at? That's the same area code as Iowa."

I said simply, "Well, yeah."

"What's she doing down there?" he asked.

I replied, "Well, Doug, we sent her there for some business."

He pressed on, "Well, I was just wondering, because I could have gone there for you."

I looked him in the eye and said, "We found out where Jancita is at and sent Annie Mae down to talk with her."

He was taken aback, "Wow, I could have done that for you."

I called Annie Mae later on. She told me, "I have made contact with Jancita and she says she would agree to make a statement. She is still fearful to deal with this, but will consider making her testimony."

I said, "Annie Mae, you've got to get a commitment from her. It is crucial for her to take the stand."

Annie Mae called back that same evening saying, "Guess what! That goddamn bastard, Doug Durham, called me. I don't want anything to do with him. I told you that. How does he know I'm here?" I told her that he happened to intercept her message to me. She said, "He told me that we'll both visit Jancita and fly her back to Minneapolis over the weekend."

I didn't think this was such a bad idea. I said, "Why not go ahead and ask her if she would come up here. Maybe Doug can fly her back."

Eventually, Annie Mae agreed, "Okay, but I won't fly back with him. I'll come back on my own." When she arrived at the airport, I picked her up. She said, "Dennis, I don't trust Doug Durham. I don't trust him. *I don't trust him!*"

I said, "Well, listen, Annie Mae, you have done everything very well. You found Jancita, and going to court is the next step."

"Well, alright," she said.

Doug flew down to Des Moines and brought Jancita back. After Jancita arrived and got settled, I finally began to form a friendship with her. At first she did not want to testify, but in the end she decided to do it. I noticed that Doug was always hanging around her. It seemed to me that there was a relationship beginning between them. It didn't disturb me then; it was none of my business. Just the same, I told Annie Mae to watch her, and Annie Mae stayed at Jancita's side.

Each day in the late afternoon, Jancita and I would talk. I told her that I was going to ask her some questions about the incident that might be embarrassing and difficult to answer. She said, "Okay, I can handle it."

I asked her, "Jancita, when we go to trial, are we going to prove that a certain man raped you at gunpoint?"

She said, "Yes."

I continued, "And the man who raped you, was that man William Janklow?"

"Yes," she answered quietly.

"Alright," I said then, "we are going to trial."

Often Doug would come into the office to take Jancita to breakfast or lunch or something. Of course, he never included Annie Mae because she absolutely refused to be seen with him in private or public. She felt sure he was betraying us, but I still could not believe I could be so misled by him.

Jancita finally had her day in court. During questioning, she was a little hesitant to answer me. I don't think she wanted to describe to me and to the court the embarrassing and intimate details of what Janklow had done to her, but she testified about the main facts in the case. Judge Mario Gonzalez ruled that there was enough evidence to try Janklow on rape and other charges. He issued a subpoena to Janklow to appear as a defendant. The trial opened on October 31. On November 2, Janklow was elected Attorney General of the state of South Dakota. He ignored the subpoena. Neither he nor his lawyer appeared in court.

Janklow vowed to put all AIM leaders either in jail or six feet under. He, and white South Dakotans in general, depicted the trial as an attempt on the part of AIM to discredit him in his bid to become state attorney general and, some years later, to further discredit him in his campaign to become governor. This was untrue. I had become involved in Jancita's rape case before anybody knew that Janklow would run for office.

The court convened without Janklow. Jancita had agreed to undergo a lie-detector test. In all, she was on the stand for two hours, both before and after the lunch recess. She had more to say than she had been able to tell me before. Bill Janklow had taken her home and, when they were almost there, he had pulled over at a deserted place, ripped off her blouse, and raped her.

After hearing all the witnesses, the judge called three times for Mr. Janklow, who, of course, was not present. The court called in the BIA police, asking whether they had, in fact, delivered Janklow's subpoena to the U.S. marshal who would serve Janklow the papers. They said that they had. They had a written notice from the marshal stating that he had delivered the subpoena to William Janklow. When Janklow still failed to appear, the judge issued two warrants: for "carnal knowledge of a female under sixteen (years of age)," and "assault with intent to rape." Those two warrants were still outstanding as of today.

Gonzalez ordered Janklow to be arrested if he set foot on the Rosebud reservation. All efforts to try him in federal court were squashed. Most documents relating to the case against South Dakota Attorney General William Janklow simply disappeared.

In the meantime, it became clear to me that Jancita and Douglas Durham had become intimate with each other. This was none of my business—at least under normal conditions it shouldn't have been. Annie Mae told me that Jancita had been back in Des Moines, that she had begun drinking, and that she was with Doug all the time. Annie Mae said, "Dennis, Doug is abusing Jancita. He beats her up."

I did not want to believe this. I had not seen Jancita with a blackened eye, cut lips, or bruises, so it was hard for me to accuse Doug face to face. Annie Mae told me, "He's made her his woman and he's abusing her sexually." I didn't know what to say. I had no firsthand knowledge about it, but I confronted Doug.

I said, "Listen, Doug, I think you ought to let her go. It's not right. There's something between you two that is not working. You argue all the time." But I never saw him physically violent with her. Others saw it, but he hid it well from me.

Still another voice was raised against Doug—this time by Eda Gordon, a white legal aide, friend, and trusted supporter of AIM. She helped us in any way she could. On one occasion, I told Eda to work on a project with Doug Durham. She told me, "I absolutely will not. I distrust him. I am sure he is an informer."

I said, "Eda, that was an order!" which I realize now was out of line.

She said, "I'm here as a volunteer. I don't take orders. I just won't have anything to do with that guy, but I will be here for you in any other capacity." Still, I remained unconvinced that Doug could betray us.

Toward the end of 1974, I was confronted by something that stunned me like a bolt of lightning from the blue. I was in LA visiting Marlon Brando, who had long been involved in Indian issues and had become a friend, when I got a call from Vernon Bellecourt who said, "I have some very, very important news but I cannot give it to you over the phone. I am here with Clyde, and we need to talk with you immediately."

I said, "Alright, I am coming." Marlon kindly picked up a ticket for me, and I flew back at once to Minneapolis.

As soon as I met Vernon, he said, "Look at these papers, Dennis."

What he showed me was a report by an informer working for the FBI. When an agent makes a report on an assignment, he or she fills out what is known as a "302 form." The one I was looking at was signed "Douglas Durham." It had been given to us by Ken Tilsen, one of AIM's lawyers. It came to Ken as a consequence of my friend Herb Powless having been arrested in Phoenix, Arizona, on a firearms violation. Herb's trial involved a closed "in-camera" hearing, during which an informant testified against the defendant. Only attorneys are allowed to be present during this particular examination of a witness—who was none other than Doug Durham.

The FBI obviously thought that the proceedings of this in-camera hearing in Arizona would never come to our attention in Minneapolis, so they accidentally blew Durham's cover. Herb was told the name of that witness and got a description of him. And, of course, it was Doug, the man I had named as AIM's security chief. Ken Tilsen, as Herb's lawyer, requested a copy of the 302 that I now held.

Vernon called a meeting. There were seven or eight of us present—Russ and his brothers Ted and Bill, Clyde and Vernon Bellecourt, Herb Powless, and Annie Mae. We studied the papers and concluded that all the evidence was there. Doug was an agent—no doubt remained. In discussing the situation, my friends never pointed a finger at me or said, "Dennis, we were right and you were wrong. We told you so." They never even hinted at that. I was very touched, feeling so close to my people as I sensed their friendship and love for me. Instead of coming down on me, they gave me strength.

We talked about what to do, trying to estimate the damage Durham had done to AIM. And I must speak the truth in saying that some of those present suggested that we kill him. One of our group, expressing his rage, said, "We ought to just take him out and shoot him, and go bury him someplace." Everybody gave free rein to their outrage and anger, cursing "that dirty bastard" and saying "what a fucking slime!" and so on.

Annie Mae said, "I was the first to suspect Doug. It's up to me to take care of this. I'll take him out if you want me to." And she absolutely meant it.

I was determined to turn my friends away from such impassioned ideas of vengeance. Vernon came to my rescue in his agreement with me. He said, "We know that he's not the only infiltrator. Let's watch Durham, let's track him, let's see where he leads us as he might be working with somebody. Let's see who else within AIM turns out to be a rat." Everybody immediately agreed that this was the best plan. We would monitor his calls. There were only two phones at the AIM office, and we were able to monitor these calls with little difficulty. So without knowing it, the tables were turned on him. It was now *us* shadowing *him*.

Having to face the fact that Durham was an FBI operative shook me up, not because the FBI had gotten into our organization, but because of *how* it had been accomplished. I could have accepted the situation easier if some guy had simply stolen documents from us, or if they had tapped our phones. We knew that happened all the time. But the manner in which this man had completely fooled me into believing he was my friend—so that I accepted him as such—really hurt. Floyd Westerman, Bojack, Herb Powless—these were some of my true friends who have my confidence and a place in my heart. To such friends I could expose my true feelings. In the same way, I had come to accept Doug. I confided things to Doug Durham that I would only tell Floyd, or my brother, Mark.

The knowledge that Durham merely had been a spy crushed me. It was a bad time for me. Bit by bit, I apologized to those close to me for having been so blind to their warnings, particularly Annie Mae. Our main objective was to expose him in public and to his face at just the right time, to make him admit that he was a spy for pay. But we would not do it right away. We first had to watch him in hopes that he would lead us to his fellow informants. So we had to hide our feelings in his presence and pretend that nothing had changed, which was not easy to do.

On January 1, 1975, Doug Durham told me there was a confrontation going on in Gresham, Wisconsin, where members of the Menominee Warrior Society had taken over a long-abandoned novitiate belonging to white monks, the Alexian Brothers. The Menominees had asked if we would come to Gresham. They had taken possession of the abandoned buildings because they were in need of facilities. The Menominees only hoped they would be allowed to claim the property for use as a hospital and an education famility, but—of course—the locals were enraged by the takeover. The situation up there was critical, and the Menominees needed help. Their warriors were armed and ready to fight. I called Ron Petite and told him about it, saying that we would be going there. I also told Kamook. Then I passed the word around to everybody, saying, "Get ready, we're going to support the Menominees."

We had a black van at the time. Doug drove for us with Jancita at his side. Of course, he still did not know that we were on to him. As expected, he tried to provoke us with his usual bullshit—trying to get us into hot water, asking, "Shall we get some guns? Shall we take heavy weapons to that place? What about kidnapping the governor?"

I said, "No, Doug, we're going there just to mediate. We want to avoid violence."

He went on and on, "I think we should take heavy weapons along."

We stopped at the AIM office in Milwaukee to discuss with Ted Means and Herb Powless how we should proceed. By coincidence, the office of Patrick Lucey, the governor of Wisconsin, had just put in a call for Dennis Banks, asking if I would come and help negotiate a peaceful settlement. I had planned on going anyway as AIM's representative to assist in drafting a list of concerns the Menominees might have and finding ways in which the Indians might acquire the old vacant buildings to fulfill the tribe's needs for a hospital and a school. I was prepared to handle it. My first demand was that nobody would be charged for the occupation. While Ted, Herb, and I discussed strategy, I told Doug, who was in the black van ahead of us, to "go on up there and get us a room. Set up a command headquarters."

Outside the novitiate, we were met by members of the Menominee Warrior Society and some press people. I tried to assess the situation. Forty-five warriors were holding the 225-acre complex made up of a twenty-room mansion and a sixty-four-room building. The Menominees' justification for holding the site was the old agreement with the U.S. government that allowed reclamation by tribes of abandoned sites situated on Indian land and for such sites to revert back to Indian use. The Alexian Brothers were willing to give the land up, but for a steep price. So there was a standoff.

Annie Mae soon arrived from Lincoln, Wisconsin. She was packing a gun because she considered the situation to be pretty tense, what with the armed warriors inside and law enforcement people outside.

We started negotiations and set up a committee, while the law enforcement people set up theirs. Our committees would meet almost every hour under a white flag of truce. I went inside the novitiate to talk to the warriors. Herb Powless and Ted Means came in with me; it gladdened us to see old friends in there from AIM. My friends told us, "Okay, Banks, here's what we want. We would like this whole abbey turned back to the Menominee people. We want it to be converted into a hospital, a cultural center, and a meeting place for Native people. It must be given back to the tribe."

We went back outside and met with the Alexian Brothers. They insisted, "No, we are not giving it up. It is for *sale*. The price is $750,000. If you can come up with that amount, you can move in right now."

Both sides were serious, and the conflict was growing dangerous. The hundreds of law enforcement officers surrounding the buildings were soon joined by vigilantes who were members of a so-called concerned citizens committee and called themselves "WHAM" for White American Movement. The sheriff was a John Wayne-type who was ready to use armed force. His deputies had sealed off the area surrounding the abbey, cut power lines, and severed telephone communications with those inside. Extremists whipped up hysteria and spread the rumor that among the Indians were heavily armed Russian communists. That claim was absurd. There was gunfire—not as heavy as at the Knee, but a sporadic shot now and then. Every two or three hours a shot would go off and tensions would rise. Then things would calm down again.

Cy Griffin, a red-bearded white supporter who looked like John the Baptist, set up a radio station in a motel room. We broadcasted on this station to communicate with the men inside, as the phone lines had been cut. Later we set it up on the top floor of the tallest building in Gresham. It was an underground station; we did not have a license. Our broadcasts could be heard by people throughout the county. At first, Doug Durham tried to take over this operation, but we quickly put Annie Mae in charge. Durham by this time was strutting around introducing himself to the press as "AIM's Public Relations Director." We let him—anything to keep him away from where serious matters were being discussed and to prevent him from entering the abbey.

Matters improved when Governor Lucey sent in the National Guard—two hundred fifty men strong—to replace the local police forces. The guard was led by Col. Hugh Simonson, a good man determined to avoid bloodshed. He did not allow his men to carry loaded weapons. He restored telephone service and electricity to the abbey and reduced the number of checkpoints from twenty-two to eleven. He announced, "We're not on either side. We love everybody." He also said of the Menominees inside the abbey, "They are all sacred souls. I want them to come out with their heads up and take up a normal way of life."

Still, as long as the conflict with the Alexian Brothers remained unsolved, a siege was maintained. The white community of Gresham did not take kindly to Simonson. They wanted the novitiate tear-gassed and stormed. They sent a delegation to the governor, complaining that Simonson was "mollycoddling" rebels and renegades. The white population's fears were obviously based on money. If the Menominees could get away with obtaining the abbey for nothing, then *their* private property could be in danger. I continued trying to break the deadlock. After a time, it seemed as if the Alexian Brothers were beginning to soften their position and that they might just give us the abbey. Negotiations started to lean in that direction.

I had told the leaders of the warrior society about Durham. I had warned them to be on their guard if ever they met him. One particular evening at the novitiate, my old friends John Waubanascum and Neal Hawpatoss wanted to know if they could have a private ceremony with me. They wanted to have a sweat lodge and asked me to run it. I said, "Sure, I'll do that." I told Colonel Simonson, "We are going to have a sweat lodge ceremony inside the novitiate. I want to go back there this evening."

He shook his head, "Dennis, there's a curfew. There can be no movement at night after 8:00 P.M."

I said to myself, "To hell with the curfew!" I phoned Neal, "Go ahead and build a fire for the sweat. I'll come back in tonight." Annie Mae was organizing food to be backpacked in by way of a secret route. She was very good at that sort of thing. That night I drove around the back of the novitiate with Annie Mae and John. We hoisted the back-packs of food and other supplies, walked about five miles, and managed to get inside unseen. We had a very strong ceremony that night, which lasted until three o'clock in the morning. We all felt good and refreshed. In the early morning, Annie Mae, John, and I walked back out, got in our car, and drove to the motel where we were staying. I went to sleep knowing that the warriors would stick it out, no matter how long it might take.

In the end, we wore down the Alexian Brothers. They deeded the whole abbey to the Menominees for *one dollar*. We left Gresham after having been there for twenty days. Shortly before our last day, Doug and Jancita disappeared without a word. Maybe Doug had an inkling of what we knew about him. The warrior society of the Menominees left the novitiate on February 3, 1975 after occupying it for thirty-four days. They were immediately arrested, handcuffed, and transported to jail in Shawano, Wisconsin. All during the night in their cells, they chanted their Native songs. In court the next day, they were cheered by over a hundred tribal people. They were released soon after. Although there was some indignation among the warriors over being arrested at all, they looked upon this as a great victory. They said, "We have made the reservation bigger by two hundred and twenty-five acres. We have forced the white man to give something back."

I found out that Doug Durham and Jancita had gone to Des Moines very briefly, then up to South Dakota. We got ahold of Doug and told him to come back to Des Moines. We showed him a 302 FBI document without revealing the signature. He said, "What have I been telling you? There's a pig in the movement who has infiltrated our organization." He pretended to be very angry and repeated, "I told you this before!" Then Vernon uncovered Doug's signature at the bottom.

Vern said, "Okay, Doug, read this one then."

Doug said, "But I looked at it already."

Vern said, "Look at the bottom."

Doug stared for a moment at his own signature, turning white as a sheet as the blood drained from his face. He stammered, "Well . . . what do you want to know? Do you want me to admit that I work for the FBI? *Yes*, I *do*. I work for them, and I have done so for a long time." We asked him a lot of questions and made two cassette tapes of this confrontation in which he admitted everything. At last he asked, "Can I go? Are you holding me? Can I leave now?"

I told him, "Doug, this hurts me right here inside me. I always thought you were my friend."

He blinked and looked down. Then he said, "Well, what can I say? I work for the FBI. That's my job. That's what I get paid for."

I said, "Well, you can go anytime you want to."

And Vern said, "Yep, you can go."

We watched him walk out the door and down the hallway. We gathered at the window and saw him get into his car and speed away, tires screeching. I stood there thinking about his dyed-black hair and brown contact lenses, and the false avowals of friendship he had made for so long.

We decided that Vern Bellecourt would hold a press conference in St. Paul about Douglas Durham, about who he was and what he had done. We had the address and phone number of Doug's wife in Des Moines, so we called her to say that we would meet with the media and identify Doug as an operative for the FBI. He received word from her and called our office, saying, "I would like to come and admit what I did." As I remember, the press conference took place at the Minneapolis/St. Paul Airport.

Doug told the news people, "Yes, I do work for the FBI." He boasted, "Inside AIM, during the trial, I exercised so much control that you couldn't see Dennis or Russell without going through me. You couldn't contact any other chapter without going through me. And if you wanted money you had to see me." He also said that he was paid eleven hundred dollars a month for spying on us.

For a while after that, Durham made a living as an anti-AIM lecturer. He soon became a public speaker for the John Birch Society and other right-wing organizations. He came up with such absurdities as accusing Richard Nixon and Nelson Rockefeller of being secret communists who were selling out the USA to Russia. As for AIM, he said it was "communist-infiltrated and paid for," a revolutionary organization "planning to create chaos." He mentioned national monuments and government or law-enforcement buildings as being among our likely targets. State governors, he claimed, were on our list of those to be assassinated. He said, "Mt. Rushmore is going to be bombed, and bombs have been planted in a number of oil-company storage-tanks."

After we exposed him as an FBI operative, Durham and Jancita Eagle Deer disappeared from view. We heard they were hiding out somewhere around the Rosebud Sioux reservation and that friends were concerned about Jancita. On April 14, 1975, according to her brother, Albert, a dark-haired man in a blue Chevy picked up Jancita from her home near Valentine, Nebraska, forty miles south of the Rosebud reservation. Jancita was next spotted at least two hundred forty miles away in Aurora, Nebraska, on a lonely dirt road, trying to hail down a speeding car.

It was reported that she appeared to be staggering and "not quite all there." The car hit Jancita at such speed that she was thrown some distance from the impact and killed instantly. We sent a representative from AIM to investigate the tragedy. The coroner said physical evidence showed that she was probably beaten and/or perhaps pushed out of a fast-moving car before she was hit. Because of the severity of her injuries from the collision, this could not be proven.

Up to this point, Jancita still had hoped to get the rape case against Janklow into federal court. After Jancita's death, her stepmother, Delphine Eagle Deer, tried to take up her case. About three-quarters of a year later on a winter night out on a desolate reservation road, Delphine was beaten to death by a BIA policeman who pleaded drunkenness as his defense. Delphine's body, her legs broken, was found lying in the snow with her tears frozen on her face. The man who killed her was never charged.

Note: Bill Janklow has finally been held responsible for his actions. On Monday, December 8, 2003, a South Dakota jury declared Janklow guilty of all charges against him for an August 16, 2003, wreck in which motorcyclist Randy Scott was killed. Janklow was convicted of manslaughter, failing to stop at a stop sign, speeding, and reckless driving. Janklow immediately resigned his seat in the U.S. House of Representatives, effective January 20, 2004—the date of his sentencing, which could include up to ten years in prison.

CHAPTER 20

Fields of Terror

*An extraordinary number of unresolved homicides and incidents of
terror and violence have unfortunately become commonplace on the
Pine Ridge Reservation.*

—Arthur S. Fleming, U.S. Commissioner on Civil Rights

Sometimes I am surprised at being alive. From 1972 to 1976, the Pine
Ridge reservation was a killing field, and I spent a great deal of time
there. More than three hundred people are reported to have met a violent end in this place of fear and suppression. I have a list of sixty-two
confirmed murders. The vast majority of these victims were killed by the
BIA police, FBI agents, and Dicky Wilson's goons. Most of the victims
were members of AIM or sympathizers, adherents of OSCRO, the
Oglala Civil Rights Organization, or traditional full-bloods who had no
liking for Wilson's way of ruling the rez. Over 90 percent of the killings
and other violent hate crimes were never even investigated.

Pine Ridge in those days was described as a place of shootings,
knifings, beatings, firebombings, and every other kind of assault. Since
I was at the top of Wilson's hate list, as well as on that of the FBI and
State Attorney General Janklow's, I was a prime target for being "wasted."
I thank the spirits and my luck for being alive to write this story.

Basic rights taken for granted everywhere else in this country had
been suspended on the reservation by Wilson's order. I myself, an American Indian, was forbidden to set foot on Pine Ridge land, and so—at

times—was Russell Means, though he was a member of the Oglala tribe. Wilson once stated publicly that he would "personally cut off Russell's braids" if he should dare to come to the rez. The tribal president had a crude poster on the wall of his office that stated, "ONE OF RUSSELL MEANS' BRAIDS CUT OFF—FIVE DOLLARS, TWO BRAIDS—TEN DOLLARS, MEANS' WHOLE HEAD PICKLED—ONE HUNDRED DOLLARS."

One local Indian newspaper, the *Shannon County News*, described the situation:

> Mr. Wilson, our local goof-ball, who set himself up as the Hitler of Pine Ridge, has denied Indian people freedom of the press, guaranteed under the First Amendment of the Constitution. He has denied our people freedom of speech and freedom of assembly. The question now is: will all of our Sioux who oppose him be escorted to the reservation lines to be forced into exile? If this local bully continues, it may come to that.

This was written at the beginning of Wilson's rule before it turned deadly. A clipping from the *New York Times*, dated July 6, 1975, describes the situation at that time in this paper's manner of cautious understatement:

> There have been at least eight killings on the reservation so far this year along with uncounted fights, beatings, and outbreaks of shooting. Some of the incidents are still unexplained, but added together, they have created an atmosphere of terror between Mr. Wilson's mixed-blood supporters, universally known as "the goon squad," and the supporters of the American Indian Movement, allied with the full-blood traditionalists. . . .
>
> The United States Civil Rights Commission said in a staff report that the tribal election, in which Mr. Wilson won a narrow victory over AIM leader, Russell Means, was marked by irregularities in that perhaps a third of the votes were improper. Mr. Wilson, a jaunty man with a large paunch who habitually wears dark glasses, has run matters with such a "firm" hand that one previous BIA reservation superintendent was fond of saying that he, himself, was a "puppet" to the chairman's domineering personality. His opponents have often

charged that he ran a corrupt and dictatorial administration, backed up by the intimidation of the "goon squad," most of whom hold government jobs.

In addition to his salary, Mr. Wilson lives in the relative luxury of federally subsidized housing, is raising cattle, horses, and alfalfa, and has a trucking operation.

In the 1974 election for tribal chairman, Wilson won a narrow victory over Russell Means, though Russ actually won more votes, through widespread election fraud. Wilson forced his council members to watch a film, *Anarchy USA*, which suggested that communism was using AIM to bring about a worldwide communist takeover. The FBI and BIA supported Wilson in his anti-AIM campaign. Government money paid for his goons and for their weapons.

Everything else paled, though, when it came to the actual murders. Respected conservatives and former council members began fleeing the rez, choosing to live some place outside rather than become targets for tribal police and goon violence. One of my dearest friends, Pedro Bissonette, was one such victim. On October 17, 1973, he was brutally murdered by BIA police. The news of his death struck me hard. The thought that I would never see him alive again seemed unbearable to me. Pedro had created OSCRO, which opposed the Wilson dictatorship. He was a spokesman for the traditional full-bloods who resisted the regime. He supported AIM and was a thorn in Dicky Wilson's side. So he was set up to be killed.

Pedro had been under surveillance since Wounded Knee. He had a carefree attitude and shrugged off all warnings to be watchful. Friends had warned Pedro never to drive alone, but he just laughed and told them not to worry. One night Pedro stopped for a beer at a bar in Whiteclay, Nebraska, just a few miles south of the rez. A white man tried to provoke Pedro into a fight, cursing and physically attacking him. Pedro, who had been a boxer in his youth, knocked the fellow down and walked out. The instigator immediately pressed charges for assault and battery against Pedro. The court obligingly issued a bench warrant for Pedro's arrest, describing him as "armed and dangerous" with orders to "shoot to kill."

Pedro was waylaid by two or more BIA policemen on a lonely Pine Ridge road. One of them was Joe Clifford, a personal enemy and goon.

The other was Del Eastman, a special agent for the BIA and a confirmed Sioux-hater from the Crow reservation in Montana. Pedro died from multiple gunshot wounds to the chest. He had been shot point-blank at a range of two feet. There was never an investigation of Pedro's death.

I wanted to be with Pedro's family for his funeral, but I could not do so because I would have been arrested as soon as I set foot on the rez. I told AIM's lawyer and friend Ramon Roubideaux to relay my deepest prayers and condolences to the family. I felt low and devastated. But even though I could not go to Pedro, *he came to me.* His family arranged for the funeral procession to come to the reservation border, where I would be waiting a few feet short of the boundary line. Ramon drove me to the border and we stopped right in front of the BIA police cars sitting on the other side. We waited for fifteen minutes, then in the distance saw the lights of many cars slowly coming toward us. There were at least a hundred of them. The procession came to a stop.

I stood in silence as Pedro's friends brought the casket out and carried it over to a spot near me. They opened the lid and let me see Pedro's face for the last time. It was one of the saddest moments in my life. With tears in my eyes, I fumbled in my pocket for the AIM patch I had brought. I placed it on his heart and I held him for a moment before I sprinkled some sage into his coffin. I told the hundreds of people who had come about Pedro's gentleness; his sense of humor; his compassion for the poor, the sick, the children, and the elderly; how he always managed to provide food for the hungry and a roof over the head of the homeless. I talked about his courage in the face of death. I said, "Pedro was small of body, but he had a heart as big as the universe." The coffin was closed and placed in the hearse. The cars made their U-turns and drove slowly back the way they had come. I waved farewell to them until they were out of sight.

With Pedro's murder, the real terror began. Violence and bloodshed became almost daily events. None of the attackers ever worried about concealing their identities—they were under Wilson's protection. As a result, their names and crimes became common knowledge. In June 1973, BIA police shot Clarence Cross and his brother, Vernal, while the brothers slept in their car parked on the roadside. Clarence was killed outright; Vernal was severely wounded. Both were AIM members. In the fall of 1974, goons were firing M-16s into the home of the Little

Bear family when one of the bullets shot out the eye of four-year-old Mary Ann Little Bear. During the same period, Helen Red Feather was attacked by goons. They sprayed Mace in her face and brutally kicked her in the side, though she pleaded with them that she was four months pregnant. On November 20, fifteen-year-old Allison Little Horse was found dead in a ditch, a bullet through his heart. All of these victims were AIM members or their children. Jeanette Bissonette was shot and killed by a sniper as she returned from a wake. She was Pedro's sister-in-law. Nobody was safe.

The outrageous violence culminated on February 27, 1975. A group of four lawyers, two legal aides, and a Wounded Knee defendant arrived at Pine Ridge to investigate the civil rights abuses on the reservation. They landed at the Pine Ridge airport in a private plane, then went by car to interview people on the rez. When they came back to the airport, they found the plane shot full of bullet holes. They unloaded the plane, put their bags into the car, and prepared to leave. At that moment Dick Wilson arrived with about a dozen vehicles full of goons. These thugs kicked in the windshield of the investigators' car and actually tore off its roof to get to the people inside. The goons dragged the passengers out of the car and asked Wilson, "Dicky, what shall we do with them?"

He said, "*Stomp them!*"

The goons at once attacked the lawyers and legal aides, knocking them to the ground, kicking and trampling them while also beating them severely. One went after Roger Finzel, one of the young lawyers, with his knife, slashing at the lawyer's face and trying to hack his hair off, because the hoodlum "thought it was too long." Eda Gordon, one of the two legal aides, threw herself across Finzel in an attempt to protect him. Her hand was badly cut by the goon's knife. Wilson threatened to kill his victims if they ever came back to the rez. All members of the legal team wound up in the Rapid City hospital.

That was not the end of the violence, even though one event seemed an answer to our prayers—Dick Wilson had finally been defeated. He lost his bid for a third term as tribal chairman by a three-to-one margin. The winner was a former BIA superintendent and longtime Wilson opponent, Al Trimble. Unfortunately, Wilson had two months left before he had to relinquish his office, during which time he wielded absolute power. One newspaper quoted a Pine Ridge resident as saying,

"Dick Wilson is very angry about his election loss. He has promised death and destruction to those who worked against him."

The little reservation town of Wanblee, South Dakota, was Al Trimble's home. Its inhabitants were mostly full-bloods, who had voted overwhelmingly for their home boy. Wilson told his henchmen that "Wanblee has to be straightened out." Shortly after that, on January 31, 1976, several carloads of heavily armed goons drove into the town. They wore government-issue bullet-proof vests and were armed with AR-15 rifles. They began by firing into the house of AIM sympathizer Guy Dull Knife. Even though witnesses positively identified some of the goons, the FBI took no action against them. Instead, they arrested Dull Knife and his wife, Pearl.

Then the goons fire-bombed the home of Charlie Abourezk, the son of U.S. Senator James Abourezk who had on several occasions criticized the tribal chairman. Later, Wilson threw Charlie off the reservation. Even a senator's son was not safe from Wilson's vindictiveness. It was clear Wilson felt sure the government would support him no matter what crimes he committed.

Byron DeSersa was a tribal attorney and an AIM supporter who had been with us at Wounded Knee. Seeing the goons shooting out windows and fire-bombing homes and knowing he was a target, he decided to leave Wanblee. His car was overtaken by goons as they riddled the vehicle with bullets. Three shots tore through DeSersa's leg, almost severing it. He dragged himself into a ditch. All the other passengers in his car fled except George Beltelyoun, who tried to help the attorney. DeSersa told George to run like hell and save himself. Byron DeSersa bled to death while the goons chased the other occupants of the car. His life probably could have been saved by a simple tourniquet.

Random shooting continued throughout the night at Wanblee. Neither of the two FBI agents who had arrived at Wanblee that afternoon nor the BIA police made any effort to put a stop to the vigilantes running amuck. An FBI spokesman justified this by saying "the agents had no authority to act in a protective capacity," even though people had appealed to them for help.

In spite of the obvious danger during these terrible times at Pine Ridge, Kamook and I lived on the reservation in the little settlement of Oglala, South Dakota. Not only did we have strong family ties to the rez, but also I felt that our people there needed a strong AIM presence to give them some measure of protection from the goons. The Oglala community welcomed us, having asked AIM to stay nearby after Wounded Knee because they were afraid of the goons. The people at Oglala were mostly traditional, Lakota-speaking full-bloods and, for that reason, were constantly harassed by Wilson's henchmen.

I had become very close to the Jumping Bull family. They had a big hall at Oglala called the Jumping Bull Hall where lots of AIM events took place. The family owned at least fifty acres of land, including a large wooded area with a creek. I asked Cecilia Jumping Bull if the AIM people could stay on their land. It was clear that we needed space for an AIM camp instead of crowding into people's homes and possibly putting them at risk. She got together with her family and they agreed, saying, "You can camp on our land if you want to, maybe down by the creek."

We scouted for a good location and decided to establish our camp in a place people called the "dam area" on the lower part of the Jumping Bull property. A ravine snaked through it, but the land above the ravine walls was flat. We put up four tipis and a number of tents. We had a pretty good idea of what we wanted to do with the surrounding two or three acres, like raising some crops in a big garden. In the spring we plowed up about three acres using a truck to pull a handmade, improvised plow back and forth over the field. It was a crazy method but it worked.

Soon we had formed quite a community there. People started coming down from Pine Ridge. Kamook's sisters dropped in and stayed a while, as did many other friends. Some came on the weekends when we drummed and sang. At any given time we might have thirty, forty, or fifty people spending an evening with us. The camp had become very popular. Among the people who came to live there was my old friend, Leonard Peltier, a Lakota-Anishinabe from the Turtle Mountain reservation, four miles north of Belcourt, North Dakota. His joining us forever changed his life.

In 1975, I was once more a defendant, this time in a trial at Custer, South Dakota, some fifty miles west of Oglala, for my role during the confrontation at the Custer Courthouse after Wesley Bad Heart Bull was murdered. I was out on ten thousand dollars of bail. The trial started June 16. My pre-trial motions were heard in a heavily secured courtroom. Spectators were forced to give their names and addresses, told to empty their pockets, purses, and briefcases, and then made to walk through electric sensors. Even a baby was subjected to having his diaper scanned. The courthouse windows and the judge's bench were reinforced with quarter-inch steel plates, and forty South Dakota police officers were brought in to "guard" the proceedings.

An additional squad of armed volunteers—including the local sheriff's deputies; state troopers; and State Game, Fish, and Parks employees—increased the number of law enforcement personnel. All of these "protective measures" had been carefully orchestrated by William Janklow. Clearly he hoped his security circus would increase fear and apprehension of AIM in the jurors and the public. Janklow was by then the State Attorney General, the highest law enforcement official in South Dakota.

From the first day of court I could see that I could not expect a fair trial at Custer. Judge Marshall Young imposed a gag rule on the press. He forbade reporters covering the trial from "giving out any information except that which occurs in open court, adduced only in evidence and arguments." This meant, for example, that if someone had shot the judge inside the courtroom, the reporters could not mention it. It was a ridiculous situation. The judge also forbade all "extra-judicial statements or any release of any leads, gossip, or information obtained outside the court." The gag rule also barred reporters from giving their own interpretation of the trial, speculating on the merits of the case, or mentioning the credibility of the witnesses. It was pointed out to me that the gag order would also protect the jury from outside influence and, that in consideration of the prejudice white South Dakotans had against me and AIM and the influence such people might have on the jury, it would be favorable to my defense. I did not see it that way.

Janklow had decided to try me personally, making the trial a face-off between two men who, in the purest form, represented the opposing views of two races. Janklow himself read the charges against me. The prosecution claimed that my trial was merely an ordinary criminal case, and neither a political nor a "sociological experiment."

While giving my own opening statement, I made it crystal-clear that this was a purely political trial, and that, in trying me, they were trying AIM. I told the jury that "the state of South Dakota had created an atmosphere that led directly to a police riot, and that the question was not whether I was guilty or not, but a question of whether we would find the state guilty or not." I acted as my own attorney because when I questioned jurors for selection, I was able to get underneath their veneer of impartiality to the racism hiding beneath it, like lifting a rock to expose a mass of slimy worms. During the entire trial, I strove to keep my face impassive and to speak quietly even while making witnesses squirm under my questions. I managed to remain calm even while Janklow browbeat and coerced defense witnesses. Janklow was petulant. He whined and complained when he did not get his way, and smirked and gloated when he did.

For the duration of the trial I traveled each weekday to Custer in the morning and back to Oglala in the evening, where Kamook, Tashina, and I were living in a two-room, green-painted tar paper-and-log shack we rented from the Jumping Bull family. Our home was located near the AIM camp, which had come to be known as Tent City. Harry Jumping Bull, who was then in his eighties, and his wife, Cecilia, had just celebrated their fiftieth wedding anniversary. It was also the anniversary of the Battle of the Little Bighorn where General Custer had met defeat and death.

Late in the afternoon of June 25, 1975, two FBI agents and two BIA policemen showed up at the Jumping Bull ranch. They wanted to search the house for a young Indian named Jimmy Eagle who reportedly had stolen a pair of old cowboy boots from a white youth at a party. They checked out the area, asked a few questions, and left. That night we had heavy thunderstorms and tornado conditions. Kamook and I were up during the night because little Tashina had developed an ear infection. In the morning we decided that Kamook would take her to Pine Ridge Hospital while I went to Custer for the trial. Had we remained at the camp that day, who knows if any of us would still be alive or if I would be serving out a life sentence in a federal prison.

Leonard Peltier was running the camp in my absence. He had assigned Joe Stuntz Kills Right, a young, tall, rather shy Coeur d'Alene Indian, as my bodyguard. Every day I picked up Joe early and took him with me to Custer. On this particular day, however, I gave him the day off because he had not slept well. I went down to the camp at about

4:00 A.M. to wake up two of our security people to go with me to Custer while Kamook took off for Pine Ridge with the baby.

Promptly at nine o'clock, trial proceedings began at the Custer courthouse. Sometime after the midmorning break, our defense committee's runners came in and asked the court for permission to hand me a note saying there was trouble at Oglala. A short time after that, the committee workers returned to say, "There's *shooting* at Oglala!" At that moment a state trooper whispered something to Attorney General Janklow, who rose and asked if we could all approach the bench. He explained to the judge that because there was violence breaking out at Pine Ridge, he wanted to have the trial put in recess for the day so that he could take charge of the situation. I knew it had to be Tent City that was under attack.

I was very worried about Kamook; I quickly called the hospital to find out when she had last been seen. They said she had left an hour before. I was afraid that she and the baby were already back at the camp under fire, and I was concerned for everybody out there. Once outside the courthouse, I took off immediately for Oglala.

What actually happened on that fateful morning of June 26 can only be reconstructed from what was reported by people who were there. Late in the morning two strange cars appeared on the Jumping Bull property. They stopped near the creek behind the main house. Two federal agents, Ronald Williams and Jack Coler, got out and removed a high-powered .308 rifle and a handgun from the trunk of one car. They were the same two men who had shown up the evening before on the pretext of searching for Jimmy Eagle, and the year before, the same Ronald Williams, then a member of a SWAT team, had aroused the anger of Judge Nichol at the Banks/Means trial with his gross professional misconduct.

Also near the main house was a red pick-up truck occupied by a few people from camp who were either arriving or leaving. Some of the people of Tent City were not yet awake because of the heavy storms and the babies that had cried all night before. A few young Indians leaned on a car, waiting for some hot oatmeal the women were fixing. Angie Long Visitor was in the main house washing breakfast dishes while her four small children played outside. Suddenly she heard sounds like firecrackers. She ran to a bluff behind the house to see what was going on. From there she observed two white men in civilian clothes firing guns in the direction of the camp. Angie and her husband grabbed their children and fled.

The agents were using their two-way radios to call for help. "Looks like they're shooting at us!" The next calls were urgent, "Come on, guys, come on!" Then, "We've been hit!" Coler was hit first in the arm. It seems that Williams took off his shirt to make a tourniquet to stop Coler's bleeding. Then Williams was hit. It all happened pretty fast.

Within a short time, the two agents and Joe Stuntz Kills Right, the young Indian I had given the day off, were all lying dead on the ground. Joe had been shot in the head as he ran toward a small outbuilding for cover. His death struck all of us deep in the heart. I wondered why I hadn't taken him with me that day. Now his wife and two small children would have to live without him. Joe had wanted to become a medicine man and had studied at the Institute of American Indian Arts in Santa Fe, New Mexico. Worst of all, there would never be any investigation into this quiet man's senseless death. He lay there all day and into the night while shots continued to be exchanged.

It was very strange how, immediately after the first bursts of gun-fire, the BIA and the Feds appeared on the scene with every kind of heavy weaponry. Cars sped into the area in clouds of dust. Agents were suddenly everywhere, as though they had been waiting just over the next hill. For weeks we had noticed a heavy build-up of law enforcement people on and around the rez. Sixty or more new FBI agents, most of them members of SWAT teams, had created an atmosphere of high anxiety so thick you could taste it.

The endless violence of goons with the apparent support of the FBI had fostered a hair-trigger tension ready to explode into a full-blown war. The presence of so many marshals and FBI agents only encouraged Dick Wilson's thugs to continue their murderous activities. How could the government *not* have known they were looked upon by traditional Indian people as allies of the goon squads? They *had* to know that if they ventured into AIM territory they would surely incite trouble.

Tent City quickly became a battle zone. Our people were poorly armed, but at this point there was nothing they could do but try to defend themselves and provide diversions so others could escape. Some of the men in our camp, Leonard Peltier, Bob Roubideaux (a distant relative of Ramon Roubideaux, our attorney), and Dino Butler, felt that this might be their last day. The only hope was to get out of there. They checked the only available vehicle and found it was too low on fuel to get them very far. The only way out was through a grove of trees that was fast being taken over by the Feds. They hastily gathered some supplies. Someone collected some ammunition and the rifle belonging to Agent Coler, then about sixteen people took off on foot, looking for a miracle.

The Feds, BIA police, and vigilante ranchers who had come along for the ride moved in with deadly speed using high-powered automatic and semi-automatic weaponry, M-16s, tear-gas bombs, spotter planes, helicopters, and trained marksmen scouring the area for any signs of movement. The Feds destroyed the camp—they shot up the houses, privies, garbage cans, anything at all. They wrecked the Jumping Bull home, seemingly deliberately destroying even the framed photographs of family members. They put a bullet in the head of a child's doll. The acrid smell of tear gas hung over this entire scene of desolation.

The initial arrival of the two agents at Tent City always seemed to me to be a case of calculated provocation. The FBI had wanted to create an incident that would give them an excuse to wipe out our camp. I believe, and so do many others, that the Feds set up their own two agents. Coler and Williams were used as bait. The FBI might not have intended for the two agents to die, but they deliberately put them in harm's way. The Feds apparently went looking for trouble, and they found it. They were amazingly well prepared for it. Three days before the incident, members of the goon squads had begun moving their families off the reservation into Nebraska, along with Dick Wilson's political allies. Then several hours before the shoot-out occurred, the goons had already started setting up roadblocks to seal off the highway to and from Oglala and Pine Ridge.

After Coler and Williams fell, more than fifty highly trained marksmen swarmed in, peppering the whole camp with lead. It is a wonder that Leonard and his group of men, women, and children got out of there alive. The terrain in that area consists of open, arid hills and gullies with few trees or natural places to take cover. With the overwhelming odds against the little group of fugitives, it did not seem possible that even a mouse could escape. But the Great Spirit protected them. A bald eagle appeared above them, showing them a way out. They followed it. Leonard and his people had stopped running only long enough to pray, and their prayer was answered by a truly miraculous escape involving a trek of more than one hundred miles over barren country. Wherever they knocked on a door, they were given a meal or a place to rest.

Leonard has never denied having fired in the direction of the agents from about one hundred fifty feet away. *Everybody* who could grab some kind of weapon fired it to keep the attackers at a distance. But Leonard could not and *did not* fire the shots that killed the two agents. Even now the government admits that its specialists actually do not know who killed them. Our camp came under attack by agents of the U.S. government who came in shooting. We hadn't gone out looking for trouble. We were just there. We had done nothing against the law to justify an invasion. The FBI admits they have not the slightest idea who killed the two agents, yet more than twenty years have passed and still Leonard is in prison for something he did not do. But his strength is with him wherever he is. The prison will never crush him.

For me, not knowing what was happening that day and the powerlessness I experienced were awful. I was unable to get to Oglala at all. Three of us had left the courthouse in Custer and driven like hell until we came to the first set of roadblocks. The Feds weren't letting anybody through, so we ran the first roadblock, only to be stopped at the next one the FBI had set up. We were pretty close to the camp at that point and could even hear shooting in the distance. The agents were rude and somewhat hysterical. I kept saying, "My wife and child are there. That's where I live! I need to go and find my family!"

One of the BIA officers said, "Go ahead. You're on your own. Walk on in there." The shooting was still audible in the distance.

An FBI agent laughed and said to me, "Go ahead, Big Chief, start walking!" They searched the car but still did not let us pass. We could see that there were other roadblocks ahead. There was no way to get by car to Oglala or Pine Ridge. We remained at the roadblocks, where I finally found somebody who had seen Kamook in her car with two other people. Their car had also been turned back, so she was not at the camp. The news relieved my mind a little.

Late in the afternoon I could still hear some random shots now and then but no real exchanges. Families that lived in the area were still running to get as far away as possible from Oglala. When the roadblocks finally came down, I went to Pine Ridge to see Kamook's aunt, Lou Bean. She told me that Kamook had gone to Custer to wait for me. We had a room there that we used sometimes during the trial when it was too late to travel back to Oglala. I was very relieved to find her safe with Tashina.

That night we talked about the events of the day and what each of us had heard and experienced. Kamook told me that at about 9:00 A.M., she and a nurse at the hospital in Pine Ridge were visiting together while she was waiting to see a doctor. She could see out the window a number of police cars leaving town. In those times, our people knew that when all the police cars headed out of town they were going after AIM people. Before long, even before the time that the shoot-out began, there was an announcement over the hospital PA to have all medical staff report to the emergency station to receive wounded. A few minutes later the nurse came running back and told Kamook, "There's a lot of killing going on. They're asking for body bags!"

The following day, a force of more than one hundred fifty heavily armed agents began a military-style sweep of civilian homes across the reservation. Without warrants, they entered homes, abused Indians verbally and physically, and made the people of the rez feel like victims of a foreign occupation. The FBI and wire services put out lurid stories about the shooting at Jumping Bull's property, saying that the agents had been massacred, executed, ritually tortured, and scalped.

With all the inflammatory misinformation, white South Dakotans became paranoid. It was certain that under these circumstances I could not get a fair trial. The trial continued anyway. Within a month, on July 26, I was found guilty of assault and riot charges for what had taken place at Custer in February 1973 in front of the same courthouse I now found myself being tried in. I was told to show up on Tuesday, August 5 for my sentencing. I faced up to fifteen years in the penitentiary. Judge Young allowed me to remain free on a pre-sentencing bond of ten thousand dollars. He stipulated that I was to check in every day with the local sheriff's office until the day of sentencing.

Janklow threw a fit. He said I was likely to jump bail, and he was right. I thought about it long and hard, and concluded that once I had left the courthouse after sentencing, I would be in the hands of my enemies. My life wouldn't be worth a plugged nickel. I did not appear in court on August 5. The day before, a bench warrant was issued for my arrest; Kamook and I had become fugitives with every hand raised against us.

CHAPTER 21

Outlawed

When all the weaponry was finally still,
Two special agents of the FBI
And one young Indian upon the hill
Had been the victims found to fall and die.
The rest of the beleaguered outlaw group
Escaped the eyes that watched their hopeless flight
By following an eagle's sudden swoop
Until they reached the safety of the night.
Although the flight began from mutual dread,
The only ones to face a jury's say
Were those accused of shooting agents dead
And not the man who blew Joe Stuntz away.
The law, it sadly seems, will always be,
From time to time, applied selectively.

—Anonymous

They looked for me everywhere. A nationwide search for me was conducted by local, state, and federal officers. My friends joked that every
Indian male with long hair between thirty and fifty years of age was liable
to be stopped and questioned. I heard on the radio that police *almost* got
me twice, once in Kansas and once in Oregon. They broke into a sympathizer's apartment in Sioux Falls. I wasn't there. They looked for me in
regional AIM offices. I wasn't there either. They searched for me in the
WKLDOC office in Rapid City and laid siege to the National AIM

headquarters in St. Paul. Helicopters hovered overhead, and reporters yelled to the people inside, "Where is Dennis Banks?"

In an action like a Keystone Cop comedy, a state trooper pursued a vehicle driven by an Indian with braids. The Indian turned out to be Vernon Bellecourt. Later, state patrol officers, helicopters, and FBI agents tracked down Vern's car and searched it. Vern told them, "As you see, Dennis isn't in the car, but you can look under the hood if you want to."

Leonard Peltier and his group of sixteen followers had evaded the FBI dragnet and made it to Crow Dog's Paradise at Rosebud, where they found shelter among hundreds of Sun Dancers. At the end of the month, I also arrived at Crow Dog's. Kamook was there, too. We didn't know that one of the people there, someone we trusted, was an FBI informant who regularly reported on our activities to his bosses. But we had our ceremonies and were united for a time. We all pierced, giving our bodies to the Creator, and felt strengthened by it.

Leonard and I were fugitives from justice. We thought it best not to bring the hunt down on the Sun Dancers, so we decided to keep moving until we found a place of safety. We left Kamook and Tashina at Crow Dog's because I thought it too dangerous for them to travel with Leonard and me.

Kamook joined a group of young AIM people, headed by Bob Roubideau, traveling in an old, decrepit Mercury station wagon. The men were transporting rifles and ammunition for use by the people in Pine Ridge to defend themselves should it become necessary. Kamook, her sister, Bernice, and of course little Tashina were among the passengers. They were driving along the Kansas turnpike when someone yelled, "Hey, this thing is starting to smoke back here!" Everybody piled out of the car. Bob Roubideau was trying to find out what was wrong when the old clunker blew up.

The explosion was terrific. Bits of asphalt were flung into Bob's face, temporarily blinding him. He rolled away from the car just as the rounds of ammo went off. Then the exploding gas tank blew the roof off the old station wagon. Kamook was hit in the arm by shrapnel and cut badly. A farmer stopped to help, got suspicious, and called the police. The whole group wound up in a Wichita, Kansas, jail. Kamook was charged with transporting illegal weapons across state lines and sentenced to three years of probation. She did her probation time in

Rapid City while staying with her mom and dad. When the police rummaged through the charred wreck of the car, they found the .308 rifle used by Agent Coler during the shoot-out at Tent City and pieces of another rifle that they claimed had killed the two agents.

Leonard and I were still the subjects of a nationwide search. Wherever we went we found support and a place to hide. On the doors of many reservation homes, and even on those of some white sympathizers, people posted signs that read: DENNIS BANKS WELCOME! It was a way to make their thoughts known and to mock those who were hunting for us. We kept close contact with Kamook and other AIM people.

I got a message about a meeting to be held at Oglala by Loud Hawk, the headman there. The elders had told him, "We need help. Our young men have no weapons or ammunition to defend the people, and we need some explosives. If the goons and FBI come near us, we need some means of scaring them away. We need to be prepared this time."

We went to Oglala to meet with them. I was not worried about going into the lion's den—Oglala was the last place the FBI would be looking for me. The elders asked me, "Can you go and find this kind of stuff for us?"

I said, "Alright, I will try," and I talked it over with Leonard Peltier. I had heard that explosives could be found in logging camps.

Then friends told us, "We can get you what you need in the Seattle area."

I do not consider myself a violent man. On the contrary I hate violence and have always tried to avoid it. I often had persuaded our men to resolve conflicts peacefully, but Pine Ridge had become the scene of a life-or-death struggle. It seemed to me that I should gather arms for our people to defend themselves since the law would not protect them. Even if the guns were used only for show, perhaps the goons would realize that resistance was gathering momentum. I found myself caught in a web of events that might easily lead to violence.

We drove to Los Angeles and went to Marlon Brando's place. Marlon pointed to Leonard and asked, "Who the hell is this?" When I told Marlon, he said, "Goddamn, you've got some nerve! But it's okay." We helped Marlon unpack the motorhome he had just driven home from a trip.

I told him, "Marlon, we're going to leave tomorrow because it is too hot for us to stay around here. Leonard is wanted under a federal warrant and so am I. We don't want to put a lot of heat on you, so we're going to leave."

He said, "Don't leave. Let's talk about getting you some legal counsel." Still, I felt that we needed to keep moving. We had dinner with Marlon and talked for hours about all of the events and issues we were grappling with. The next morning, Harry Belafonte, who was in town for a movie deal, showed up. When I told him that we had gone underground, he hugged me and wished us good luck. As we were leaving, Marlon asked what we were traveling in.

"Well," I said, "we have that car. It's outside."

He looked at it and said, "Dennis, this car isn't going to make it very far. I'm going to give you this motorhome. Do you know how to drive it?"

"Well, I can learn," I said.

"You'll have to," Marlon said. Then he asked, "Do you need any money?"

"That's why I came here—to get some gas money," I said.

"You're going to need more than gas money. How long do you think you'll say underground?" he asked.

"I don't know. A lot depends on what they are going to charge us with," I said.

Marlon left the room and returned in a short while. He handed me an envelope, saying, "Dennis, here's some money for gas and food."

I thanked him as Leonard and I left. I could tell by the feel of it that there was a good amount of money in that envelope. As we got to the bottom of Mulholland Drive, I counted the money and told Leonard, "Look what Marlon has given us!" Our "food and gas money" was ten thousand dollars! We headed out in the motorhome.

We wanted to get some rifles. We bought ten of them right there in Los Angeles, where we could buy them over the counter without having to register them. Leonard and I drove back to South Dakota because I knew that Kamook needed money. When we got there, we had to be careful not to be seen. We parked the motorhome during the day near Rushville, Nebraska, then drove it during the night into Pine Ridge and

Oglala. We made contact with Kamook and our many friends there. We had a ceremony that night with our friends. I told them about Marlon, what we had done, and where we had been. We left three thousand dollars and the rifles with them. They were good rifles—.30s and .60s, all brand new.

We took off again, this time for the Northwest Coast to get more weapons and the explosives. Kenny Loud Hawk and Russ Redner, a Western Shoshone, came along. We asked Annie Mae Aquash to join us because we needed someone who was not wanted by the law who could go around openly buying whatever we needed as we traveled. The five of us drove across North Dakota and Montana to Portland, Oregon, then to Puyallup and Yelm in Washington State, where we stayed with friends for four days.

We put the word out that we needed explosives for Pine Ridge. Three different groups of supporters brought us what we needed. We wound up with about two hundred sticks of dynamite and ten assault weapons. We had some concern because the weapons were automatic and, of course, illegal. I don't know why we worried about that considering all the other things we were wanted for. We decided to protect the people who had supplied them by filing off all of the serial numbers so the Feds could not trace the source of the weapons.

While we were staying in Nisqualliy and Puyallup country, we held sweat lodge ceremonies. Many people came to support us. They brought us ammunition—boxes of 12-gauge shells, boxes of .22s, and boxes of .30-06s. We ended up with about five to six hundred rounds of assorted ammunition. We bought a station wagon because we wanted to carry all of our explosives in a separate vehicle. I called Kamook, who said she wanted to join us. We bought her an airline ticket and she flew to Seattle, where one of our supporters picked her up and brought her to us. She had Tashina with her and was visibly pregnant again. It was a good reunion for all of us.

On our last day there, a small single-engine plane buzzed us three or four times. We realized that we were under surveillance and had to leave. That night we got out of there. I was driving Marlon's motorhome with Leonard in the passenger seat, while Kamook, Tash, and Annie Mae slept in the back. Kenny and Russ were behind us in the white station wagon. About six miles down the road we ran into one of our supporters, a beekeeper named David. He gave us several large jars of honey to sweeten our journey.

We arrived in Portland in the morning. Leonard phoned the place we had been staying about some things he mistakenly had left behind. Whoever answered the phone said, "The police are here!" and hung up. On a hunch I called up David, the bee man, and he whispered, "The police are all over the place, and the FBI. You guys got out at just the right time." That was all he said before he hung up, too. That day we drove out of Portland on the interstate, determined to get the weapons to those who needed them. We sensed the danger all around us and had an eerie feeling of something closing in on us.

When the FBI raided the place where we had been staying, they discovered that we had left the night before. Having spotted us from the air, they knew that we were traveling in a white motorhome and a white station wagon. They sent out bulletins with a description of our little caravan. A police officer in Portland notified the highway patrol via Teletype that he had seen us driving east on the main highway, describing Leonard and me as "armed and dangerous." The bulletin instructed police and state patrol officers not to stop us when sighted because the FBI reserved the right to arrest us. The bulletin concluded with, "Repeat! Do not stop these vehicles!" The FBI was setting up their own road block somewhere ahead of us in order, as I am still convinced, to blow us away.

We were driving along Interstate 84 near the Idaho border, the motorhome in the lead with me in the driver's seat and Russ and Kenny a quarter-mile behind me in the station wagon. It was November 14 and night had fallen. Somewhere along our route, a state trooper by the name of Ken Griffiths was having his coffee and studying the FBI bulletin. He then went on his rounds patrolling a section of I-84, and just as he got on the freeway he saw our two vehicles drive by. He instantly realized that we were the fugitives and followed us. He managed to slip between me and the station wagon. I heard Kenny over the CB say, "Dennis, look out! The pigs are behind you!"

The trooper was flashing his lights for us to pull over. We slowed to a stop. I was thinking fast. The trooper already had his gun out as he leaped from the squad car. The cop was looking us over, making sure we were the ones the FBI were looking for. Now, here we had a state trooper who had received orders *not* to stop us but was doing it anyway. We will never know what he really was doing—whether he was looking for a moment of glory for himself or if it was all a mistake.

Meanwhile, some fifteen miles down the road, the FBI was waiting for us. They had already put out warnings to the police in the area that there was likely to be a massive shoot-out. State Trooper Ken Griffiths unwittingly saved our hides that night. I look back upon him, bumbling into this situation, as Coyote—the trickster of legend who sometimes helps Indians when they are in trouble. At that moment, however, he did not seem like a lifesaver to me. He was pointing his shotgun at us, hollering, "Get out, everybody! Get out with your hands up! One false move and I blow your heads off!"

It was about eleven o'clock at night. Leonard had been dozing beside me in the passenger seat. Kamook, Tashina, and Annie Mae had been sleeping in the back. The commotion woke everybody up. By this time another trooper, Clayton Kramer, had appeared. In the rearview mirror, I saw Kenny and Russ leave the station wagon and Kramer force them down at gunpoint, their faces to the pavement. Kamook, carrying Tashina in a blanket, got out of the motorhome followed by Annie Mae and Leonard. Soon everybody was lying prone on the ground under the troopers' guns. Kamook was in an advanced stage of pregnancy, so making her lie on her stomach was unnecessarily cruel.

I had no intention of joining the party. The engine was still running. I shifted quietly into gear, revved the engine, and took off. I could hear Trooper Griffiths screaming in anger. I heard shots and stepped on the accelerator. Glass shattered as a bullet crashed through the windshield. I fired two rounds to scare him off. He was firing like a maniac by then, hitting the motorhome again. While Griffiths was busy firing at me, Leonard saw his chance, jumped to his feet, and was hit by heavy buckshot in the back, through the right shoulder. It was a large wound that bled heavily, but he ran on into a field and made good his escape.

I was in a desperate situation. I knew there would be roadblocks somewhere. I had a very good chance of being killed. I didn't want to risk it. I realized I had to get out of the motorhome fast. I was on a slight downhill grade, so I steered the vehicle on a straight course. Slowing down to about 30 MPH, I grabbed my parka, opened the door, and jumped out while the motorhome was moving along. I hit the ground and rolled a few times, scrambled to my feet, ran to the side of the road, and threw my firearm into the bushes. I went over a fence and ran as fast as I could into the woods.

While running blindly in the darkness, I stumbled into a couple of barbed-wire fences and was badly cut. In the excitement and my eagerness to get away from the road, I paid no attention to my wounds. I glanced back for a moment to see the motorhome still going straight down the interstate all by itself for a quarter of a mile. Then it veered off onto the median, where it got bogged down and just stopped between the eastbound and westbound traffic.

The engine was still running when the police arrived. I could hear sirens wailing as I scrambled up a nearby ridge. From there I could see Brando's motorhome below me. There were squad cars all over the place, and I could hear a lot of shooting. The police and FBI were there in no time at all—because they had been waiting for us. I was too far away to hear their voices, but, according to police reports, they were hollering for the occupants to come out with their hands up or else. Of course nobody came out, so they started firing. At least twenty law enforcement officers pumped round after round into the motorhome. The vehicle was completely shot-up. Finally they threw tear gas into the interior and waited expectantly for survivors to emerge, but they were disappointed.

In the end, they screwed up enough courage to enter the smoking motorhome to find no one there. They seized the ammo, the weapons, and some explosives. The next day, they dragged it all into a field and blew it up, detonating the whole kit and caboodle, including the dynamite in the station wagon because they thought it unsafe to transport. They blew away all the evidence and did not even save a single stick of dynamite. So when we went to trial six months later, they did not have any proof to support a weapons charge against us.

I watched the whole wild scene from up on a distant ridge—the flashing lights and the police milling around the shot-up motorhome. It was a picture of utter confusion. Then I turned my back on this scene and went deeper into the woods. When I hit railroad tracks, I followed them the rest of the night. I was still walking early the next morning as the sun came up. This was November in the north country and it was icy cold. I didn't have gloves and was still bleeding from my left hand.

My right hand was punctured by barbed wire, and I had deep scratches on my chest and knees. The bleeding did not concern me, but my hands were painful and stiff. I could not move my fingers.

I came to a creek with tall reeds and a beaver's lodge. It seemed like a good place to rest. Hidden from view, I stayed there among the reeds out of the wind for about two hours. I noticed a farmhouse with a barn about a quarter-mile away and knew that I would wind up in that barn. It looked so inviting, but I thought, "Not right away. I better wait." I heard some dogs barking in the distance and saw four men with rifles walking toward me. There was a little reed hut nearby, like a duck-hunter's blind, which I crawled into. No snow had fallen yet, but it was as cold as a refrigerator in there.

As the men came nearer, I could hear them talking. They were just some hunters looking for deer. I could hear the dogs barking outside. Luckily for me, they were neither pointers nor setters, but just ordinary dogs. As they ran off, a thought occurred to me. Years ago I went out hunting, I would come to a reed hut like this one and fire off some buckshot into it on the chance that I might bag some water fowl hiding inside. I thought, "Oh man, what if they start shooting and kill me, then walk on. I would be lying here forever, and nobody would ever know what happened to me."

But the hunters went on their way and nothing happened. I guess the situation had made me overly apprehensive, so for the rest of the day I stayed inside that icy hut. Later someone else came by. Judging by the sounds, it was just a little kid.

That evening as it was getting dark, I walked over to the barn and cautiously went inside. I pulled three bales from the middle of a big stack of straw bales, and where they had been I made a place to sleep. I was shivering badly and my hands were hurting like hell. I had two pairs of socks on because my boots were a little big on me, so I took one pair of socks and used them to warm my hands. I had a wool cap on when I ran into the woods but it was gone, maybe stuck on a branch somewhere along the way. I had the light hood of my parka, though. I slept that night burrowed in the hay.

The next morning, the sound of someone talking woke me with a start. It was the farmer, and he was talking to his dog, saying, "What's the matter, girl? What is it?" The dog kept barking, but the owner dragged her away. That afternoon the dog came back, sniffing around. I saw the animal standing there, growling at the spot where I was hiding. The owner came in once more, trying to calm the dog, "Come on, girl, there's nothing here." The dog persisted, but the man dragged her away. I was afraid that the farmer would come back and start checking around, so I went back to the reed hut and watched the farmer return to the barn with his dog, rummage around in there for about a half-hour, then disappear into his house.

For four days I went back to the barn to sleep at night in the hay; during the day I hid in the hut. I was ravenously hungry, having survived only on water that I licked from icicles. I saw the farmer pumping water into a gallon jug from an outdoor pump. Then he put the jug down beside the pump and went back into the house. I waited for a while, then made a run for the jug. I took it into the reed hut and drank deeply from the pure water.

During all of this time I was worried sick about Kamook and little Tashina. It was torture not knowing what had become of my family and Annie Mae and Leonard. The fear that they had been hurt was gnawing at me. I knew that most of the shots had been directed at the motor home, but the uncertainty was driving me nearly mad. A thought went through my mind, "Did I do the right thing? Did I abandon my people just to save myself?" Feelings of guilt overwhelmed me. I had to have answers.

I noticed the farmer was loading up his hauling trailer. Other cars were coming and going. What I didn't know, and was to find out later, was that the farmer was being joined by the rest of his family, and they were all moving away from the farm. This was their last day on the place, and it was my fifth day since escaping from the interstate. I decided to come forward and show myself. I had a story ready to tell him about being lost in the woods after some kind of accident.

The farmer was standing by the trailer. I had planned what I was going to say. If he went inside and grabbed the phone, I would have to run. I called out to him, "Hello? Hello there." He walked over to me, and I said, "Look, I got lost from my group a couple of days ago, and I have been out in these woods ever since. I was wondering if you could give me a lift to town, or if you could let me use your phone, or—"

He stopped me from going any further, saying, "You're Dennis Banks, aren't you?"

I looked him squarely in the eyes and said, "Yes, I am."

He burst out, "Man, oh man, you'd better watch yourself! There are hundreds of police looking for you. You're the big story on TV!" He went on, "My wife and I met you some time ago in Lincoln, Nebraska. You and Marlon Brando were making a speech. You asked for donations that night, and I didn't have a single dollar to give you. I'm so glad I can be of some help now."

I was stunned. Of all the thousands of people I could have run into that day, I find this man who turns out to be a friend. The odds of it happening must have been a million to one! I asked my new friend, "Do you know what happened to my family and the people they were with?"

He told me, "Well, according to the reports on TV, there was a big shoot-out with the troopers, and they shot up this motorhome, which they say is owned by Marlon Brando. They arrested your wife, one other woman, and three men, but one guy got away. They think it's Leonard Peltier."

I asked, "Was anybody hurt?"

"No, they're all fine."

It flashed through my mind that my taking off in Brando's motorhome had served as a distraction that might have enabled Leonard to get away safely. Otherwise he might have exchanged fire with the trooper, and somebody could have been killed. This new thought made me feel a lot better.

The farmer went on, "There was another follow-up report about a shoot-out between some farmer and the guy they think is Leonard Peltier, but nobody was hurt. That guy stole a pick-up and got away. It's on the news right now."

I said, "Listen, I need a ride. I have to get out of here and get in touch with people who can pick me up."

He asked, "Where are you going?" I told him I wanted to go to California to get in touch with my friends from AIM. He said, "I'm heading east, but I could make a detour and go south. I could drop you off then, but you will have to ride in the back of the trailer, because they have roadblocks all over the place. If they stop us and see you, we'll all get arrested. Are you hungry?"

I said, "I sure am."

He went inside the house, came back out, and drove off. About thirty minutes later, which seemed like an hour, he came back. I trusted him, but only to a point, so I kept looking for any squad cars that might be heading this way. I was prepared to bolt and run. Finally, he came back with his wife. He was holding a bag of sandwiches. He said, "I told my wife who you are, and we're going to help you."

She poured me some hot coffee in a Styrofoam cup and said, "This is our last day here. We're moving on."

Her husband opened the back of the trailer, showed me a box I could sit on, and said, "Hop in."

They took me all the way to Winnemucca, Nevada, where they put me up in a motel. I had my first chance in a long time to see my reflection in a mirror. I was shocked at what I saw. I was a mess. My head and hands were caked with blood. I took a long, hot shower then had a good look at my injuries. I had deep gashes on my forehead and on both legs above the knees where I had hit the barbed wire. I had not noticed the wire in the darkness and had grabbed it to stop myself from falling. The barbs had punctured my hands, and to this day I still have the scars.

After I got dressed, the wife of the farmer said, "Well, Mr. Banks, we've got to go now. So I guess this is good-bye and good luck."

I thanked them for all they had done for me and asked them one last favor, "Could you go to that pay phone over there and call this number in San Francisco? Ask for John Trudell." I watched until he motioned that he had someone on the line. I walked over and grabbed the phone, saying, "John, this is Dennis."

John said, "Wow, where are you at? Man, the whole country is looking for you. Is Leonard with you?"

I said, "No, he isn't. I don't know where he is." I told him where I was and said, "John, I need you to come get me. I've got just enough money for one night up here."

He said, "Okay, I'll be up there as soon as I can get a car. That should be sometime tomorrow morning."

So I waited and rested up. I was worried that at any moment the police would get a lead on me, or that they would find out I had been traveling with that farmer, or that the motel-keeper would get wise and turn me in. The farmer had told him his "guest" would be staying until noon the next day. I spent a fitful night and got up early the next morning. I had fifteen dollars left to my name. I walked down the road, got some rolls and coffee, and went back to the room.

John showed up at 10:00 A.M. I was overjoyed to see him. He filled me in on all the news. Kamook, Tash, Annie Mae, Kenny, and Russ were alive and uninjured, but unfortunately they all were in jail. Leonard was on the run, but nobody knew where he had gone. I was very concerned about Kamook and about what had happened to our little girl, Tashina, but the first thing was to get me to a safe place. John took me to Reno, Nevada, and we stayed there with some supporters for two days.

I had real long hair then. I knew the police would be looking for somebody with long hair, so I braided my hair in two thick plaits and cut them both off. I later heard that the people I stayed with in Reno kept my braids for years. I did not want to hide or go into that paranoia of having to look behind every tree for cops. I had never been that way and did not want to be that way now. Even when Leonard and I went underground after the Sun Dance in August 1975, we never hid ourselves. We openly walked around and did our shopping; we only disguised ourselves by wearing sunglasses.

John Trudell and another friend, Darrel Standing Elk, took me from Reno to the Bay Area. I stayed with them for a few days then called my friend Lee Brightman and asked if he and his wife, Trudie, would put me up. They agreed, so I stayed the rest of November and all of December with them. I was safe at last—that is, until the next major crisis. So ended my Oregon adventure.

When I look back at all the tight spots I have been in, I realize that the closest call was when that state trooper stopped us on the interstate because of the many shots that were fired at the motorhome. And that trooper intercepted us just by an odd chance, against orders. Had he done what he was supposed to have done and let us pass, we would have run into a whole army of FBI and police waiting to let us have it. We all might have been killed, and the children that were to come later would never have been born. That and the way I was befriended by the farmer and his wife makes me feel that the spirits were protecting me and Kamook.

Maybe the Creator is an AIM-lover.

CHAPTER 22

Exile

The Creator took a bit of thunder and made it into a drum. The drum is the thunder and rain. The American Indian Movement is like a drum that speaks all languages and makes people understand. The drum is sacred.

—Henry Crow Dog

I had settled down at Lee Brightman's place in El Cerrito, a suburb of Oakland, California. I felt as though I were a part of Lee's family with his wife, Trudie, and his two young boys, Crazy Horse and Gall. I knew I was still being hunted nationwide, but I had become over-confident because luck had been with me so far. As the weeks passed without any sign of the Feds closing in, I relaxed.

I was sad, however, because Kamook was in a Wichita, Kansas, jail on a charge of interstate transportation of unregistered firearms, and our little daughter, Tashina, had been placed in a foster home. The charge against Kamook stemmed from the incident on the Kansas turnpike when Bob Roubideau's station wagon blew up. She had been charged and quickly tried. The court was lenient with her because of our daughter and because she was eight months pregnant with our second child. She had been given probation, but that was immediately revoked when she was arrested during the Oregon shoot-out. The law sent her back to Wichita for parole violation.

While staying with the Brightmans, I tried to live as much of a "normal" life as was possible under the circumstances. I would take their car out and do the grocery shopping for them. I would go jogging every morning with Lee or take a stroll in the park. I never really hid myself. Instead I was on the street, always in the open, meeting people I felt I could trust. I never disguised myself while I was on the run, except once. That happened shortly after I escaped from Wounded Knee. I put on an afro wig and dark glasses and a sort of Caribbean shirt, trying to transform myself into a Chicano. I felt so ridiculous that I gave up the disguise after three days.

Every Tuesday night Lee would go to a bar in San Francisco named La Roca to play cards. There were always six to eight regulars who would sit in on a game. Sometimes they would play all night. I would have a hot-water-and-lemon drink or a 7-Up—something nonalcoholic. It was an all-men get-together, and I got friendly with those guys. They asked me what my name was and I said, "Dennis." That's all I told them. The fourth time I went there I lost about ten or fifteen dollars and thought, "Well, I'll sit out a few."

Another one of the guys did the same and we started chatting. He told me his name and asked, "What do you do, Dennis?" I told him that I was working with Lee on American Indian concerns. I never went into details, keeping the talk vague and light.

I asked him, "What do you do?"

He said, "Don't tell anybody. I am with the Drug Enforcement Agency. I'm a narc."

The hair on the back of my neck stood straight up. I thought, "My God! I'm playing cards with a federal agent!" I calmly asked, "Have you ever been in on any great drug busts?"

He answered, "Yeah, several."

I said, "Isn't that a scary business to be in?"

"Naw, not really. There's two other guys I work with here, too—guys we're playing with, Jim and Danny."

Holy cow! Here I was playing poker with three federal agents. One of them turned out to be a cop with the San Francisco Police Department. Later that evening when we were driving home, I said, "Lee, man, do you know what these guys are doing for a living?"

He said, "No, I never asked them. I think they have some sort of government jobs."

I burst out laughing. "Lee, three of them are federal agents."

Lee sat there bug-eyed and said, "Oh Jesus!" He started to laugh too, but he was concerned. "What do we do? Stop going there?"

I said, "No, you've been a regular fixture there for a long time. If we stop coming, they'll ask themselves, 'Why?' Besides, it's always safest to be closest to your enemy, where he never suspects you to be."

We gambled with those guys two or three times more. Later, after I got busted and Lee was out on bail for harboring a fugitive, he went back to La Roca one night. When those agents saw him, they gave him a hard time. "Lee Brightman, you son of a bitch, was that Dennis Banks you brought in here to play poker with us?"

Lee laughed and laughed, "Yes, that was him, the most wanted guy in the country, right under your noses."

"Lee Brightman, you mean, lowdown bastard, you better not tell anybody about this."

Word had somehow leaked out that I was staying with Lee and Trudie. I had started to get phone calls at Lee's home, and I said to myself, "Uh-oh, this is not good!" One day I was there alone when the phone rang. The caller identified himself as an employment agency looking for Lee. I said, "Well, you can call him at his office."

He asked, "Well, who is this?"

I said, "I'm his brother."

"Which brother?"

"What does it matter?"

Then the guy said, "I'd like to know who I'm speaking with." A few minutes later he called back again to ask, "What time did you say Lee will be back tonight?"

"He gets off work at 3:30 P.M." I hung up with a funny feeling about this strange phone conversation. That night I told Lee about it.

Lee said, "I have a job. I don't know anything about an employment agency. We'll just have to wait and see what that's all about."

Two days later, early in the morning, Lee shook me awake. "Dennis, Dennis, the FBI is outside. They want us to come out with our hands up." I looked out the window and could see a number of agents surrounding the place.

Lee and Trudie were rushing around, very excited. They called to me, "Hurry up, get dressed!" Then Lee said, "Trudie, you go out first. Take the kids and go out now!" She went out and the Feds pulled her and the boys over to stand on one side.

Lee was about to go out. I knew that I would be taken to jail so I said, "Lee, I want to take a book along."

He said, "*What?* Come on, man, let's go. The police are out there, and the FBI. Just look at them. Let's not give them any excuse to get rough. They've all got guns drawn and they are waiting."

I said, "I'd like to have some reading matter with me," and I took one of Lee's books. It was by Gore Vidal, I think. I don't recall the title. I guess Lee thought I'd gone crazy, bothering about reading matter in that situation.

I stepped outside with the book in my hand, and the agents began shouting at me, "Put your hands up! Drop the book, drop it now!" So I did. Then one of them yelled, "Turn around, put your hands behind your back!" I did as I was told. Then the same guy yelled, "Get down on your knees, down on your knees!"

I was not going to resist them, but at the same time something within me would not let me go down on my knees. I felt it was something I just couldn't do. That guy kept screaming at me, "Get down on your knees. Lie face-down on the ground!" I just stood there not moving an inch.

Finally an older agent walked up to me. I still had my hands in the air. He said, "Put your hands down!" I did. He said, "Mr. Banks, put your hands behind your back." I did and he handcuffed me. He said, "Come on, let's go."

I said, "Can I get my book?"

He reached down and grabbed it. He repeated calmly, "Come on, let's go." He put me in a squad car. I watched these FBI agents, all young kids except the one who had handcuffed me. They looked scared and green.

They took us to jail in El Cerrito to book us. They didn't take Trudie, just Lee and me. They held Lee on suspicion of harboring a fugitive and charged me with unlawful flight to avoid prosecution. We stayed in jail for one night. Lee was released on his own recognizance but was told he would be charged for harboring me. I was transferred the next day to the county jail in San Francisco. While I was there,

Marlon Brando, Vine Deloria, and Harry Belafonte came to visit me. That was a morale-builder.

Finally I was arraigned on a charge of "unlawful flight to avoid prosecution." Unfortunately, that was not all. I was also being held for extradition to South Dakota. This was serious. I had no illusion of what would happen to me once Janklow had me in his power.

I was arraigned on the fugitive charge and remained in jail for about three weeks. My bail was set at one hundred thousand dollars. A friend of mine, Fred Lane, who was executive director of the Indian Center in San Francisco, came to visit me. He put up the Indian Center as collateral for my bail. Oddly enough, the judge accepted the center as bail security and announced, "Defendant is released on bail." I was released the same day and had a good reunion with all of my friends, sharing that evening with the whole Indian community.

Temporarily at least, I was at liberty. It seemed as though I was the only one free at the time. Annie Mae was in a South Dakota jail on a different charge. Leonard Peltier had made good his escape to Canada but was on the run. Russ Redner and Kenny Loud Hawk were being held on one hundred thousand dollars bail each. And sadly, Kamook was still behind bars in Wichita, Kansas. Her bail was only twenty thousand dollars, but that was still a lot of money.

A man in San Francisco contacted me, offering to help raise Kamook's bail. It was Jim Jones, an evangelist, called by some a cult leader. His church, the People's Temple, had a big following. I had met Jim Jones earlier when he raised some money for the Wounded Knee defense effort. He was himself part Choctaw and very sympathetic to the Indian cause. This was the same Jim Jones who later committed suicide with some nine hundred followers in Guyana, however, when I met him he showed no signs of the paranoia that would later destroy him. I gladly accepted his offer.

Kamook was in difficult times. The state officials had taken Tashina away and put her into a foster home. On December 30, 1975, Kamook went into labor. Prison officials refused to release her from custody for her delivery, so she gave birth by cesarean section in a prison hospital. We called our new daughter Tiopa Maza Win—"Iron Door Woman"— because she was born in jail "behind an iron door." The prison doctors tried to persuade Kamook to let them sterilize her, pointing out that, in her situation, she should not have any more children. She of course told them to go to hell. Then they presented her with a bill for over $2,700.70 for the surgery. Prison conditions were very harsh. I was worried sick about her since I couldn't be there with her.

Kamook sent me a letter telling me about her love for me and for our movement. She spoke of her determination to maintain the struggle for as long as she lived. She told me about her feelings for Tiopa Maza Win, and how prison officials would not allow her to hold her own tiny infant or to breastfeed her. It was a heartwrenching letter. Kamook closed it with, "But we will survive even under these rotten conditions." I have quoted her letter many times. And we did survive.

Simon Ortiz, the famous Indian poet from Acoma Pueblo in New Mexico, wrote a poem, "The Father of Iron Door Woman." It reads, in part:

> At the Unitarian Church,
> he brings his child to us.
> She is swathed in blankets,
> and he holds her tiny face
> to us, and he says,
> "This is Iron Door Woman.
> From here on, I want to be known
> as the Father of Iron Door Woman."
>
> Iron Door Woman was born
> behind the iron doors of jail,
> and the father tells us,
> "All these years, we have been
> knocking on iron doors—all of us,
> not just Indian people."
> The tiny girl moves in his arms,
> and her eyes shine.
> It is possible then to see
> the life which includes us all.

It was arranged for Kamook's sister, Bernice, to take Tiopa and our firstborn, Tashina, with her while Kamook waited out her jail time.

Somehow, we all became stronger through the pain inflicted upon us. If one does not become mean because of it, becoming an enemy to oneself, then pain can give strength to a person and add a feeling of victory to mere survival.

When I met with Jim Jones, he was very upbeat about Kamook. He told me, "We've got to do something to get your wife out of jail." He arranged for a big gathering at his temple, which was regularly attended by a huge crowd.

First Lee Brightman spoke; I followed with a ten-minute speech. I said how happy I would be if we could raise the money for Kamook's bail. Then Jim described Kamook's suffering. He was very charismatic, skillfully playing on the emotions of his congregation. He was so persuasive that I felt like going into my own pocket to give to our cause. He even orchestrated part of his sermon with soft music, a choir in the background accompanied by the old cathedral organ. People kept giving and giving. Jones asked if there was anyone in the audience who could come up with twenty thousand dollars. When nobody stood up, he asked for ten thousand dollars. A woman stood up and said, "I can give five thousand dollars toward this bail."

After that we were able to raise the whole twenty thousand in checks and cash within half an hour. I was so happy that I burst into tears. I told the crowd, "If only my wife could witness all that is happening here!"

Early the next morning Jim and I went to the bank and changed the checks, money orders, assorted bills, and loose change into large bills, which we took to the Justice Department office. They notified the U.S. Attorney's office in Wichita that the bail money had been secured and that Kamook could be released at once. I stayed around until everything had been confirmed and I had proof that Kamook had been told of the good news.

There was still quite a bit of money left in excess of the bail, so Jim said, "I'll take care of Kamook's flight tickets." I had planned to meet Kamook at the airport but Jim said, "No, no, Dennis, wait at the church for her." Always the PR man, Jim didn't want to deprive all the people who had contributed bail money of the thrill of seeing Kamook and me reunited.

I told him, "This is *my* wife. These are *my* children. I haven't even met my youngest yet. I should be the first person they see as they step off that plane!"

But Jim prevailed. A few of his people brought Kamook right from the airport to the temple. I met Kamook at the door where we hugged each other before the big event took us over. On that Sunday the temple was packed with more than three thousand people. Music blared out a welcome for us. A lot of American Indians had come, and they had the drum going strong. They brought Kamook and the little ones up to the stage. People were screaming and yelling. Kamook began to cry. She wanted to thank the people for their help but could not get the words out. She could only sob. I went up on the stage and proudly stood by her. There was another big roar and Indian war whoops.

When all the noise began to die down, Jim Jones asked for quiet. He said, "One week ago we made a pledge that we were going to have Kamook in this temple, that we were going to raise the money to get her out. We did that. And she is here tonight with her newborn baby and reunited with her husband." The people began yelling again as though they were beside themselves with joy. That was the beginning of our relationship with Jim Jones.

When I first met Jones he was very upbeat and positive. He had a lot of strength and shook hands firmly. I liked the way he presented himself. As time went by, his character seemed to change. He was still upbeat in general, but I sensed a kind of paranoia creeping in.

Suddenly Jim no longer wanted to talk with people over the phone. He began to be haunted by the thought that people were spying on him. He preferred to meet privately with people. He started to build security fences around himself, using a protective shield of followers acting as his bodyguards. Each time I visited him he seemed worse. His paranoia was becoming obvious. He perspired all of the time, frequently taking off his glasses to wipe the sweat from his face. He got himself a pair of very dark sunglasses so people couldn't see his eyes. He was popping pills all of the time. He spoke in undertones so softly that I could hardly understand him. He was afraid to be overheard.

He would whisper to me, "Dennis, did anybody come here with you? Did anybody follow you? Did you check your rearview mirror?"

I would tell him, "Jim, nobody followed us."

He would whisper back, "You can't trust anybody. The FBI, the CIA, they're all over the place. They've got my phones tapped. They're infiltrating the temple!" He would go on and on like that. He told me he was going to Guyana, that some of his people were already there.

He said, "I'll lead them into the jungle where we will be safe. In Guyana I'll rebuild my temple and create a community. I'd like you to come with me. You can build your sweat lodge down there and do whatever you want, but I need your help. I need your spiritual support. All of these people are leaning on me, depending on me as their spiritual guide. I can't carry this burden by myself. I need you as a friend. Remember, I'm Choctaw, so you must do this for me. I'll build you a home down there, and you and your family will never have to worry about money for the rest of your lives."

It was hard for me to say no to him because I owed him a debt of gratitude. But I definitely did not want to stay with him in Guyana. I tried to make him understand that my work had to be done in America—not in some foreign country—and that my place was with my people, not with his. He did not want to hear it. He went to Guyana and took half of his hundreds of followers with him.

Jim got in touch with me a few times after that, always urging me to join him. "I have three flight tickets for you, Dennis."

I told him I might visit him sometime, that I would think about it. And that's where we left it. Some time later, I got a call about nine o'clock one night from a friend in San Francisco, saying, "Dennis, Dennis, did you hear the news?"

I said, "No, what news?"

He said, "Something happened in Guyana. Jim might be dead. We don't know anything for sure yet, but they say there are hundreds of dead people down there at his camp." He went on to say that there had been some shots fired. According to reports coming in, a congressman from California had been killed. I turned on the TV and, sure enough, there was the news coverage of a mass suicide, a shoot-out at the airport, and reports that everyone at the camp was dead, including Jim himself. I had thought Jim had some three hundred people down there, but it turned out that more than nine hundred people were dead, mostly by poisoning.

I think Jim Jones had been on a road of self-destruction for some time. He had been suffering from delusions that everyone was after him. During the three months he had been in Guyana, he had become like a snarling wolf held at bay. I heard stories of physical abuse at the camp, of children having been beaten. There were rumors that he had reserved a number of women for himself, even married ones. I was told his behavior had become bizarre in the extreme.

Kamook and I often talked about what might have happened had we gone to Guyana. If we had been there and Jim had ordered us to drink a glass of cyanide, I am sure we would have refused. Would he then have ordered some of his men to shoot us, as had supposedly happened to a few who did not want to join him in death? Somehow, I don't think so. I believe that even in his worst delirium he would have recognized me as a friend.

After my reunion with Kamook, I still had to wage a desperate battle to find sanctuary in California. I was a fugitive from justice, and it was essential to prevent my extradition to South Dakota. As state attorney general and later as governor, Bill Janklow used his considerable influence and the resources of the whole state of South Dakota to get me back under his power. I fought back with my own campaign to avoid extradition. This was not only my battle for survival, but also a very personal, intense duel of Dennis Banks versus Bill Janklow.

I started the ball rolling by holding a press conference on February 28, 1976 in San Francisco. I told the press that I could never get a fair trial in South Dakota and that Janklow once had publicly proposed putting a bullet through my head. I also spoke of plans to gather a million signatures on a petition to Governor Brown to grant me asylum and deny my extradition. We canvassed the state from top to bottom. Marlon Brando helped by calling on many of his celebrity friends to lend their moral support.

The battle went on for three long years. Finally, I had a face-to-face interview with Governor Edmund Brown, Jr., in the state capitol—just the two of us. He told me, "Well, Mr. Banks, when we leave here I am going to sign a letter to Governor Janklow denying your extradition to South Dakota. I would appreciate it if you would put in your newsletters that people stop writing me letters in your behalf. I am positively inundated by letters and telegrams in your support."

I replied, "Governor Brown, thank you, sir. I'll gladly stop this flood of mail."

In a one-page statement, Governor Brown explained the reason for his decision. He stated that he was convinced bodily harm, or even death, might come to me if I were sent back to South Dakota. He also said polls indicated that racial prejudice was rampant in South Dakota, a fact that would prevent me from getting a fair trial there. He said that not one single fact alone had led to his decision, but that the total picture made him fear for my life if he let me be extradited.

Janklow, of course, was outraged. He started a lawsuit in California to have Brown's decision reversed. The Third Court of Appeals ruled in Janklow's favor, determining that I had to be sent back to South Dakota. Brown promptly challenged this ruling before the California Supreme Court, which concluded that only the governor had the right to decide extradition matters, *not* the courts. Two days later, Brown officially notified South Dakota that he was denying extradition.

Janklow did not give up. He somehow managed to send ninety-three convicted criminals to California instead of to prison because, as he put it, "California seems to welcome outlaws." In the meantime, he waited until Brown was replaced by another governor. I would be safe only as long as Edmund Brown, Jr., was governor of California.

After Kamook and the children joined me, I felt that we no longer should burden Lee and Trudie, that we should get our own place. We moved to Davis, California, northeast of San Francisco, where I enrolled in the D-Q University. The "D" stands for Dekanawida, the prophet and statesman who formed the Five Nations Iroquois Federation. The "Q" means the Aztec god Quetzalcoatl, the Plumed Serpent, healer and bringer of corn—the food that enabled humans to survive. The university, which occupies some six hundred forty acres of what had once been an army communications center, chose this double name to symbolize the unity of North American and Mesoamerican Indians, an area of study that D-Q University specializes in.

I knew that I might have to live in California for a long time. I spent a total of eight years in exile there. Although my stay was enforced, the time in California was very fruitful for me. I enrolled at D-Q for a two-year course of study. Besides the basics, I took some electives: social studies, world history, Native history, ecology, and other subjects that interested me.

I felt the need to establish a sweat lodge at D-Q. Darrel Standing Elk and I put one up, and from then on we had sweats regularly. I was a Sun Dancer but could not leave California to dance in South Dakota. I thought, "If I cannot go to the Sun Dance, maybe the Sun Dance will come to me." I asked the university board whether we could hold a Sun Dance at D-Q. They designated a place in the northeast corner of the campus for it, but at that time there was no one in California who could conduct a Sun Dance. Then Leonard Crow Dog came out to visit me. I offered him tobacco and we smoked the pipe.

I asked him, "Crow Dog, is it all right to hold a Sun Dance here, so far away from Lakota country?"

He said, "Absolutely! Even if you are the only dancer and you have only one singer, you must do it." He pointed to one particular spot and said, "Do it right here." Darrel, my brother, Mark, and I prepared the Sun Dance ground on that very spot. We began watering that bit of ground thoroughly, and in about three weeks the grass was coming up. We knew we would have a good area for our Sun Dance.

Two medicine men from South Dakota, Charlie Kills Enemy and Archie Fire Lame Deer, the son of John Fire Lame Deer, came to D-Q to help Crow Dog run the dance. At first it seemed as though we would have to make do with only six dancers, but soon we had over thirty men who would fulfill their pledge and dance at D-Q. We had women dancers as well—Carol Standing Elk and Pearl Brandon among them. People from the Pitt River reservation near Vancouver, Canada, and Klamath Indians from Oregon arrived to take part in the first Sun Dance ever held in California. In the end, about five or six hundred people gathered around the Sun Dance circle. It was a beautiful dance that is still remembered.

The university became a place of spirituality as well as learning. Sweats were conducted, Indian-style marriages took place, naming ceremonies were held. Young people began to connect with their Indian religion.

I had to make a living, so I lectured at other universities and made speaking engagements. I also started teaching a course at D-Q called "Tribal Federal Law," as I was a registered tribal attorney on the Rosebud reservation and had become familiar with the subject. It wasn't too long before I became an assistant vice president of the university. In the spring of 1979, I was offered a chance to teach a course called "The Media and the American Indian" at Stanford University.

That same year D-Q was looking for a chancellor. They had never had a chancellor before. I was the only candidate, and they hired me for $12,000 a year. I was responsible for developing a long-range curriculum, overseeing spiritual ceremonies, being in charge of political gatherings, making the public aware of D-Q, and raising money. I was the last chancellor at D-Q, and maybe from a technical point of view I still am their chancellor, since I was never fired or terminated. For six years I was an academician and found that I enjoyed it.

Life usually doesn't give us one thing at a time, but a whole banquet of things at once. Kamook and I were blessed with another little girl five years after Tiopa was born. This child was the first one I actually saw come into this world. When it was Kamook's time to give birth, the doctor asked me if I wanted to go into the delivery room. At first I thought, "No, I'll just be in the way."

But the doctor said, "Come on, it's alright." He showed me how to scrub down and put on a cap and mask, apron, paper pants, and little coverings for my shoes, even rubber gloves. It was going to be a cesarean birth, so Kamook was given an injection to deaden the nerves in the lower half of her body.

There were about five doctors around her. They asked, "Well, Mr. Banks, are you ready?"

I said, "Okay."

The head surgeon made an incision. It must have been about eight inches long, from Kamook's belly button on down. There was a little blood, which was suctioned away. Another incision was made through a clear film surrounding the baby. I was utterly fascinated by what I was observing. The doctor said, "There she is, Mr. Banks, just inside there. We are going to bring her out." He reached in and pulled out the baby. It was moving and crying, making little noises and stretching already. There was a big, long navel cord attached to her and to Kamook, and I watched the doctor sever it. Then the baby was placed on a scale. She weighed ten pounds! That's why we nicknamed her Chubbs.

I leaned over to speak with Kamook. She was pretty groggy as she asked, "Are they through yet?" I said yes. Then she wanted to know whether it was a boy or a girl. I told Kamook that we had a lovely ten-pound girl. Kamook kind of sighed. I gave her a kiss and she went to sleep. The wonderful experience of watching our baby come into the world was so precious to me, it gave me a new awareness of what birth-giving involves. It was an unforgettable moment for me.

Kamook was amazed when she was able to hold her baby for the first time and said, "Oh, she's so chubby! Wow, she's *really* a chubbs!" So that nickname stuck. Chubbs's real name is Tokala, meaning Kit Fox, but nobody calls her that. She has been very close to me over the years, and I think it began when I saw her for the first time coming straight into the world from her mother.

In 1982, Edmund Brown, Jr., decided not to run for governor of California again. Republican George Deukmejian, a hard-nosed law-and-order fanatic and former attorney general of California, was elected governor. He made it known that, if he received a request for my extradition to South Dakota, he would honor it. I prepared for the worst. I knew there was a sixty-day grace period for me between the election and the swearing-in ceremony when Deukmejian would take office. I would have to use that time to figure out whether Kamook and I would leave the country or find another state to seek sanctuary.

In the end we settled upon New York. The governor, Mario Cuomo, was a progressive democrat. He had shown himself to be sympathetic to Indians and had invited representatives of the Six Nations to be present at his inauguration. Also, as New York Secretary of State, Cuomo had supported the Mohawks during their controversial Moss Lake takeover. So New York was our best bet. I made some preliminary calls to my old friend, Chief Oren Lyons, faith-keeper of the Onondaga Nation in upstate New York. He promised me sanctuary on his reservation.

I phoned my lawyer, Bill Kunstler, who told me, "Dennis, if you choose to come to New York, you are going to get a good reception. I can guarantee that. You will not only have my legal support, but also that of the whole Center for Constitutional Rights of which I am the head." So I decided to go first to New York City, submit to arrest, fight extradition, and see what Governor Cuomo would do. Kamook was to come later so as not to arouse suspicion that I was planning to flee California.

Kunstler was able to find out from one of the people in Deukmejian's office that an extradition warrant for Dennis Banks had arrived from South Dakota and that Deukmejian planned to execute the warrant as soon as he was sworn in on January 2, 1984. I decided to get out of California on December 26th.

Kamook, the children, and I lived at that time in a little rented house in a subdivision of Dixon, California, just a few miles from Davis. Already we had noticed a police car stationed around the entry streets to our area, and we knew why he was there. In addition to the watch on our home, we assumed that our phone was tapped. I told Kamook, "It's time. We've got to get out of here!"

I went into the garage and packed two suitcases full of things that would last me at least a month. We kept these bags ready so I could leave at a moment's notice. I had to make sure that Kamook and the children were out of the house in case the law enforcement people stormed our place with guns blazing, so I arranged for my family to be in Sacramento at the time of Deukmejian's inauguration.

During the night of December 25, we secretly passed the suitcases to a friend who would help me to get away. My plan was to go about my daily chores—driving to hardware store, the laundromat, and the grocery store—as if the last thing on my mind was to go on the lam. At the grocery store, I parked and went inside. The police car that had followed me from a distance stopped, turned around, and drove back to his usual observation post, assuming that everything was on the up-and-up. I called Kamook from the store, saying that I would be home about three o'clock. I was pretty sure that our conversation would be overheard. Then I slipped out a side door and got into a car with some friends who were waiting there for me.

We drove nonchalantly over the state border into Nevada where other friends were waiting to transport me further. We stayed in Reno for about six hours, doing a little gambling. I lost about twenty dollars that night. Later, I was picked up at the MGM Grand Hotel and taken to Salt Lake City, where I transferred to yet another car. That vehicle took me to Minneapolis. My sister Mary Jane and a friend, Fred Short, had agreed to drive me the last leg of the journey from Minneapolis to New York City. We drove toward Chicago, traveling on Interstate 80 bound for Manhattan. At Chicago, Interstate 80 is joined by Interstate 90, which later heads up through Pennsylvania into upstate New York.

Fred drove most of the way—too long, as a matter of fact. He was so tired that Mary Jane had to take the wheel away from him, and he fell asleep in the front passenger seat almost immediately. I was resting in the back when, all of a sudden, Fred came out of his sleep and grabbed for the wheel. The car lurched out of control for a few seconds, but we had not been going that fast and the roadway was straight with no turns. Mary Jane had to slap Fred's face to wake him up. He just looked blankly at her, let go of the wheel, and went back to sleep.

Later on, when Fred took his turn again driving, I reminded him, "Take I-80 all the way into New York City."

He said, "Okay, Dennis." Mary Jane and I dozed off.

I woke up at about eight o'clock in the morning and the first thing I saw was a sign: "NEW YORK—200 MILES." I said, "Fred, where are we at, man?"

He said, "Just coming into Syracuse."

"*Syracuse!* Fred, we're way off course! We're not supposed to be up here. Right now, we're supposed to be getting into New York City!"

He just looked at me and said, "Jesus, I got on the wrong highway!"

We stopped for coffee and sat there in silence. I did not want to get into a conversation with Fred while I was upset and neither did Mary Jane. It occurred to me then that we were close to the town of Nedrow on the Onondaga reservation, the home of my friend, Chief Oren Lyons, who I was supposed to meet in New York City. He was probably waiting there for me already. I told Fred and M. J., "Let's go to Onondaga and see Alice Papineau. She is a clan mother there and an old friend of mine."

So we got back on the freeway. Before long, I was knocking on at Alice's door. She opened it and exclaimed, "Dennis Banks! What are you doing here? Don't just stand there. It's cold. Come on in!"

She immediately started heating something up for us to eat. We drank coffee, laughing and talking about old times. Fred and Mary Jane went into the next room to sleep. Alice asked me, "Where are you headed?"

I said, "I'm on my way to New York City to turn myself in to the authorities there."

Alice said, "Why don't you stay overnight? You're all tired out and its snowing." So it was. She gave me Oren's number in New York.

When I called Oren, he said, "Dennis, what on earth are you doing in Nedrow? Listen, I'll be coming back up there tonight. Stay there."

I watched the snowflakes swirling in the dark sky and decided to get a good night's sleep. As fate would have it, I never made it to New York City.

CHAPTER 23

Onondaga

Our old men have frequently taken a single arrow and said, "Children, see how easily it is broken." Then they have tied together several arrows with a single cord, and our strongest man cannot break them. This is what the Six Nations means. Divided, you may be destroyed by a single man. United, you are a match for the whole world.

—Canassatego, 1775

It was snowing really hard the next morning in the Onondaga hills. Alice said, "Dennis, maybe you shouldn't go to New York. It might turn out badly for you there. Nothing is going to be done over a weekend anyway."

Saturday passed and Sunday did, too. Alice was concerned for me, fretting about the situation I was in. She said, "Maybe you should fight from here against your extradition."

On Monday morning I was gathering up my stuff, ready to go to New York City, but Alice had already invited the Tadodaho, Head Chief of All the Six Nations, to come to her house to talk with me. The Tadodaho is a respected leader of the Onondaga and likewise of the Great Council Fire of the whole Iroquois Federation, which is situated on the Onondaga reservation.

At that time, Leon Shenandoah was the Tadodaho. He was a great man who died shortly before I began writing my story. His death was mourned not only by his own tribe, but by Indian people all across the country. Alice asked him, "Why couldn't Dennis be given sanctuary in the Long House?"

The Tadodaho looked at Alice for what seemed to me a long time. Then the two of them spoke to each other in the Onondaga language. Leon lit his pipe, nodded, and said, "Um-um, um-um." Finally he turned to me, speaking in English, "Well, Dennis, even though I am the Head Chief of All the Six Nations, I just can't give you sanctuary all by myself. There is a certain process that we have to follow. You have to ask sanctuary from the whole membership of the Long House. It has to come from the people, and it first has to go to the clan mothers. From them, it goes to the chiefs of the Onondaga Nation, then they give it to the Grand Council of the Six Nations Federation. But I will gladly begin that process."

I thanked him. Later I called Bill Kunstler in New York City. "Bill, what do you think of my staying at Onondaga and fighting extradition from here?"

He immediately concurred, "Brilliant, Dennis! The best idea yet!"

I asked Alice, "May Kamook and I stay here a while?"

Alice smiled, "Yes, of course."

Meanwhile, Kamook was still at our former house in Dixon. I had someone call her, saying, "The package has arrived. Thanks for the Christmas present." That was our code, meaning that I was safe and in good hands. Later on, I managed to get word to her about where I was staying.

On January 2, 1984 at nine o'clock in the morning, Deukmejian was sworn in as California's new governor. He lost no time. At ten o'clock the same morning, our house in Dixon was surrounded by police. They entered and searched the entire place looking for me. A few moments later, Kamook and the kids came back from shopping. The police went after her with a vengeance. "Where is your husband?"

She told them, "I don't know where he's at. Maybe he'll call." They couldn't get anything more out of her.

At Onondaga I went from house to house soliciting support from the chiefs. They took me to the Long House to debate the matter. The Long House is the heart and soul of the Iroquois, and this particular one is also where the Grand Council of All Six Nations is held. The building itself is about one hundred feet long and sixty feet wide, a single-story structure with high ceilings of beautiful cedar logs. It is divided into two parts: the mud house and the long house—the so-called two houses of government. The entrance is at the exact center of the building. All the chiefs have a designated spot to sit on the left side, while the clan mothers occupy the right side near the entrance. The young children are given their place there, too. The Tadodaho sits in back of the stove where the sacred fire is kept burning. Everything is done in a ceremonial manner.

In the evening when the sun goes down and no more business can be conducted, the benches are dragged to the center of the Long House. There are usually two or three of them, and the singers straddle them, pounding on them with their turtle-shell rattles while they sing. Sometimes the singers sit opposite one another across the aisle of benches, shaking their rattles. There are always ceremonies going on in the Long House—winter ceremonies, spring rituals, summer rites, green corn ceremonies, ceremonies for the young ones.

The chiefs took me into the Long House and had me sit in the center. They debated my case back and forth, speaking in their own language. From time to time someone would explain to me in English what was going on. Finally I was told, "We want to help. We are going to put it to the clan mothers. We don't know how long it will take, but we will call them together. Tobacco will be burned each day as medicine. That is how we do these things." My case went to the Clan Mothers, who discussed it thoroughly, going over the details again and again.

The chiefs had warned me to stay away from the media. They wanted no reporters coming to Onondaga. I strictly obeyed them in this matter, but the press somehow found out and hung around the border of the reservation. One photographer snapped a photo of me from far away with an extra-long telephoto lens. Soon after, there were headlines on the front pages of various newspapers: "DENNIS BANKS AT ONONDAGA!" The cat was out of the bag. As a result, the chiefs got a lot of pressure from the outside. The FBI, sheriffs, and local police made threatening noises. Fortunately the FBI could do nothing, as the reservation was under state jurisdiction and Cuomo had declared that he would respect the sovereignty of the Onondaga Nation. Of course, an extradition warrant from South Dakota arrived at Albany, New York, but the State of New York never acted on it. All this meant I was safe as long as I stayed on the reservation. On January 10, Kamook and the children came to join me. My family was together again.

In late March the clan mothers made the decision to grant me sanctuary. Then they brought the matter before the chiefs who, after a full day's session, joined in providing a safe haven for me and my family. The Chiefs of All the Six Nations were invited to come to Nedrow to support the Onondaga position. So the heads of the Grand Council of the Iroquois League came together. They met for two days in the Long House to talk about my case. I was allowed to sit in as an observer, though I could not understand what was said because most of the speeches were made in the Iroquois language. Finally, the chiefs made their pronouncement, one by one, "Yes, sanctuary is granted."

The Tadodaho asked me to stand up. He said, "The chiefs have given their full support for you and your family to stay on Six Nation land. You now are safe under the wings of the Onondaga Nation." I wanted to jump up and shout for joy, but in respect for the solemnity of the Long House atmosphere, I restrained myself, remaining quiet and reserved. I looked over to Kamook and we both had tears in our eyes.

Finally the Tadodaho said, "We are going to close the business with a dance tonight." They brought out the turtle-shell rattles and began to dance and sing. All at once the Long House was filled with the sounds of music and the laughter of children. They asked Kamook and me to stand with our own children as the clan mothers came, clan by clan, to greet us and shake our hands. All the chiefs did the same. Chief Oren Lyons had the last word as he announced, "Dennis Banks and his family now sit under the Long Leaves of the Great Tree of Peace planted at Onondaga long before the white people came to our shores." Kamook and I were to live in Nedrow for the next eighteen months.

At first we stayed with Alice Papineau, but her house was already crowded with members of her own family. I did not want to impose upon her hospitality any longer than necessary. We were happy and thankful when the tribe made available to us a large log cabin on a hill. Kamook and I were so happy to be safe again that we gladly made the repairs the old cabin needed.

One day when we were redoing a wall, we discovered old newspapers dating back to 1914 that had been used as wallpaper. When we built a new wall, I placed a whole contemporary newspaper wrapped in plastic inside the wall, adding a note, "To the occupants who open this up in the future, Dennis Banks and his wife, Kamook, lived in this house in 1984 and put up these new walls." The note went on to explain why we were in Onondaga at the time. Many years from now, unless the cabin burns down or collapses, perhaps someone will again repair the wall and come across my little historic item.

The reservation was small, consisting of about 7,300 acres. Only some 3,500 people lived on it at that time. It was up to me to keep busy and to find things to do. To keep in shape I would run every morning, weather permitting. During January, when I started, it was still very cold with the roads iced over. Blizzards and snow storms blew through frequently. In such cases, I would wait until afternoon to run when it was a few degrees warmer, or I would wait until the storm blew over.

By February the weather was slightly warmer. A couple of seven- or eight-year-old boys started running with me then. They had watched me for some time and decided that running was fun. Soon there were seven kids jogging along with me, so we started a running club. I told them they had to run all the way to the dam, about a mile away, and run back to where we had started from. Some of the younger kids could not do that, so we started running from one telephone pole to the next, then walking to the one after, running to one, walking to the next. That way the youngsters were all able to keep up with the group. That was the way I trained them.

By March, I had fifteen kids running down the road. We generally met at Alice Papineau's. We did our warm-ups and stretching exercises there. More and more parents brought their children to join us. They kept coming, and we ended up with about forty kids participating. From among them, we formed a pretty good cross-country team. I had jackets made for twenty-five of them with a logo that said: CROSS-COUNTRY EAGLES—ONONDAGA NATION. From this group, I began to train a special team made up of eighth, ninth, and tenth graders, also called the Eagles.

We organized a run for them from New York City to Los Angeles to participate in the Jim Thorpe Games that were named after one of the greatest athletes of our century. Jim Thorpe was an American Indian of Sac and Fox descent. In the 1912 Olympic Games in Stockholm, Sweeden, Thorpe won the decathlon and pentathlon, but was deprived of his gold medals because he had already turned to professional baseball in 1911. In 1982, Jim Thorpe's family was finally given the gold medals from the 1912 Olympic Games, something that thousands of American Indians had urged the Olympic committee to do for years. The Eagles were a great success in the Jim Thorpe Games and were written about in the newspapers.

As Kamook and I began to settle in with our new community, I found I wanted to learn as much of the Onondaga way of life as I could, even a little of their language. I was interested in all the aspects of their traditional way of life. One day I discovered three good-sized mud turtles belly-up. An Onondaga friend showed me how to cut them open, scoop all the meat out for soup, and make the shells into large turtle rattles. I learned how to cook Onondaga-style and began to eat strange foods, which at first seemed repugnant to me.

For example, 1984 was the year of the locusts. After seventeen years of living as grubs and larvae, the locusts emerge from deep in the earth. Alice Papineau told me, "We've got to get up early in the morning to gather them, because later, after they have eaten their fill of leaves, they are no good for *our* eating. Then they are too mushy and spoiled. But if we get them early, they are empty and good to eat. We catch them and fry them up. If you eat locust, it is said that you will have seventeen years of good health and happiness. Want to try some?"

I was game for it and so was little Chubbs, who was then about four years old. She wanted to see what they tasted like, but Kamook and our older girls refused. So Chubbs and I got paper bags and brushed the locusts right off the trees, each of us catching a hundred or more. All of these creatures were jumping around in our bags when we brought them in to Alice, who was heating some butter in a big frying pan. She said, "Just open the bags and shake them out into the skillet!"

We did and she slammed the lid on tight. There was a crackling noise like corn being popped. After stirring it all up, Alice brought it to the table and filled our plates with stir-fried locusts. Chubbs and I were crunching away while the others watched us. The taste was quite good. Tashina said, "Ohhh, Daddy, no, no. Eating insects is gross!"

Chubbs just smiled and said, "Yummy!" Since then, almost another seventeen years have passed, and we *have* lived, as they say, a healthy life.

Chubbs and I have shared a wonderful father-daughter relationship. She liked to pal around in those years with her daddy. I remember that at Onondaga it would get so cold at night, sometimes below zero. Chubbs would need to use the outhouse and would ask me to walk her out there. So we would venture out under the stars and sit on the old two-seater overlooking the lights of Syracuse. It would be cold as blazes, and she would chat away with me about little things as we sat out there. She liked to go to the Long House, where she learned to dance at an early age. She is still my queen. Of course, I love Tash and Tiopa as much as Chubbs.

In 1985, a fourth baby joined our family. This time Kamook gave birth to a little boy. He was born in Syracuse, New York, five years after Chubbs was born. He was later given a special name by Grandma Jumping Bull at a big naming ceremony: Chanupa Washte, meaning Good Sacred Pipe. I am very proud of all of our children and of Kamook, who was a deeply devoted mother and partner.

We did not know then how long we were to stay at Onondaga, so we put Tashina in school there. She was so excited, telling Tiopa, "Guess what! I am going to *school!*"

We got her a little lunchbox and a shoulder bag to keep her schoolwork in. We even made her a nameplate that read, "HELLO. MY NAME IS TASHINA." On the morning I was to take Tash to her first day of school, we held a little ceremony and burned some sage for her. I explained to her, "This is your first day. I am going to leave you for a few hours and won't see you until I pick you up this afternoon."

She asked, "But, Daddy, how long is *that* going to be?"

I told her, "Five or six hours."

I drove the van to school and parked it in front of the playground. As we got out, I noticed tears welling up in Tash's eyes. I took her hand and we went inside to meet her new teacher. I said, "So long, Tash, I'll see you after a while."

"No, Daddy, I don't want you to leave me."

I said, "Alright, Tash, we'll go to school another time." I told the teacher, "When Tash feels better, I'll bring her back."

We went to a little café where I ordered some coffee and an orange juice for Tash. After a time she looked up at me and said, "Well, I'm ready. You can take me to school now." That night she came home all smiles and told us the names of the kids she had met. Even at bedtime she was still telling Tiopa about all of the nice new friends she had met at school.

Later, when hunting season began at Onondaga, I told Kamook that I was going to go hunting the following Saturday. Tash, who was about nine at the time, heard me and asked, "Daddy, can I go with you?"

I said, "Sure. We'll be out hunting deer."

At school she told all of her friends that she was going hunting with her dad. She was so excited, just counting the days. On Friday night I told Tash, "Tomorrow we'll get up early before the sun comes up to go hunting."

Early the next morning, Kamook fixed us a big breakfast with hot oatmeal. She packed lunch for us with a thermos bottle of hot coffee, and off we went. A friend of mine had lent me his .30-06. I drove up to the top of a hill where I knew deer were abundant, parked the car, and we started up the hill with Tash carrying the lunch bucket. I told her, "We've got to be very quiet. We can't talk because that would spook the deer. We only whisper."

Suddenly, I saw two deer through the woods. I said, "Shhh. Stop. Put your lunch pail down. Just watch."

I loaded up the rifle and Tash asked, "Dad, what are you doing?"

I said, "What do you mean? I am going to shoot the deer."

At that she started crying loudly. "No, no! Dad, you can't do that!" And she went on sobbing, "I don't want you to shoot the deer!"

I said, "You were looking forward to going hunting with me. What did you think hunting was about if not for getting meat for food?"

She cried, "You didn't say anything about killing the deer."

Of course, the deer had run away when they heard Tash crying. So two deer were saved that day because of one little girl. To her, hunting meant that we were just going to watch our four-legged relatives. I said, "Okay, okay, I won't shoot any deer. We're just going to have a nice walk today and watch them." Then she stopped crying.

When we got home, Tash ran happily inside and said, "Mom, we hunted two deers! And you know what? Dad wanted to *shoot* them, but I wouldn't let him."

I could not step one foot off the reservation for fear of being arrested, but friends arrived all the time to visit me—Russ and Ted Means, Bill Wahpepah, Clyde Bellecourt, and others. The whole AIM leadership came to see me. Over time, people came from all over the world to show support for the Onondaga Nation and me.

Above all, my time at Onondaga was a time of learning. Here among the Iroquois, I saw Indian ideas of wisdom and brotherhood put into practice. Here the concerns of the "least fire" found their way to the Great Council Fire, where the concerns of the humblest became the concerns of the greatest chiefs. Here, public concerns were solved in a solemn, age-old manner. In the Long House, all decisions had to be unanimous. Discussions continued until every person was persuaded and satisfied to give his assent, or until all arguments were exhausted and a plan was abandoned. Then, in the evening when the concerns of the day were behind us, it was time to offer thanks to the Creator with tobacco for the morning sunrise and to enjoy our families together.

What I learned from my Onondaga friends was that you must always leave room for debate, whether it is a matter of high political confrontation or a family dilemma. The knowledge has helped me in my own life every day since then. I will always remember the help and friendship of the Onondaga people, of their open homes and hearts. But in September 1984, my enforced stay on the Onondaga reservation came to an end.

CHAPTER 24

Freedom

The absence of freedom must never make us forsake the path of human love for the path of caged fury.

—Dennis Banks, 1984

At Onondaga I was free, but also not free. I could not leave the reservation without facing arrest. Onondaga was becoming a prison for me—a friendly, loving one but a prison all the same. I was cut off from my life's work, from places that were sacred to me, from so many of my friends, and there was only one way to once again live a meaningful, satisfying life. I had to give myself up and surrender to South Dakota authorities. I talked it over with Kamook.

I said, "I don't want to be a fugitive from justice forever. This is not the kind of life I had planned for us. Janklow is no longer governor, and I think that if I give myself up now, I might get the minimum jail time. I could serve maybe two years and put the whole nightmare behind me. Then we could really be free."

Kamook and I had the concerns of four little children to consider, but I knew that through various support networks my family would get some help if I was serving time. Finally, Kamook agreed. The first two people we told of our decision were Chief Oren Lyons and Leon Shenandoah. They tried hard to dissuade us. "Going to South Dakota is like sticking your head into the lion's mouth," they said. "Don't do it. Stay here where it's safe."

Then we told Bill Kunstler. His instant reaction was, "Are you out of your fucking mind?" But we remained firm. Our exile had to end even if I had to serve a prison sentence, so I set the process in motion.

We started negotiations with Marshal Young, who would be the judge sentencing me, and with Dee Glasgow, the sheriff of Custer County. I had to be sure of getting a light sentence before I gave myself up. What if Young decided to give me the maximum sentence of fifteen years? Kunstler and Oren talked with the judge over the phone. Young wanted to know about my daily activities. They told him about my work with Indian youth, about my policy of no drugs and no alcohol, and about my training Onondaga kids in various sports, giving the judge a kind of report card on me. After considering this information, the judge indicated that he would go easy on me. I had to trust him and take the plunge.

I let Bill Kunstler and Bruce Ellison, our Rapid City lawyer, work out the terms of my surrender. Still, I was uneasy. I had some options—either to drive there or fly. But what if I got arrested on the way out? I called Dee Glasgow, telling him that we were, in fact, coming in, but I didn't say when or how. I told him that we would meet him at the airport, either in Rapid City or in Pierre, and that we would let him know more later.

We drove to Rapid City and stayed for a day or two in Wanblee on the Pine Ridge reservation at the home of medicine man Richard Moves Camp. We had a sweat lodge ceremony, and Moves Camp burned sage and sweetgrass, prayed, and fanned me off with his eagle wing. I called Sheriff Glasgow to tell him that I would surrender to him the next day at the Rapid City airport. Word got around fast. There were about two hundred reporters and media people present when Glasgow greeted me and put the cuffs around my wrists. Kamook stayed beside me, giving her strength to me as we stood there, letting our love for each other be seen.

People came from many places, even from Europe, to be character witnesses during my one-day trial and sentencing at Custer. By sheer coincidence, many of them wound up in the same plane flying from Denver, Colorado, to Rapid City, South Dakota. John Trudell sat next to Darrel Standing Elk. Behind them sat Richard Erdoes with Claus Biegert, a supporter who had come all the way from Munich, Germany. Across the aisle sat Janet McCloud, an elder from Washington State, and a French photographer friend of mine, Michelle Vignes. In front of them sat Oren Lyons and Clyde Bellecourt. The whole plane was full of friends from across the world who were coming on my behalf. There was a lot of laughter when they found themselves on the same 747 jet. It was almost as though they had rented the plane for a private "support Dennis Banks" party.

The trial was held on October 9, 1984, at Custer—not in the old, picturesque courthouse where I had been tried before, but in a new, plain courthouse. Since dawn on that day, two Japanese monks and a nun had been chanting and drumming to support me in spirit. The nun, Jun San, was a close friend who had visited Kamook and me at Onondaga. The two monks came from Massachusetts, where they had built a peace pagoda.

What took place was really not a trial but a sentencing. The trial had been held years before in 1975 when a prejudiced jury had found me guilty. Before I was sentenced, my friends and supporters were given a chance to speak on my behalf as character witnesses to persuade the judge to go easy on me. Bill Kunstler and Bruce Ellison again acted as my lawyers on this occasion. One after another, my friends took the stand. I was touched by their concern for me, which they showed by traveling long distances at their own expense to help me. I still have a copy of a letter I wrote to one of them. It reads in part:

> Thanks for your words of encouragement and what you did for me. For a moment I thought you were Jesus Christ come back to speak up for me . . . but of course you didn't have any holes in your hands or feet.

At the end of the testimony the judge gave me three years. It could have been worse. The proceedings should have ended at 3:00 P.M., but testimony was still rolling on at 6:00 P.M. Some of my friends who had planned to fly back home on the same day missed their flights. They all got together at a nearby church where Father Garvey, an old-time supporter, acted as host. The day ended with Jun San drumming to the chant of her prayer.

I served one year and two months of my sentence. At first I was incarcerated in the South Dakota State Penitentiary at Sioux Falls, a maximum security prison. When I arrived, the warden came down to greet me, asking if I still wanted to do my time in a state other than South Dakota. I told him I had changed my mind about that. If I went to jail in another state, my wife and children would have to travel long distances to visit me. I would do my time in South Dakota.

I went through the usual routine—two weeks of orientation and processing, medical examinations, x-rays, blood tests, and so on. Then I was assigned my permanent cell. All the Indians in the joint were watching my back, alert to any move that might threaten me, whether it be from an inmate or a guard. It was a good feeling to have brothers determined to keep me from harm. I was also glad to know that Indian religions were finally recognized in the prison and that some ceremonies were allowed.

Christmas Eve 1985 was happy and sad at the same time. At 10:30 P.M., an inmate tried to "hang it up," that is, commit suicide. He was screaming and working himself into a frenzy. He couldn't stop. He was in his cell and hard to get at. He told the guards that he wanted to talk to me. By this time, all the inmates were yelling at the guards to hurry it up before the man killed himself. The whole cellblock was in an uproar. The guards fetched me from my cell and brought me to the would-be suicide on a tier above me. When I got to his cell, four guards were already inside and four more were standing in the hallway. The poor guy was sweating and shaking like a leaf.

As soon as he saw me, he broke into tears and sobbed uncontrollably. It was pitiful to see a human being reduced to this state. I stuck my hand through the bar. He grabbed it and held onto it as if it were a life preserver. He said that he wanted to talk to somebody "who was real, who would listen." He told me he didn't want to stay one more minute in this terrible place. He had been in prison for five years and could not take it any more. He went on and on in this vein, but eventually became calmer. I lit some sweetgrass, smudged him up, and purified him. After we did this, he stopped sweating and wanted to lie down. Before I left, I asked him if he intended to try again to hang it all up. He said, "No."

At this time, I myself felt close to breaking down. How could I help him? Here was a young man about to take his life. He wanted to die so that he would not have to spend his life in prison. For him death was the road to freedom. I hoped that I had convinced him to go on living, but was his spending a lifetime in prison any better than dying? I didn't know the answer. He finally said, "Thanks. Thanks a lot." He shook my hand and lay down on his bed.

Christmas Day was different. After the evening meal, trustees handed out popcorn balls, peanuts, walnuts, apples, and oranges, while inmates sang out the usual Christmas songs. The singing was great. Even though we were separated by cells, everyone just started singing together like one big choir. It wasn't loud, but kind of soft and deep, lasting about two hours. Then some shouts arose, "Merry Christmas, you guys." The cellblock grew quiet as each of us began thinking our own thoughts, remembering those we missed.

In January I was transferred to the Springfield Correctional Facility, a minimum security prison in Springfield, South Dakota. It was a *coed* jail! Possibly the only one of its kind in the country, it had once been some sort of technical college, which had been closed four or five years earlier. The State of South Dakota converted it first into a women's minimum security prison. It had no walls around it, only a large fence. The state legislature then transformed it into a coed facility in what was described as a "social experiment." I was part of that first group of forty inmates sent there. I wrote Kamook that this was a big change for the better, because she and the kids would now be able to visit me every two weeks.

My inmates were thrilled at the news. Everybody was talking about the coed prison, even those who would stay behind at Sioux Falls. The guards woke us up at four o'clock in the morning. We packed up everything we had and took our stuff downstairs. I took my radio and my bed linen. I felt a great stirring inside me. It was still dark when we checked out of the main building. We were getting transferred to another place, and that in itself was exciting. It meant that time was being chipped away. I was going through another phase that would eventually lead me back out of prison. I was to be reclassified.

Leaving the prison we had to pass through four electronic gates, which slammed shut behind us with a loud metallic clang, marking off our passage from the maximum security areas of the penitentiary to the minimum security areas. Each time a gate opened for me, I began to understand the reality of moving out of that confinement. As the last gate clanged behind me, I was outside with the wind blowing in my face. We all boarded a Greyhound bus. There was nothing to indicate that it was a prison bus carrying inmates. The ride took us close to three hours; and it was about 11:00 A.M. when we arrived.

As we pulled in, we saw all these women standing in front of the dining hall. There were some thirty of them waving and cheering, looking happy to see us. As we got off the bus, the women were smiling, laughing, and making suggestive remarks, "Oh wow, I'll take *that* one!" "The one over there is the one for me!" It made us laugh and feel good. So we waved back at them, blowing kisses and whistling at them as they whistled back at us. Even though we all knew we were social guinea pigs, we didn't mind. We just felt good.

We were taken inside for a half-hour orientation session, then they told us, "We'll go through the rest later, after we eat lunch. There will be women in there eating with you at the same table. You can shake hands with the women when you meet them, but this will be the only time when you *ever* touch a female inmate. There will be no fooling around!" I went in with two pals, Antelope and Brings Plenty. We went through the line with our trays and looked for a place to sit. There were three or four women at almost every table. Three tables were empty.

"Well," I said to myself, "there's no sense sitting at an empty table." Three Indian women were sitting at one table, and I joined them, followed by Antelope and Brings Plenty. I introduced myself as did my two pals, and we chatted between mouthfuls. We felt as if we had been reborn into human society. And that was the beginning of my stay at Springfield Correctional Facility.

It would be difficult for someone who has never been inside a prison to understand what I felt and thought at that time. Springfield, as I said, was an effort to bring minimum and medium security male and female inmates together to find out whether prisons could be made less dehumanizing. If you are a man in a man's prison, you are surrounded by men all the time. You take showers with them, play softball and football with them, and smell the sweat of a hundred guys. You never see a woman, never come into any physical contact with one. So you begin to lose focus on yourself as a member of the community at large. You live in a kind of psychological desert. The people who thought up the idea

of Springfield tried to change this. I don't know if the experiment succeeded or if it lasted, but it did a lot of good for me at that time. I was
there for nine months in 1985, from January to September.

While I was at Springfield I went through a home-building course.
They taught me how to put up a house, roof it over, wire it, and do the
cabinetry. I was so proud of my first cupboards that I carved my name
in the back of them with the date and year. The first house that was
constructed by the men and women of the correctional facility was sold
to a private party. I was released on parole just as the very last nail was
driven into a roof shingle of the house I helped to build.

In April 1985 while I was still at Springfield, my paternal grandfather died. He was one hundred three years old, the oldest Anishinabe
on our reservation. His name was Bijah, but we called him Pops. I tried
to remember him through my small boy's memories. I recall that every
day he had his snuff. And he had a cigarette that he would puff on then
lay down to burn out on its own. He would take just one puff and then
forget about it. He never bought his cigarettes in packs but had a large
pouch of loose tobacco to roll his own. Bijah was a lumberjack and
involved in logging all of his life. After I had grown up and left the
reservation, I visited him a few times—not as often as I should have
and even less after the movement started. He would always listen when
I told him about the struggle, and he would talk about not giving up:

> Never give up. That's how I run my life. And I stay close to nature.
> During the sugaring time, it is important to recognize that one can't
> take all the sap away from the tree. We have to leave enough so that
> the tree can survive and thrive, otherwise one might make a mistake
> and take the tree's life force away. So we must think the Indian way if
> we are going to survive.

That was Grandpa Bijah. In my mind I always see him sugaring, chopping wood, hauling water. He was a grand old man who left a legacy as
simple as it was clear. I was very sad when I heard that he had passed away.

I made an application to go home for his funeral. Because he died in
Minnesota, I would have to leave South Dakota to attend. The warden
and the governor had to approve the application; however, I had jumped
bail in South Dakota and been a fugitive for eleven years, and Janklow

was once again governor. I prayed that I would be allowed to go, but I expected him to deny my request. He had always been hard on me, but the day after I was notified of my grandfather's death, about 4:00 in the morning a guard woke me up to tell me, "Mr. Banks, the governor has approved your leave to go to the funeral of your grandfather."

I thanked the Great Spirit for answering my prayer. And I was surprised that Governor Janklow had, for a while at least, wiped away the hatred that had existed between us for so long and let me go. He knew that once I stepped over the state line, he had no more jurisdiction over me—particularly on the rez—so this was no small thing for him to do. If I went on the lam there, he could have done nothing about it except issue another warrant for my arrest. I thought of what must have been going through the governor's mind and the struggle it would have cost him. I respected him for what he had done and was grateful to him for this.

Two guards took me to Minnesota. As part of the agreement, I had to pay for the car and gasoline, and for the time the guards were on duty with me. They were not dressed in uniforms, but in civilian clothing as I was. All through the funeral, they never let on who they were.

When the burial took place, we put a tin of snuff in grandpa's coffin along with his tobacco pouch and rolling papers. I met many of my old friends and felt very sad that I had not been able to share his last years with him. I felt left out of what would have been an important part of my life with my dad's father. As I looked at him lying in his coffin, I felt the power that he had passed to my dad and to me. I thought of what a fine man Bijah had been, a man who had worked hard, never looking for an easy way in life. A strong, traditional, wonderful man—that is how I remember him.

All through the time of my imprisonment, I sent out newsletters to my many friends. On September 13, 1985, I had been in jail for one year. That day I wrote:

As long as there is blood running through these veins of mine and warming this cold prison cell, I will think of freedom. I must do at least one more day. And when the sun rises tomorrow, if there is a flower growing someplace in this world, I want to be there to smell its fragrance. When a baby is heard crying, I want to be free to comfort its cries. As long as the sound of the drum is beating, I will sing the songs of my people. . . .

While it seems dramatic as I read it again now, that's how I felt when I was not free.

After I had finished half of my sentence, I was eligible for parole. On August 6, 1985, the parole board granted me my release on the condition that I would find a job on the outside. I received job offers from many places around the country, but I applied only to the Lone Man School on the Pine Ridge reservation. I wanted to be close to Kamook, her family, and so many of our old friends. At first I asked for a teaching position, but I lacked the necessary qualifications. Then I applied for the positions of drug and alcohol counselor and running coach. I filled out the forms and fired them off. One question on the application asked, "What experience do you have as a running coach?"

I put down, "I ran from the FBI for eleven years and they never caught up with me." Of course, I also mentioned the work I had done with the Onondaga Eagles. The school board must have had a sense of humor, because I was accepted.

As they were aware of my longtime association with Honeywell, a multi-business group of Japan that had long supported my efforts and had once employed me as a recruiter for minority workers, the Lone Man school board asked me if I could help develop a plan to create work for the many unemployed in the community. I began working on this as soon as I arrived. We compiled what we called a "skills bank" that determined how many people were available for various types of work. Then I contacted Honeywell in Minneapolis, Minnesota, requesting that some of their people come to us in Oglala. After several meetings with us, Honeywell agreed to move the production facilities for their computer circuit boards to Oglala. They arranged to provide training and wages for at least one year. After that the Lone Man School would independently own and operate the enterprise. That is how we founded the company called Lone Man Enterprises.

Kamook was busy working, too. She organized a large sewing project employing twenty-five women in quilt-, shawl-, and skirt-making.

They produced about fifteen quilts a month and sold them just as fast as they could finish them. Thus we both created jobs for the folks in the Oglala area. I was happy about that, and I was free at last. I never again found myself behind bars. A new, untraveled road stretched before me.

CHAPTER 25

Suddenly I Am an "Elder"

Life is like a circle.
You walk and walk only
To find yourself at the
Place you started from.

Henry Crow Dog

They call me an elder now, or Granpa. I still have to get used to that. I'm past sixty but the spirits have been kind to me. I am in good shape. I'm still vigorous. My hair is still dark. But will it be one year from now? So many of my old friends in the struggle are now hobbling along on a cane, had triple bypasses, suffer from emphysema or diabetes. Old age is creeping up on us.

So how are we doing now? We still are part of the struggle. I will be part of it as long as there is breath in me. I still live life to the fullest, but things have quieted down. The days of armed confrontation are over, at least for now. Many young kids nowadays have never heard of Wounded Knee. We try to keep the memories alive.

I have promoted legislation that makes trading in items from Indian graves illegal. I have organized "walks for justice" to free Leonard Peltier—unfortunately without success. I organize protests against the practice of digging up and displaying Indian remains. I support the fight against baseball teams giving themselves names like the "Cleveland Indians" or the "Atlanta Braves." I struggle to keep AIM alive. I mourn the absence of so many of warriors who have passed on to the spirit world.

There have been great changes in my personal life. Kamook and I broke up. Of all the women I loved, I loved Kamook the best. She shared my life for seventeen years—the good and the bad. She stood by me through years of danger and exile, went to jail for the sake of AIM, and was braver than the bravest warrior. She gave me four children—three girls and one boy. Our breakup was my fault; I was away too much, involved in too many Indian causes, leaving her alone with the kids. She moved to Albuquerque, New Mexico, with two of our children—my son, Chanupa, and my youngest daughter, Chubbs. Tashina and Tiopa have themselves become mothers, and Chubbs is also having a baby soon. I see them often. I will never forget what Kamook has done for me and for the American Indian Movement.

After Kamook, I had one more long relationship. In 1989 I led a protest against the digging up of Indian graves. We stopped the desecration and reburied the bones of these ancestral people. The event was covered by an attractive white photographer by the name of Alice Lambert. Once our talking gave way to an animated conversation, the inevitable happened. I moved into her Newport, Kentucky, house, which became my home for almost ten years.

At this time, I was organizing my Sacred Runs. Groups of runners, most of whom were American Indians, would go with me to meet people all over the world. We staged "teach-ins," during which we would talk about Indian history, culture, and civil rights struggles, while in turn learning about the culture and history of the country we were visiting. We were particularly eager to meet with other indigenous people—Australian Aborigines, Maoris from New Zealand, the Scandinavian Sami people who are sometimes called Laplanders, Inuits of Alaska, and Ainus of northern Japan. We ate strange foods such as kangaroo meat and wiggly white grubs in Australia, and moose-nose soup in subarctic North America. Alice became the director of the entire operation. She ran the computer, made all the arrangements, and saw to the details.

On October 10, 1992, Alice Lambert gave birth to a baby boy in Newport, Kentucky. When he was born, the woman who registered his birth wanted me to give him a name right away. I said, "No, a medicine man from South Dakota is going to come and we are going to have a naming ceremony."

She said, "That's good that you people are still carrying on these traditions. What time will he be here with the name?" She thought the medicine man was going to be there that afternoon.

I told her, "No, we won't have the ceremony until next year."

She said, "Oh, no, he has to have a name today before I leave. I have to send this vital statistic information today to the state capital. This baby was born here, and here's a space for his name and weight and all that. If you don't have a name, he won't get a birth certificate and he won't get a Social Security card, and there won't be proof that he was ever born."

"Well, then put 'Baby Banks' on there."

"No," she said.

I said, "Well, then put 'Baby Boy Banks' on there."

"I can't do that," she said.

"Okay, would you please leave the room for a minute?" She left and I told Alice, "We're going to name him 'Hokshila' for now."

The lady returned and asked, "Did you decide on a name?"

"Yes, his name is Hokshila," I replied.

She said, "Oh, that's great. How do you spell that?" She filled out the form, placed her little stamp on it, and put it in an envelope. She came back some ten minutes later and asked, "By the way, what does this name mean?"

I said, "Boy." She got mad.

A year later in South Dakota during a traditional ceremony, our son got his final name—Minoh, meaning Good.

But my relationship with Alice was cursed like all the others: I was away too often and too long. When I returned after an absence of some weeks, I found my possessions neatly packed, ready to go. It was my fault again. Having a relationship with me is like being married to a sailor who is always at sea. Alice let me keep Minoh. In February 1999 I took Minoh with me back to the rez in Minnesota where I was born. He is ten years old now as I write my story.

I have not always been a good father. I love and enjoy children. I love to play with them, take them to the movies, and teach them sports, but I am not a twenty-four-hours-a-day father. I was most of my life an absentee parent. My children had to live not without knowing my love but without my being there for them. I told them, "I will try to always be there for you when you need me most, even when you are grown up, even in your married life, but most of the time I'll be involved in the struggle, and that means being far from home." I try to do better with Minoh.

One of the sad aspects of being an elder is that one by one, your old friends and comrades in the struggle are no longer here. So many have gone to the spirit world. Old Henry Crow Dog, who prepared for me my first sweat lodge, is gone. He opened up for me the world of Lakota belief, let me take part in his sacred ceremonies. It was Henry who always told me, "Don't look at life with the eyes of your face, but with the eye of your heart."

Gone, too, is Frank Fools Crow, the oldest and most respected of Lakota medicine men. He ran the first Sun Dance I participated in. I miss my friend, the medicine man John Fire Lame Deer, a Rosebud, South Dakota, Lakota. I miss his wicked humor. He always told me, "A spiritual leader must, at the same time, soar as high as an eagle and be as low as a worm crawling in the mud. He has to experience everything, the highest and the lowest in order to become a medicine man." When John was in his eighties, he sometimes would point out to me a grand-motherly woman smiling at him and say, "That's one of my old girl-friends from long ago. She still has that love wink in her eyes." His son, Archie, also a spiritual leader, died recently. I think he was only sixty years old, a victim of heart trouble and diabetes. This vicious disease is a particular curse of American Indians. I also think of Pete Catches from Oglala on the Pine Ridge reservation, another greatly admired spiritual man, and of Phillip Deere, a Muscogee Indian, from Norman, Oklahoma, who became AIM's medicine man after Leonard Crow Dog resigned from that position. These are some of our spiritual leaders who have gone to another world.

And there are our warriors who left an empty space in my life: Pedro Bissonette, always smiling, doing good things for the sick and the elderly, blown away on a lonely road by Dick Wilson's tribal police; Buddy Lamont, Kamook's uncle, a Vietnam vet, killed by a sniper's bullet at the Knee; Oscar Bear Runner and Severt Young Bear, who brought us the AIM song; Milo Goings and Louis Bad Wound, both Lakota. But I'd better stop before I break down.

There is an old Cheyenne proverb:

A nation is not conquered until the hearts of its women are on the ground. Then it is done, no matter how brave its warriors nor how strong their weapons.

And so I want to honor our women warriors who have left us. Lou Bean, Kamook's aunt, who covered for us at Wounded Knee while I made my way out of the perimeter, passing in secret through a ring of marshals and FBI agents. She was a nurturing woman who never let you go from her house unfed. And Gladys Bissonette, who told us, so long ago, "Let's go to Wounded Knee, and if you men won't do it, then we women will." I think of Mary Gertrude, Henry Crow Dog's wife, a strong, traditional woman, a good bead-worker and moccasin-maker. I mourn Nilak Butler, Inuit, a strong fighter in the struggle who died recently after a long bout with cancer. Gone, too, is Grandma Cecilia Jumping Bull, who witnessed the great shootout in which two FBI men and an Indian, Joe Stuntz Kills Right, were killed.

Finally, I grieve for Annie Mae Aquash, a Micmac from Nova Scotia. She was petite, but her heart was big as the sky. She was brave as a lion and had dedicated her life to the struggle. I remember her radiance at Wounded Knee, where Wallace Black Elk married her—Indian-style— to Nogeeshik Aquash, an Ojibwa.

Annie Mae was shot in the back of her head, execution-style. On February 24, 1976, her body was found in the snow alongside a Pine Ridge road. She wore just a light jacket, jeans, and tennis shoes.

It was during a meeting in Los Angeles, California, that John Trudell came over to me and said, "Annie Mae's body has been found." The news devastated me. It was only the presence of so many people that prevented me from bursting into tears. There was absolute silence in the committee room. I left in order to regain my composure. Annie Mae was truly a great warrior. In my mind she had earned a sacred eagle feather for her bravery. It took time for the finality of her death to sink in.

Annie Mae's murderers have never been identified but, some people, former goons and FBI-lovers, have tried to reopen the case. They try to put the blame for her death on AIM. They will not succeed. It was her strength that killed her, because she was perceived as a threat by the goons and the government. She told me once:

> I know that I will be killed. They won't let an Indian like me live. The FBI has put a jacket on me. When I refused to cooperate with them, they spread the rumor that I was one of their informants. One FBI agent told me, "You won't be around anymore next year." So I think that my life will be short. I have accepted it. It is better to die young, having done something for your people, than to grow old never having done anything. But remember, it doesn't matter if the FBI kills me or whether my life is snuffed out by one of our own people who believes the rumors the Feds have spread about me. It always will be the FBI who murders me.

My mind is crowded with thoughts of those warriors who stood, fought, and died for us. They were brave men. They were brave women. I shall not eulogize their deaths. Instead, I shall draw on their life memories and be strengthened.

I am sorry to inform my readers that on February 5, 2004, Kamook took the stand in Rapid City, South Dakota, in a trial against AIM security personnel Arlo Looking Cloud and admitted that she has been a paid FBI informant since 1988, that she had worn a wire to record conversations with AIM people and others, and that she had been gathering information against the American Indian Movement. My emotions as described earlier still stand—she was a good mother to our children. History may judge her differently.

CHAPTER 26

Looking Back

With age comes wisdom—sometimes.

—Dennis Banks

The weather was terrible, as terrible as winter in South Dakota can be. With the windchill factor, the temperature was down to sixty below. Icicles dangled from our hair, eyebrows, and beards. Breath turned into white clouds. A bone-chilling storm was sweeping over the land. It blew some areas bare and piled up huge snowdrifts in other places. Swirling snow cut visibility down to a few feet. Roads were covered with black ice; cars spun out of control, burying themselves in the snowbanks on either side of the road. It was February 27, 1998, the twenty-fifth anniversary of the takeover of Wounded Knee—a day of remembrance.

We had to fight our way through the blinding blizzard, mile by mile, to get to the Knee. It was a great gathering, a day of great emotion. In spite of white-out conditions and the cruel cold, some seven hundred people had forced their way through the storm to join this celebration of our struggle for freedom and self-determination.

We started out with a ceremony at Oglala, in the western part of the Pine Ridge reservation, at the grave sites of Joe Stuntz Kills Right, Annie Mae Aquash, and Gladys Bissonette. Those three had given their lives for the movement. We sensed the haunting feeling of their presence as we said prayers, sang, and made tobacco offerings to their spirits. So many memories swept over me at that time.

About forty of us stood at the grave site, including my old friends Clyde Bellecourt, Ellen Moves Camp, and the photographer Kevin McKiernan, who had been at Wounded Knee with us in 1973. More than half of the people standing there praying were under twenty-five years old, brought to this place by their fathers, who wanted to connect them to a past they had never known. It felt good to see the young people next to us old-timers. I resolved to tell them of what had happened at Wounded Knee before they were born, to tell them of what their fathers and mothers were doing in those wild and glorious days of '73. It occurred to me then that I myself was an elder—a grandfather, an old relic, an artifact. An old part of my life ended then, and a new, unfamiliar part began. We all embraced, shook hands, sang the AIM song, and, as they had seen us do, the youngsters sprinkled sacred tobacco on each grave.

The snow came down hard. Visibility was down to almost nothing. We progressed to Calico Hall, the place where Wounded Knee had began. The family of my old friend Pedro Bisonette was there to welcome us. Pedro, a civil rights leader and one of the finest men who ever lived, had been brutally murdered by tribal police. His wife and children had hung pictures of Pedro on the walls of Calico Hall. They had also prepared a lot of food for us—hot coffee to warm us up, sandwiches, fruit, and juice. They also provided lots of food and hot drinks for the runners and walkers.

It had been decided to have sacred runs from four different directions join up at Wounded Knee. We even had teams of horseback riders, who made a fantastic sight outlined against the milky whiteness of a landscape shrouded by clouds of swirling snow. Calico was one of the starting points. We went outside to see the runners off, singing songs and burning sweetgrass in honor of Pedro. Clyde Bellecourt took the feathered staff, ran it out to the road, and gave it to the lead runner. A fierce storm was upon us, but the runners took off and just kept going. No one was falling behind. We also had relay teams of eight or nine guys who passed the staff to new groups of runners a mile at a time.

We formed a caravan of about twenty-five to thirty cars, vans, and trucks. Our headlights were on and emergency lights were flashing.

The sight reminded me of that night twenty-five years before when we drove through Wounded Knee while goons and FBI agents on the roof of the tribal council building trained their machine guns on us. Dicky Wilson stared at us in disbelief, clutching a loaded .38 in his fist. Things were different in 1998. People came running to wave at us, shouting words of encouragement even though the sounds were swallowed up by the roar of the storm.

We drove east at a snail's pace along U.S. Highway 18 until we came to the junction with the road that leads north toward Wounded Knee and Porcupine. There we were joined by another group of runners and walkers powdered with snow, coming from the east. Among them were Kamook, Charlene Teeters from Santa Fe, and my teenage son, Chanupa. I was proud of them as I saw them bent forward, straining their bodies against the wind.

We drove alongside the walkers at about five miles per hour. About twenty-five cars were in front of me and suddenly I noticed that as many were behind me. More and more people and cars were joining us in spite of the storm.

We arrived at Wounded Knee about 1:30 P.M., and parked at the foot of the hill. A mass of cars was parked among tipis that some people led by Tom Cook had set up. Tom was a remarkable man, a Mohawk from upstate New York along the Canadian border who spoke his Iroquois language. He had come to us at Wounded Knee while still very young, and he had never gone back east. He married a Lakota woman, Loretta Afraid of Bear; they had lived among the Sioux and he became a road-man of the Native American Church.

Someone had made a big fire around which people were warming themselves. Walkers came in from Denby and Porcupine, and a group of horsemen emerged from the white fog looking like ghosts—an unforgettable sight. Runners came in with flags and eagle-feather staffs. Young girls arrived wrapped in brightly colored Pendleton blankets, forming brilliant silhouettes against the surrounding whiteness. A huge crowd of people milled around me, and my heart swelled with pride that so many had come in spite of the raging blizzard.

I looked at the weather as a blessing, because it reminded me to tell the children around me about the women and children slaughtered here by Custer's cavalry on a day like this in the winter of 1890, their bodies frozen solid like blocks of ice. And I would tell them of the wind that sometimes brings with it the wails of the ghosts of the dead, buried up there in the ravine, so that we might hear their voices. I would describe to them as well some of the coldest days in February of 1973, when we were encircled by an army of marshals, goons, and FBI. And I would point out to them the little Lakota boys, who were then riding horses amid the tipis in their flimsy clothing, to show how unmindful they were of the cold. I told some of the young people, "The Great Spirit has given us just the kind of weather we needed."

I was happy to have my wife, Alice, sharing this experience with me, as well as our little boy, Minoh, who was still too young to understand the meaning of this gathering. I told Simone, a young Oglala girl, to take Minoh back to the van, which was warm and cozy. Then I began walking up the hill to the grave site, that long trench in which almost three hundred of Big Foot's band were buried. Alice was holding on to my arm. The ice was covered with fluffy snow and was very slippery.

On the way up, I met people I had not seen in years. People were yelling, "Banks! Banks!" Behind me someone shouted, "Hey Dennis!" I turned around and, oh God! It was Bill Zimmerman, who had organized the airdrop of food and medical supplies for us during the siege, enabling us to hold out a few weeks longer. We were laughing with tears in our eyes, hugging each other. Bill said he had a plane ready to do another airdrop to remind those who had come of the one on April 17, 1973. Unfortunately, the weather made this impossible. He had brought with him another of the airdrop pilots, Larry Levin, so there were more handshakes.

I saw Richard Erdoes, as usual busy with his camera, wading knee-deep in snow. The day before Richard had slipped on a patch of ice, falling flat on his face and breaking his nose. The upper half of his face was swollen, and his nose was somewhat out of shape. But here he was at age 85, one of our oldest friends. His son Erich was also taking photographs, following in his father's footsteps.

Then I came upon Allan Cooper, a white supporter who had been with us at Wounded Knee. I had not seen him in twenty years. Al was wearing the same old Levis jacket with the Wounded Knee ribbon he had worn twenty-five years before. It still fit, though it was a little tight across his chest. His young son, Malcolm, was hanging on to him.

"Man, oh man! Am I happy to see you," Al said as he embraced me. My adrenaline was surging. I was so elated to see all these old friends; it did my heart good. It was a very emotional moment for me that I will remember as long as I have breath.

Finally we stood at the grave site on top of the hill. So many memories were washing over me. Clyde was speaking to the crowd. His brother, Vernon, stood nearby, looking emaciated after a triple bypass surgery. The years had taken their toll on us.

We held a ceremony to honor those who had passed on to another world. I said a prayer for them, then we walked down to the place where the Negotiation Tipi had stood. It was there we had argued about so many things with the Feds. There stood Edgar Bear Runner, the son of Oscar Bear Runner, and Milo Yellow Hair, opening their arms wide in welcome. Milo was now vice chairman of the Pine Ridge tribe. What a contrast he made to the goons we had faced in 1973. I hugged people and shook hands. I even hugged people I did not know. I felt so good inside. I had no words to express my feelings, but I know that I almost broke down. More prayers were offered, the AIM flag was raised, and people sang. Five men with rifles fired a salute for the dead warriors and a thanksgiving salvo for all who had come. After that we all walked together to our cars and took off to meet again at the day school in Porcupine where we would continue our celebration.

Inside the big hall at the school, there was a mountain of good, warm food and Indian-style coffee—hot as hell, black as the night, and so thick a spoon would stand up in it. There were more embraces with people who had not been at the grave site—Regina Brave, Carter Camp, Leonard Crow Dog, Margo Thunderbird, Lorelei DeCora, John Trudell, Bob Free, and so many more. I went over to Russell Means, who I had not seen in five years, and shook his hand. We started joking and kidding each other as we had always done. The years were wiped away, as if we had been doing that only yesterday.

People approached me, "Hey, Banks, this is my daughter." "Here, look at this picture of my little grandson." And, "How you doin', Dennis? Remember me?"

I looked at all of these many young faces, teenagers laughing, and I thought, "These are the children of AIM, who will take our place, who will pass on the flame."

We had two days of powwows filled with dancing and singing. There were welcoming speeches and give-aways. Babies were crawling on the floor, so you had to watch your step. The crowd got bigger and bigger. We had meetings with visitors from faraway places—aborigines from Australia, Zapatistas from Chiapas, Mexico, Tibetans—many oppressed peoples, some of whom had suffered much, languishing in prison as we American Indians had done. There was no difference between these people and us. We were as one.

McKiernan, Erdoes, and Bancroft had brought slides, which they had put together and projected on a big screen. And, oh God, there we saw ourselves, so much younger: taking over the BIA building in Washington, D.C.; demonstrating in Rapid City, South Dakota, and Gordon, Nebraska; facing the armored cars at Wounded Knee; being taken away in handcuffs. But what really shook us up and made tears come to the eyes of many of our old veterans was seeing those who had been taken away from us, who had gone to the spirit land. So many were gone who had fought the good fight alongside us. We also remembered those whose lives were taken by untreated diseases, by diabetes and alcoholism, by sheer despair. This was the most emotional moment of our get-together.

The widow of our chief movement lawyer, Bill Kunstler, was honored in his stead. Our other great lawyer, Ken Tilsen, was at that moment undergoing heart surgery. It made the older men among us reflect on their own mortality. Only the rocks and the mountains last forever, but out of the cracks in the rocks grow small flowers, life renewing itself. A medicine man got up on the stage and admonished us, "You AIM leaders, some of you have been feuding, harboring bad thoughts against each other. You all shake hands now and embrace." We did so, some with enthusiasm and some with uneasiness, but there was a renewal of old friendships that wiped out old quarrels.

The next day at the little reservation town of Kyle was a repetition of what had taken place at Porcupine. I had put together a band of drums, the heartbeat of our people. John Trudell spoke truth to us, I was one of the drummers, and Steve Emery played the guitar. Once Steve had been a fierce, slim, young warrior. Now he was a tribal judge, no longer slim with short-cropped hair, but he strummed his instrument in high spirits. That night we were totally snowed in. It was impossible even to get as far as Pine Ridge. Many slept on the floor of the school.

February 29 was the day of saying good-bye, a day of joy and sadness. People asked me, "What did you men and women of 1973 achieve? Are Indians really better off now?"

I told them:

> We were the prophets, the messengers, the fire-starters. Wounded Knee awakened not only the conscience of all Native Americans, but also of white Americans nationwide. We changed an attitude of dependence on the BIA and the government, of "give me a handout," to "I can do it, you can do it, we can do it!" We changed our people's lifestyle. People replaced neckties with bone or bead chokers. We resurrected old beliefs and ways of life, blending them with the demands of modern life, with what we needed to survive. We created a new culture, wiping out old stereotypes. Out of AIM came a new breed of writers, poets, artists, actors, and filmmakers. We no longer needed whites to "interpret" our culture.

> We created alternative schools, teaching history from the Indian point of view. We have not achieved all that we wanted. We only have made a dent in solving our many problems. We leave much to do for the new generations coming up. But we are Medewin people, the Corn Maiden people, the Sun Dance people. As the FBI and the marshals at Wounded Knee found out, we are still a strong people.

The twenty-fifth anniversary of Wounded Knee celebration completed one cycle of my life. I went back to the old rez, to Leech Lake, to the spot where I was born. I have my young son Minoh with me. I fish and I hunt. I have started a wild rice and maple sugar business. My story ends where it began.

Afterword

Since moving back to Federal Dam, Minnesota, where I was born, my son Minot and I have had a great beginning with each other and with the many cousins I never knew. We started a small business with wild rice and maple syrup. He attends Bug-a-nay-ge-shick School and K-12 Anishinabe Controlled School. He is learning the Anishinabe language and often comes home to teach me. We set nets, trap, hunt, and snare rabbits. We make canoes, drums, and birch bark baskets. We harvest wild rice and tap the maple trees. It is a good life up here.

I want to thank Masao Yamamoto, Takeo Koshikawa, and Senchi Tanaka for their loyal friendship. Masao and I have become spiritual brothers. To Fred Morgan I owe my good health. My life has been enriched by my children and by the American Indian Movement. I shall always remember those who fell along the way. One of my closest friends, Leonard Peltier, remains in prison—twenty-eight years for a crime he didn't commit.

Jun-San of Nippon-Myohoji remains my closest spiritual sister; she and I will walk this good road forever. Robby Romero and Kenny Brown are still by my side.

My daughters Darla, Glenda Jean, Denise, Tiopa, and "Chubbs" are living close to me, and one of my sons, "Buff," has moved up here. He and Minoh are great together. My brother, Mark, remains my closest friend, and Audrey, who stood by me during rough times, is still here. Charolette, our youngest sister, comes to visit often. My Wahpeton friend, Floyd "Red Crow" Westerman, is still my friend and is doing good in Hollywood.

I wish to thank Horst Rechelbacher, who has been a tremendous financial help for the past ten years. My efforts in starting up my small business have introduced me to Terry Robinson, Tracy Gale, and Larry Goose—all from Battle Point, Minnesota—and to Mutt and Lila from Cass Lake, Minnesota.

I thank the American Indian Movement for being strong. AIM will always be strong because it is a spiritual movement. Every day we receive calls of distress, and every day we offer tobacco ceremonies for those in need. Right now this earth, our mother, is in distress. She needs our help. Can we—all of us—respond? I don't know, but I am convinced that if we don't respond, we will be in peril and our future will lay in question.

Today I look around me and see the animals of the forests and lakes. Every day, eagles fly by our home overlooking Leech Lake, and to the eagles, the bears, and the porcupines, I say *me-gwitch* for a good life.

> Me-gwitch Leonard Peltier
> Me-gwitch Buddy Lamont
> Me-gwitch Annie Mae
> Me-gwitch Bug-a-nay-ge-shick

DENNIS BANKS
Anishinabe Territories
Leech Lake reservation
Where the Great Spirit lives